Regionalism, Trade and Economic Development in the Asia-Pacific Region

Regionalism, Trade and Economic Development in the Asia-Pacific Region

Edited by

Dr M.A.B. Siddique

Director, Trade, Migration and Development Research Centre
School of Economics and Commerce
The University of Western Australia

Edward Elgar
Cheltenham, UK • Northampton, MA, USA

Published by
Edward Elgar Publishing Limited
Glensanda House
Montpellier Parade
Cheltenham
Glos GL50 1UA
UK

Edward Elgar Publishing, Inc.
William Pratt House
9 Dewey Court
Northampton
Massachusetts 01060
USA

A catalogue record for this book
is available from the British Library

Library of Congress Cataloguing in Publication Data
Regionalism, trade and economic development in the Asia-Pacific region /
edited by M.A.B. Siddique.
      p. cm.
   Includes bibliographical references and index.
   1. Asia—Commerce. 2. Pacific Area—Commerce. 3. Asia—Economic policy.
   4. Pacific Area—Economic policy. I. Siddique, Muhammed Abu B.

   HF1583.R443   2007
   382'.915—dc22   2006013236

ISBN 978 1 84542 503 6

Printed and bound in Great Britain by MPG Books Ltd, Bodmin, Cornwall

Contents

Figures

Tables

Contributors

David Allen
School of Accounting Finance and Economics
Edith Cowan University
Perth, WA, Australia

Inkyo Cheong
Professor
Department of Economics
Inha University
Incheon, South Korea

Christopher Howe
Professor
School of Oriental & African Studies
London, United Kingdom

Nazrul Islam
Agriculture and Resource Economist
Department of Agriculture Western Australia
Perth, WA, Australia

Kenneth E. Jackson
Director
Centre for Development Studies
Anthropology Department
University of Auckland
Auckland, New Zealand

William E. James
Professor and Trade Economist
Growth through Investment and Trade
USAID, Jakarta, Indonesia

Emma Kopke
Department of Agriculture Western Australia
Perth, WA, Australia

Lee K. Lim
School of Accounting, Finance and Economics
Edith Cowan University
Perth, WA, Australia

Donald MacLaren
Department of Economics
University of Melbourne
Melbourne, VIC, Australia

Rahul Sen
Regional Economic Studies (RES)
Institute of Southeast Asian Studies (ISEAS)
Singapore

M.A.B. Siddique
Director
Trade, Migration and Development Centre
School of Economics and Commerce
The University of Western Australia
Perth, WA, Australia

Larry A. Sjaastad
Professor
Department of Economics
The University of Chicago
Chicago, IL, USA

John Stanton
Agricultural and Resource Economist
Department of Agriculture Western Australia
Perth, WA, Australia

Andrew L. Stoler
Executive Director
Institute for International Business, Economics and Law
University of Adelaide,
Adelaide, SA, Australia

Jose Tongzon
Department of Economics
National University of Singapore
Singapore

Trent Winduss
School of Accounting, Finance and Economics
Edith Cowan University
Perth, WA, Australia

Yanrui Wu
School of Economics and Commerce
University of Western Australia
Perth, WA, Australia

Ippei Yamazawa
President
International University of Japan
Japan

Preface and acknowledgements

The book is based on invited papers from scholars in the areas of trade and development presented at an international conference on 'Free Trade Agreements in the Asia-Pacific Region' at the University of Western Australia, Perth, Australia during July 2004. Contributors are internationally recognized academics whose main research interests centre around the impact of regional trade agreements (RTAs) on economic development in the Asia-Pacific region. The conference focused on the following major issues:

1. RTAs – theoretical perspective
2. RTAs, the World Trade Organization (WTO) and exchange rates
3. RTAs, East Asia and the Pacific (APEC)
4. RTAs and Southeast Asia
5. RTAs and agriculture
6. Future outlook of RTAs in the Asia-Pacific region.

The papers were reviewed for rigour and quality.

As editor, I wish to sincerely thank all the contributors without whose co-operation it would have been impossible to publish this volume. I am also indebted to a number of senior colleagues who extended their generous help to me in organizing the conference. I owe a special debt of gratitude to the ex-Head of School of Economics and Commerce at the University of Western Australia (UWA) Professor Paul Miller who played a significant role in raising funds for the conference from both within and outside the University. Organization of the conference and publication of the volume would not have been possible without his direct help. I am also thankful to our current (2006) Head of School, Associate Professor Iain Watson, for his constant encouragement and inspiration in publishing this volume. I also wish to thank the Head of Economics Programme (at UWA) Professor Ken Clements for his invaluable advice in relation to the publication of this book. Special thanks are also due to my good friend Mr Colin Campbell-Fraser, Director of Public Affairs at The University of Western Australia who greatly helped in promoting the Conference. Mr Ben Dyer, Ms Helen Reidy and Ms Aya Kelly provided excellent organizational assistance for the Conference.

Mr Nathan Blight undertook the painstaking task of producing the typescript and I wish to thank him for performing this task with his usual efficiency and sincerity.

I would like to acknowledge my sincere appreciation for the understanding and support received from my wife Naznin and my two daughters Farzana and Farhana.

Finally, neither the conference nor this book would have been possible without generous financial assistance received from: the Trade, Migration and Development Research Centre from Department of Foreign Affairs and Trade, Australian Government (Canberra); Department of State, United States of America; Department of Agriculture, Government of Western Australia; Vice-Chancellor's office, the Vice-Chancellery (UWA); Dean's Office, UWA Business School; School of Economics and Commerce (UWA); School of Accounting, Finance and Business Economics, Edith Cowan University; Faculty of Business and Public Management, Edith Cowan University; School of Economics and Finance, Curtin University of Technology; Institute for Research into International Competitiveness, Curtin University of Technology; Economic Society of Australia (WA Branch); Perth Convention Bureau; Griffin Group and Wine Industry Association Western Australia.

M.A.B. Siddique
Director, Trade, Migration and Development Research Centre
School of Economics
The University of Western Australia
March, 2006

PART I

Introduction

1. Regionalism, trade and economic development: theories and evidence from the Asia-Pacific region

M.A.B. Siddique

INTRODUCTION

Regional trade agreements (RTAs) are formed with the aim of minimizing trade barriers in order to increase the flow of total trade between the participating countries. RTAs bring the signatory countries one step closer to establishing a global village with fewer trade barriers. The main arguments put forward in favour of establishing RTAs are based on the theory of comparative advantage (initially developed by Adam Smith in 1776) to bring about an increased standard of living, increased employment, increased global understanding and so on. There are two main geographical facets of RTAs: regional, for example the North American Free Trade Area (NAFTA); and bilateral, such as the Singapore–Australia Free Trade Agreement (SAFTA). By November 2005 there were also three types of RTAs in force. These were free trade agreements (FTAs), which make up 84 per cent, customs unions (CUs); and partial scope agreements, which both account for 8 per cent (Crawford and Fiorentino 2005, p. 3). FTAs have zero tariffs between member countries and each country retains the ability for independent trade policy with the rest of the world. CUs are FTAs with members imposing common tariffs on non-members. This loss of independent trade policy is the likely reason for the prevalence of FTAs over CUs. Partial scope agreements have limited liberalization which dampens their appeal.

RTAs inspire much debate between trade economists, business communities and politicians. Unfortunately, there is no Aladdin's magic lamp to clearly determine the benefits and costs associated with the establishment of an RTA, because the models used to estimate such benefits and costs are based on assumptions, not all of which are realistic. Therefore a change in any given condition may significantly alter the outcome of the findings of a model.

One reason why the virtues of RTAs are hard to quantify before an Agreement is finalized and implemented, is that all agreements differ in scope and coverage, and countries have differing objectives when entering negotiations. However, some general motivations for undertaking RTAs do exist (see Whalley 1998, pp. 70–4). First, countries are more likely to partake in an RTA if its major trading partners are involved, the number of negotiators is small (and therefore the chances of success are greater) and they have become frustrated at the failure of multilateral liberalization talks. Moreover an RTA may be used to validate a strategic allegiance amongst members by promoting deeper economic integration. RTAs can also be used as a tool to guarantee market access for member countries. This is especially important for small countries entering into agreements which ensure access into larger markets. A second motive behind RTAs is the reinforcement of domestic reforms. By locking in an RTA, future changes to domestic policies will become more complicated (see also Laird 1999, p. 1191; Summers 1991, p. 300). Third, RTAs can have a tactical use: they can be used to influence multilateral negotiations (for example to pressure other countries to enter the multilateral debate), or increasing multilateral bargaining power (for example creating CUs to make talks with third parties easier).

These general motives for RTAs have demonstrated a variety of possible objectives. These will greatly influence the outcome of negotiations and the extent of the economic integration attained. When parties have very different objectives and preferences, negotiations become more complicated, making outcomes unpredictable and inefficient (de Melo and Panagariya 1993, p. 17).

RTAs AND ECONOMIC DEVELOPMENT: THE THEORETICAL BACKGROUND

Theoretical work on reform of trade policy including RTAs can be linked to economic development in a number of ways. By removing trade barriers, a country opens its markets to foreign producers. This promotes competition and efficiency. The larger market attracts new firms and forces domestic producers to pursue internal efficiency gains in order to compete (Drabek 2005, pp. 21–4). This stimulates production and leads to efficient resource allocation, specialization and transfer of knowledge, all of which have positive impacts on welfare and consumption. Also, market transparency and openness are essential for attracting foreign direct investment (FDI), which is a key ingredient for economic development, especially in developing countries. On the other hand, discriminatory trade policies resulting in cost distortions can cause misallocation of the world's resources and reduce global income (Pomfret 1997, p. 7). Governments have incentives to seek the economic improvements that free trade can offer. Multilateral free trade may be the first best option but if these negotiations fail, regionalism becomes a viable option, despite lesser gains being realized (Laird 1999, p. 1185). In this case the design and implementation technique of the Agreement become critical to its effectiveness.

The theory of RTAs was first introduced by Jacob Viner (1950) in *The Customs Union Issue*. He argued that the creation of a CU is not always welfare enhancing. Viner used partial equilibrium analysis to make this point, and described cases in which trade creation increased welfare, whereas trade diversion decreased it. The shift of imports from an inefficient to efficient source caused by the removal of tariffs represents trade creation. According to Viner, while trade creation causes no change in trade with the rest of the world, it increases trade between members, and therefore is one step forward towards free trade. Trade diversion occurs when increased trade within the union is accompanied by decreased trade with non-members. Thus it may intensify protectionism (de Melo and Panagariya 1993, pp. 6–7). Following Viner's pioneering analysis, much research was undertaken with the aim of generalizing the result into a framework for welfare enhancing CUs. For example: Vanek (1964) and Hatta and Fukushima (1979) demonstrated that a reduction of the highest tariff rate to the next highest level raised global welfare when initial trade taxes were either positive or zero, and the high-tariff good is a net substitute to all others. Hatta and Fukushima (1979) showed that an equiproportionate reduction of all tariffs raises global income. However it was soon uncovered that when preferences and realistic elasticities of supply and demand were introduced, this became more complicated. Meade (1955) in his seminal work *The Theory of Customs Unions* asserted that Vinerian theory is best suited to infinite supply elasticities and zero demand elasticities, and assessing the welfare impacts of CUs may not be as simple as trade creation and diversion. His trade theory is based on changes in the prices of traded goods being influential in welfare changes along with volumes of traded goods. This theory led to the realization that once zero demand elasticity is abandoned, even a wholly trade diverting union can be welfare enhancing (for details, see Panagariya 2000, pp. 290–3). Meade (1955, p. 52) generalized that a CU is more likely to raise welfare.

The higher the initial tariffs between member countries, the lower the tariffs are in non-member countries, the more substitutable are the member countries' goods and the less substitutable are the goods of non-member countries.

However Abrego *et al.* (2005, pp. 118–22) argue that generalizations such as these weaken when the different motivations and objectives that countries bring to the negotiating table are taken into account. Lipsey and Lancaster (1956) confirmed general results could not be applied to CUs and Johnson (1967, ch. 6) argued that the empirical circumstances of the particular case determine whether a reduction in tariffs actually improved or worsened welfare as a whole. Johnson also observes that the extension of preferences to less developed countries from developed countries can be a useful tool for kick-starting their economic growth. Conversely, Kennan and Riezman (1990) show that large countries and CUs seeking improved terms of trade through tariff reductions may refuse to agree to global free trade. Kowalczyk (1999) argues that a similar result holds for a small country which has the option of membership of multiple free trade areas.

The sustainability of trade policy and the extent of the economic gains achieved using RTAs are closely linked to the stability of macroeconomic policies (Drabek 2005, pp. 38–9). Trade surpluses and deficits are heavily reliant on national savings and investment, both of which are dependent on macroeconomic policies. Thus, the coordination of RTA members' policies is crucial to its success. Changes in trade preferences have the ability to transfer investment into or away from member countries which will affect development (Pomfret 1997, pp. 203–4). The effects on the rest of the world will depend on the change in investment and also changes in the productivity of the investment. The evaluation of a RTA's effects should include the dynamic effects on development and trade with all partners (Laird 1999, p. 1188). Trade and macroeconomic arrangements resulting from a RTA can directly influence investment and development in member and non-member countries, emphasizing the importance of their effective use.

RTAs AND THE WTO

While theories dealing with the effects of RTAs on economic development remain inconclusive, a second area of interest has emerged – where do RTAs fit into the multilateral free trade goal of the World Trade Organization (WTO), or as Bhagwati (1991, p. 77) succinctly puts it, 'are RTAs building blocks or stumbling blocks for multilateral free trade?' The General Agreement on Tariffs and Trade (GATT) provides the foundation for this argument. The aim of GATT is non-discrimination in trade amongst members – that is, all members are to grant each other Most Favoured Nation (MFN) status. From this definition it would seem that RTAs are prone to the violation of Article I of GATT. There are, however, three conditions that allow for trade preferences: (a) developed countries can give developing countries one way trade preferences; (b) developing countries can effectively give each other any trade preferences; and, (c) Article XXIV of the WTO allows the formation of FTAs or CUs (Panagariya 2000, pp. 288–9). Thus Article XXIV is the only way that a developed country can obtain trade preferences. This provision allows for the exchange of preferences given they are not partial in respect to 'substantially all trade'. The Article also states that 100 per cent of duties and other restrictive policies must be wiped out within ten years (WTO 2006b). These features of the Article are ambiguous and open to interpretation which created the opportunity for RTAs (Bhagwati 1993, p. 23).

Considering that the primary purpose of GATT was multilateral trade liberalization, the presence of Article XXIV seems puzzling. Bhagwati (1993, pp. 25–6) offers three possible motives for its inclusion. First, freedom of trade amongst any subset of GATT members produced an essential component of single nation characteristics, and the benefits of this position allowed the exception to the MFN compulsion. Second, since only 100 per cent reductions in duties were allowed, the possibility of a breakout of RTAs was small. Finally, the succession of FTAs or CUs may be an extra route to global free trade – that is, it may be a building block for free trade. Collier *et al.* (2000, p. 104) are of the view that countries can experience terms of trade deteriorations if they are left outside RTAs. This may lead to non-member countries accelerating their attempts at multilateralism. Multilateral free trade may present greater market security than RTAs by protecting against policy reversals, which can help developing countries attract FDI (Laird 1999, p. 1191).

Due to the substantial tariff cuts achieved using the GATT, barriers to trade have largely become non-tariff based. This movement provides new challenges for the WTO and policy-makers. Technical barriers to trade, competition policy, safeguard measures, anti-dumping, subsidies and countervailing duties and Rules of Origin (ROOs) are all examples of non-tariff based barriers to trade (Cernat and Laird 2005, pp. 74–85). ROOs become particularly important as countries gain membership to multiple RTAs. The resulting crisscrossing nature of ROOs depending on where the item came from has been termed the 'spaghetti bowl' effect by Bhagwati (see Bhagwati *et al.* 1998, pp. 1138–9). Differing ROOs can have negative effects on trade, at least by increasing transaction costs, and by allowing countries the opportunity to use the interplay between multiple RTAs against members and non-members (Crawford and Laird 2001, pp. 198–201). One opportunity cost of the administrative effort required to form thorough RTAs is that less time is available for multilateral negotiations. This is a larger problem for developing countries that face constraints in resources devoted to trade policy (Collier *et al.* 2000, p. 104).

Trends in RTAs

Global

Regionalism was initiated as early as 1958[1] with the entry into force of the European Common Market. Both a customs union and a services agreement were signed at the Treaty of Rome. Ethier (1998, p. 1150) observed that it might have occurred due to the failings of multilateralism advocated by the GATT at the time. The European Free Trade Association (EFTA) involving Iceland, Liechtenstein, Norway and the Swiss Confederation followed the European Community (EC) and came into force in 1960. Regionalism crossed the Atlantic when the Central American Common Market was implemented in 1961. This agreement was a customs union involving Guatemala, El Salvador, Honduras and Nicaragua. Whilst these four agreements involved many countries, regionalism did not catch on and these were the only agreements brought into force between 1961 and 1968. The successful signing of the EC may represent the beginning of 'First Regionalism' (Bhagwati *et al.* 1998, p. 1129) but with the global hegemon, the USA, still subscribing to multilateralism throughout the 1960s, negotiations were halted and regionalism stumbled. Developing countries also attempted to get involved, hoping to exploit economies of scale by opening up to similar markets. This failed as the developing countries used bureaucratic negotiation rather than trade liberalization to allocate industry, taking a narrow focus rather than a G-77 wide view (Bhagwati 1993, p. 28).

The next decade (1968–78) saw 13 agreements brought into force, including six in 1973 alone. This period set the foundations for what was to come in the next 30 years. The period 1978–90 saw only a total of ten agreements brought into action. But with hindsight, this period was the calm before the storm. From 1991 onwards, the emergence of RTAs proceeded at unparalleled rates. This period is often referred to as 'Second or New Regionalism' and this time the USA provided the primary driving force behind the take-off and acceleration of RTAs (Bhagwati 1993, p. 29). Between 1991 and 1996, 30 RTAs that were still in force at 1 November 2005 were completed. Another five years saw 42 agreements signed and from 2001 until November 2005 a staggering 84 agreements were implemented. So, up to 1990, 27 agreements were signed, and in the next 15 years 159 RTAs were executed. Put in the context of the WTO's 149 members, by July 2005, only one of the members was not part of an RTA (Mongolia), a total of 330 Agreements had been reported to the WTO (and previously to GATT) and 206 from the beginning of 1995 (WTO 2006c).[2] The growth of entry into force of RTAs is displayed in Figure 1.1.

Figure 1.1 depicts a world moving increasingly towards regionalism, aided by differences in the world trading environment since the original bout

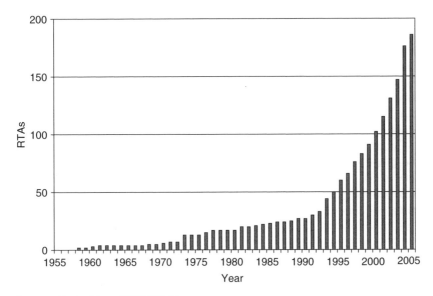

Source: Derived from WTO (2006c).

Figure 1.1   Cumulative totals of RTAs in force at November 2005

of regionalism (Ethier 1998, pp. 1149–50). A number of factors contributed
to the accelerated rate of growth. First, the trade liberalization of manufactured goods was more advanced than in the 1960s, thanks to the GATT
which caused tariff reductions. Second, most of the less developed countries
embraced the multilateral trading system and parted with anti-market
views. Third, and following on from the last point, foreign direct investment
is not only more widespread, but includes developing countries. New
regionalism may present an opportunity for an alternative entry route into
the multilateral system. Whether this is a move that is in favour with the
GATT's objectives is the subject of much debate. We will return to this question after discussing some characteristics of the new regionalism movement.

The second wave of regionalism has increased focus on institutional
coordination, along with the conventional increased trade in goods and services. This dynamism towards deeper economic integration sees RTAs
resulting in not only reduction of tariffs, but also coordination of other
economic policies, for example common legislation and standards relating
to environmental, industrial and social policies (de Melo *et al.* 1993,
pp. 176–7). This is one of the attractions of contemporary regionalism; the
ability to cover a broader range of issues and achieve more success than is
possible at the multilateral level. New regionalism also contains rather
reserved liberalization. Tariffs are likely to be lowered by only a small

proportion and certain sectors (for example agriculture) excluded all together (Ethier 1998, pp. 1150–2). Also the new wave has often brought one or more small countries together with a larger one, reflecting perhaps the importance of guaranteed market access for smaller countries. Returning to another of the motives behind RTAs, small countries that have made significant domestic reforms are regularly part of new regionalism. These countries may be hoping to attract foreign direct investment in order to become part of the multilateral trading system.

Ethier (1998, p. 1161) argues that regionalism plays a transitory role in the movement towards multilateralism. The next step in this process is crucial as these Agreements have a long timeframe. The relationship between regionalism and multilateralism raises many questions, not least being, 'Is regionalism an alternative or positive supplement to multilateralism?' Bhagwati (1993, pp. 31–3) poses two crucial questions: (a) what is the immediate impact of regionalism on world welfare? and, (b) will regionalism lead to non-discriminatory multilateral free trade by expansion of the regional blocs, or segment the world economy? Answers to the first, static question are best approached using Vinerian trade creation/trade diversion theory as discussed earlier. The dynamic time-path question asks whether regional trading blocs will move the world towards freer trade, and even accelerate this movement past what negotiations can offer. Those in the affirmative have grown impatient with multilateral negotiations and cite the 'free-rider' problem created by increasing WTO member countries as a major dilemma (Summers 1991, p. 301). Bhagwati (1993, pp. 40–3) counters this and other arguments, and uses the example of the slow transition of the European Community and the poor treatment of agricultural trade liberalization, to make his point.

Asia-Pacific region
RTAs play an important part in the opening of economies to international trade flows. The Asia-Pacific region presents a unique opportunity to study the effects of economic openness on development in a range of economies. International openness can lead to improved efficiency in resource allocation stemming from increased market access, which stimulates competition and expands product choice. Also technology and production knowledge can be transferred which leads to productivity gains. Frankel and Romer (1999) found a positive link between trade and income – an increase of 1 per cent in the trade to GDP ratio leads to a minimum half per cent increase in income per person. However, obtaining the benefits of openness is not as simple as liberalizing trade. Baldwin (2003) observes that policy-makers and developing countries often assume that decreasing barriers to trade will automatically lead to economic development. Emphasis must still be

placed on stable domestic policies and exchange rate regimes if the effects of trade liberalization are to be realized in the longer term. For Asia-Pacific economies, continued development and growth in the presence of RTAs will produce a policy challenge.

Because the Asia-Pacific region covers an extremely large area, it is helpful to break it up into smaller bodies. This has already been done with the formation of a number of sub-regions within the region. We will briefly cover three regional bodies: the Association of Southeast Asian Nations (ASEAN), the South Asian Association for Regional Cooperation (SAARC) and the Asia Pacific Economic Cooperation (APEC). Special impetus is given to APEC due to its size and relative influence.

ASEAN was founded in Bangkok on 8 August 1967 with five member countries: Indonesia, Malaysia, Philippines, Singapore and Thailand. It increased in 1984 with the accession of Brunei Darussalam, then with Vietnam in 1995, Laos and Myanmar in 1997 and Cambodia in 1999. Upon establishment of ASEAN, trade amongst members was insignificant, and this formed one of the major motives of the association. Whilst there were a number of potential barriers to the formation of ASEAN, including members' diverse historical, political and social backgrounds, and varying economic objectives resulting from the differing levels of development within ASEAN, the founding nations realized that cooperation and integration could be used to exploit any advantages their geographical proximity presented (Tongzon 1998, pp. 5–6). Also, the growing regionalism and protectionism in the world trading environment presented threats that could best be avoided through integration.

The ASEAN economies shared some common characteristics that aided their union. Tongzon (1998, pp. 13–14) observes that the ASEAN countries are based on market economies and are export orientated, and also share similar economic aspirations such as accelerated growth. Building on this, ASEAN formed two broad objectives: (a) accelerated growth, social progress and cultural development through joint endeavours in the spirit of equality and partnership, in order to strengthen the foundation for a prosperous and peaceful community; and, (b) regional peace and stability through abiding respect for justice and the rule of law (ASEAN 2005). ASEAN's cooperation in trade was enhanced with the establishment of the ASEAN FTA (AFTA) in 1992. It has yielded impressive results; in the first three years after AFTA's enforcement, exports among ASEAN countries grew from US$43.26 billion in 1993 to almost US$80 billion in 1996, an average yearly growth rate of 28.3 per cent (ASEAN 2005). This growth was driven by extensive tariff cuts. The oldest six ASEAN members (Brunei Darussalam, Indonesia, Malaysia, the Philippines, Singapore and Thailand) have brought 99 per cent of tariffs on the Common Effective

Preferential Tariff (CEPT) Scheme products down to between zero and 5 per cent. The other four economies have succeeded in placing 80 per cent of their products on the CEPT inclusion list and 66 per cent of these are in the lowest tariff range (ASEAN 2004). ASEAN has experienced considerable economic dynamism in the past 15 years and the prospect of enhanced cooperation and integration amongst itself and the rest of the world, has positive implications for the region.

SAARC was formalized in Dhaka in 1985. The initiative was first proposed in 1980. The secretaries of the seven member nations (Bangladesh, Bhutan, India, Maldives, Nepal, Pakistan and Sri Lanka) met in 1981. It was argued that the countries' geographical contiguity and historical, social, cultural and ethnic affinities presented a strong case for cooperation. In 1981 it was agreed that cooperation would focus on five broad areas: agriculture, rural development, telecommunications, meteorology, and health and population services. Further, the objectives of SAARC as set out in its charter include:

1. promotion of the welfare and quality of life of the peoples of South Asia;
2. accelerated economic growth, social progress and cultural development;
3. promotion of active collaboration and mutual assistance in economic, social, cultural, technical and scientific fields; strengthened cooperation with other developing countries;
4. increased cooperation amongst members in international forums on matters of common interest; and
5. cooperation with other international and regional organizations with similar objectives.

There are however, some barriers to cooperation within SAARC, not least being the varied stages of development of member countries and tensions between the region's two biggest economies – India and Pakistan. Obviously these are holding SAARC back from achieving its objectives and realizing the gains of further economic integration (Faleiro 2003).

A Preferential Trading Arrangement within SAARC (SAPTA) was completed in 1993 and came into force in 1995. The intent of SAPTA was to give less developed countries special treatment and ensure the benefits of economic liberalization were fairly distributed (SAARC 2006). Also, greater tariff concessions, removal of discriminatory practices and non-tariff barriers, and structural improvements were features of the Arrangement. SAPTA was one step along the path towards securing a Free Trade Area, and the South Asian Free Trade Area (SAFTA) came into force on 1 January 2006. SAFTA takes heed of the varying development stages of members and accordingly gives differing timeframes for tariff reductions. SAFTA is an important step for SAARC as the region may face the possibility of marginalization in the global economy (Faleiro 2003). It may also be a catalyst for increasing intra-regional trade which is low compared with other regional arrangements. Faleiro (2003) reports that intra-regional trade amongst SAARC is at only 5 per cent, whereas it is 62 per cent in the European Union (EU), 55 per cent in NAFTA and 33 per cent in ASEAN. Aggarwal and Pandey (1992) argue that considerable scope exists for intra-regional trade expansion, especially if members' economies continue to be liberalized. Enhanced cooperation and coordination of macroeconomic policies can only add to this and benefit the people in the region. SAARC is also undergoing negotiations with the EU to facilitate access into the large European market, which will present major opportunities for member economies.

APEC's 21 economies are home to more than 2.6 billion people (APEC 2006a). It is a dynamic region with economies at different stages of development and with vastly diverse economic objectives. APEC has been established for 17 years and has quite an impressive record of achievements. It was set up in 1989 in Canberra with 12 members – Australia, Brunei Darussalam, Canada, Indonesia, Japan, Korea, Malaysia, New Zealand, the Philippines, Singapore, Thailand and the USA. In 1991 the People's Republic of China, Hong Kong, China and Chinese Taipei joined, Mexico and Papua New Guinea in 1993, Chile in 1994 and Peru, Russia and Vietnam in 1998. APEC acts as a forum for negotiation, discussion and decision making, without any legally binding requirements on members. The forum functions as a vehicle for achieving APEC's goals and visions which were created in 1989 and have been added to since.

The initial objectives developed by the founding members were: to promote economic growth; develop and strengthen the multilateral trading system; and, increase the interdependence and prosperity of member economies (APEC 2005b, p. 3). These goals were furthered in 1994 at Bogor, Indonesia. Remembering the diversity of member economies, the leaders developed two distinct timeframes for free and open trade and investment. Developed economies were set the goal of achieving this by 2010 and developing economies by 2020. Again there are no legal requirements of this agreement for member economies. The Bogor goals were based on the open regionalism principle of extending tariff cuts to both APEC members and non-members. Open regionalism is not discriminatory towards non-members and is expected to bring greater benefits to the globe (Tang 2001, p. 64). Vamvakidis (1999, p. 44) concurs and suggests that economies should first attempt to open up multilaterally before taking the regionalism route. Substantial welfare gains are possible using RTAs, but non-members are adversely affected, and these gains are not as significant as those realized under multilateralism (Bora *et al.* 2001, p. 24). Opening up non-discriminately leads to accelerated growth and additional FDI. If one agrees with this view, then the idea of an APEC-wide FTA is a promising one. Considering the formation of APEC was partly in response to increasing interdependency between Asia-Pacific economies, and intra-APEC trade has increased since its inception, free trade could continue to bring the economies closer and strengthen the bloc's power (Tang 2001, pp. 64–6). Moreover, there is evidence that APEC members are progressively integrating further with the European Community, the largest trading bloc in the world (Dent 1998).

Global free trade could well be a realistic prospect if the two largest blocs in the world were to join forces. Even the potential for an APEC-wide FTA and the associated loss of export competitiveness for non-members may act as a 'wake up call' for multilateral negotiations (Wang and Coyle 2002, p. 564). Bora, Gilbert and Scollay (2001, p. 25) are of the view that while multilateralism is the best outcome for the world, APEC's open regionalism may provide the vehicle for finally reaching it. This may certainly be the case if non-members have an incentive to liberalize their own trade policies to remain competitive with members (Wang and Coyle 2002, p. 568). As a result of APEC's dedication to freer trade amongst members and non-members, the group broadly focuses on three main areas: trade and investment liberalization; business liberalization; and, economic and technical cooperation (APEC 2005b, p. 5).

APEC's 21 member economies have displayed impressive economic dynamism since the formation of the forum. While the region accounts for over one-third of the world's population, it produces 57 per cent of world GDP and is involved in over 45 per cent of trade (APEC 2005b, 2006a). Most remarkably however, the region was responsible for almost 70 per cent of global economic growth in its first ten years (1989–99) despite the Asian economic crisis of 1997. This value fell slightly to 61 per cent for the period 1989–2003. These excellent figures suggest APEC is doing something right. This is confirmed by delving deeper into their actions and results. APEC has been successful in reducing trade barriers – average tariffs have declined from 16.6 per cent in 1988 to 6.4 per cent in 2004, non-tariff based barriers have been transformed into tariff based, and investment barriers have diminished (AusAid, CIE and DFAT 2005, pp. 2–10). APEC economies have embraced international trade with exports of goods and services increasing from 13.8 per cent of GDP in 1989 to 18.5 per cent in 2003. FDI also benefited from this openness and grew by 210 per cent throughout the region and by 475 per cent in the lower income member economies (APEC 2006b). This culminated in real GDP in the region growing at 46 per cent and per capita at 26 per cent, from 1989–2003. This has led to the proportion of the APEC population living in poverty being reduced by 60 per cent since 1990 (AusAid, CIE and DFAT 2005, p. 27). These major benefits achieved by APEC are only contrasted by its failure to dismantle barriers in troublesome sectors such as textiles, clothing, motor vehicles and agriculture. Tariffs in these sectors still remain above average due to the high tariffs present at APEC's introduction, political sensitivity and labour intensity (AusAid, CIE and DFAT 2005, pp. 9–10). Nonetheless the significant advancements made by the APEC economies' in the last 17 years are profound. Since these have largely emanated from an increased degree of economic openness, the proliferation of RTAs has the potential to instigate further development, especially if they can target problematic sectors.

RTAs are still relatively young in the Asia-Pacific region, but they have experienced similar growth as has been seen globally.

Figure 1.2 shows that the growth rate of RTAs in the Asia-Pacific region was positive and fairly stable from 1973–2001. From this point RTAs grew at a much larger rate, with a maximum of ten signed in 2004. Tables A1.1 and A1.2 (Appendix 1.1), enhance the detail somewhat and break down the RTAs to those within the Asia-Pacific region and those involving non-members.

The first agreement involving Asia-Pacific countries occurred in 1973 with the implementation of the Protocol Relating to Trade Negotiations

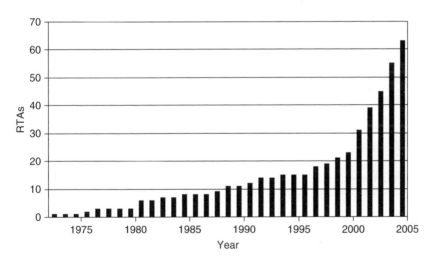

Source: Derived from WTO (2006a) and APEC (2006c).

Figure 1. 2   Cumulative totals of RTAs in force at November 2005 and involving at least one member of APEC

among Developing Countries (PTN). Members in this preferential arrangement included Bangladesh, Brazil, Chile, Egypt, Israel, Mexico, Pakistan, Paraguay, Peru, Philippines, Korea, Romania, Tunisia, Turkey, Uruguay and Yugoslavia. In 1976 a second preferential arrangement was negotiated involving Bangladesh, India, Korea and Sri Lanka, referred to as the Bangkok Agreement. This was closely followed seven months later by the Papua New Guinea–Australia Trade and Commercial Relations Agreement (PATCRA), a free trade agreement under Article XXIV, first signed on 6 November 1976 and updated on 21 February 1991. The third column of Tables A1.1 and A1.2, show that there are only three types of arrangements in force at present that involve Asia-Pacific countries – free trade agreements, services agreements and preferential arrangements. Within the Asia-Pacific region there are only two types of agreements, free trade and services, while the three types are present amongst the region and non-region agreements. FTAs account for 44 per cent of all agreements, services agreements 39 per cent and preferential arrangements 17 per cent. No customs unions, FTAs with common external tariffs, are present at all.

The Asia-Pacific region can benefit greatly from further economic integration if members' heterogeneity is recognized and embraced. The positives of openness grow when integration includes economies specializing in different sectors and enjoying varying technological advantages. The challenge for the Asia-Pacific region lies in effective policy-making, which will allow the gains to be realized.

> The slogan for APEC 2004 adopted by Chile, 'One Community, Our Future,' signals that in spite of our great diversity in cultural, social and political matters and our differing levels of development, APEC's Member Economies must work together as partners to advance towards a community based on sustainable development. *(Chilean Foreign Minister Maria Soledad Alvear V., March 2004 (APEC 2005a))*

NOTES

1. This chapter considers only those agreements still in force today.
2. These figures include Agreements that are not in force today.

REFERENCES

Abrego, L., R. Riezman and J. Whalley (2005), 'Computation and the theory of customs unions', *CESifo Economic Studies*, **51** (1), 117–32.
Aggarwal, M.R. and P.R. Pandey (1992), 'Prospects of trade expansion in the SAARC region', *Developing Economies*, **30** (1), 3–23.

APEC (2005a), *Outcomes and Outlook 2004 | 2005*, APEC. Available at: www.apec.org/content/apec/publications/free_downloads/2005.html.
APEC (2005b), *APEC at a Glance*, APEC. Available at: www.apec.org/content/apec/publications/free_downloads/2005.html.
APEC (2006a), 'Fact Sheets', www.apec.org/apec/news_media/fact_sheets/about_apec.html, 19 January.
APEC (2006b), 'Achievements and Benefits', www.apec.org/content/apec/about_apec/achievements_and_benefits.html, 19 January.
APEC (2006c), 'Member economies' FTA/RTA information', http://www.apec.org/webapps/fta_rta_information.html, 20 January.
ASEAN (2004), 'Trade', www.aseansec.org/12021.htm, 27 January.
ASEAN (2005), 'Overview', www.aseansec.org/64.htm, 27 January.
Australian Government Department of Foreign Affairs and Trade (DFAT), AusAID, Centre for International Economics (CIE) (2005), *Open Economies Delivering to People, 2005*, Canberra: Commonwealth of Australia.
Baldwin, R.E. (2003), 'Openness and growth: what's the Empirical Relationship?', *NBER Working Paper 9578*.
Bhagwati, J. (1991), *The World Trading System at Risk*, Princeton, NJ: Princeton University Press.
Bhagwati, J. (1993), 'Regionalism and multilateralism: an overview', in J. De Melo, and A. Panagariya (eds), *New Dimensions in Regional Integration*, Cambridge, New York and Melbourne, Australia: Cambridge University Press, pp. 22–51.
Bhagwati, J., D. Greenaway and A. Panagariya (1998), 'Trading preferentially: theory and policy', *The Economic Journal*, **108** (449), 1128–48.
Bora, B., J. Gilbert and R. Scollay (2001), 'Assessing regional trading agreements in the Asia-Pacific', UNCTAD/ITCD, Study Series No. 15.
Cernat, L. and S. Laird (2005), 'North, South, East, West: what's best? Modern RTAs and their implications for the stability of trade policy', in Z. Drabek, (ed.), *Can Regional Integration Arrangements Enforce Trade Discipline? The Story of the EU Enlargement*, Hampshire, UK and New York, US: Palgrave Macmillan, pp. 69–95.
Collier, P., M. Schiff, A. Venables and L.A. Winters (2000), *Trading Blocs*, New York, US: Oxford University Press for The World Bank.
Crawford, J.-A. and R.V. Fiorentino (2005), *The Changing Landscape of Regional Trade Agreements*, Geneva, World Trade Organization.
Crawford, J.-A. and S. Laird (2001), 'Regional trade agreements and the WTO', *North American Journal of Economics and Finance*, **12** (2001), 193–211.
de Melo, J. and A. Panagariya (1993), 'Introduction', in *New Dimensions in Regional Integration*, Cambridge, UK and New York, US: Cambridge University Press, pp. 3–21.
de Melo, J., A. Panagariya and D. Rodrik (1993), 'The new regionalism: a country perspective', in de Melo, J. and A. Panagariya (eds), *New Dimensions in Regional Integration*, Cambridge, New York and Melbourne, Australia: Cambridge University Press, pp.159–93.
Dent, C.M. (1998), 'Regionalism in Southeast Asia: opportunities and threats for the European Union', *European Business Review*, **98** (4), 184–95.
Drabek, Z. (2005), 'An alternative overview of regionalism', in *Can Regional Integration Arrangements Enforce Trade Discipline? The Story of the EU Enlargement*, Hampshire, UK and New York, US: Palgrave Macmillan, pp. 19–68.
Ethier, J.W. (1998), 'The new regionalism', *The Economic Journal*, **108** (449), 1149–61.

Faleiro, E. (2003), *The Secret to South Asian Success*, Asia Times Online. Available from: www.atimes.com/atimes/South_Asia/FC04Df03.html.

Frankel, J.A. and D. Romer (1999), 'Does trade cause growth?', *American Economic Review*, **89** (3), 379–99.

Hatta, T. and T. Fukushima (1979), 'The welfare effect of tariff rate reductions in a many country world', *Journal of International Economics*, **9** (4), 503–11.

Johnson, H.G. (1967), *Economic Policies Toward Less Developed Countries*, Washington, DC: The Brookings Institution.

Kennan, J. and R. Riezman (1990), 'Optimal tariff equilibria with customs unions', *Canadian Journal of Economics*, **23** (1), 70–83.

Kowalczyk, C. (ed.) (1999), *Economic Integration and International Trade*, International Library of Critical Writings in Economics. Cheltenham, UK and Northampton, MA, US: Edward Elgar.

Laird, S. (1999), 'Regional trade agreements: dangerous liaisons?', *World Economy*, **22** (9), 1179–200.

Lipsey, R. and K. Lancaster (1956), 'The general theory of second best', *Review of Economic Studies*, **24**, 11–32.

Meade, J.E. (1955), *The Theory of Customs Unions*, Amsterdam: North-Holland.

Panagariya, A. (2000), 'Preferential trade liberalization: the traditional theory and new developments', *Journal of Economic Literature*, **38** (2), 287–311.

Pomfret, R. (1997), *The Economics of Regional Trading Arrangements*, Oxford, UK: Clarendon Press.

SAARC (2006), *Regional Economic Cooperation*, SAARC. Available from: www.saarc-sec.org/main.php?id=43&t=3.2.

Summers, L.H. (1991), 'Regionalism and the world trading system', in *Policy Implications of Trade and Currency Zones*, Kansas City, MO: Federal Reserve Bank of Kansas City, pp. 295–301.

Tang, D. (2001), 'The potential of the APEC grouping to promote intra-regional trade in the Asia-Pacific region', *Journal of Applied Business Research*, **17** (4), 63–8.

Tongzon, J.L. (1998), *The Economies of Southeast Asia*, Cheltenham, UK and Lyme, US: Edward Elgar.

Vamvakidis, A. (1999), 'Regional trade agreements or broad liberalization: which leads to faster growth?', *IMF Staff Papers*, **46** (1), 42–68.

Vanek, J. (1964), 'Unilateral trade liberalization and global world income', *Quarterly Journal of Economics*, **78**, 139–47.

Viner, J. (1950), *The Customs Union Issue*, New York: Carnegie Endowment for International Peace.

Wang, Z. and B. Coyle (2002), 'APEC open regionalism and its impact on the world economy: a computable general equilibrium analysis', *World Economy*, **25** (4), 563–89.

Whalley, J. (1998), 'Why do countries seek regional trade agreements?', in J.A. Frankel (ed.), *The Regionalization of the World Economy*, Chicago and London: NBER Project Report series, University of Chicago Press, pp. 63–83.

WTO (2006a), 'Regional trade agreements: facts and figures', www.wto.org/english/tratop_e/region_e/regfac_e.htm, 20 January.

WTO (2006b), 'Regional trade agreements – GATT Article XXIV', www.wto.org/english/tratop_e/region_e/region_art24_e.htm, 23 January.

WTO (2006c), 'Regional trade agreements', www.wto.org/english/tratop_e/region_e/region_e.htm, 23 January.

APPENDIX 1.1

Table A1.1   RTAs between Asia-Pacific countries

Agreement	Date of entry	Type of Agreement	Countries Involved
Japan–Mexico	1-Apr-05	Free trade agreement	Japan, Mexico
Japan–Mexico	1-Apr-05	Services agreement	Japan, Mexico
Thailand–Australia	1-Jan-05	Free trade agreement	Thailand, Australia
Thailand–Australia	1-Jan-05	Services agreement	Thailand, Australia
US–Australia	1-Jan-05	Free trade agreement	USA, Australia
US–Australia	1-Jan-05	Services agreement	USA, Australia
China–Hong Kong, China	1-Jan-04	Free trade agreement	China, Hong Kong, China
China–Hong Kong, China	1-Jan-04	Services agreement	China, Hong Kong, China
United States–Singapore	1-Jan-04	Free trade agreement	United States, Singapore
United States–Singapore	1-Jan-04	Services agreement	United States, Singapore
United States–Chile	1-Jan-04	Free trade agreement	United States, Chile
United States–Chile	1-Jan-04	Services agreement	United States, Chile
Singapore–Australia	28-Jul-03	Services agreement	Singapore, Australia
Singapore–Australia	28-Jul-03	Free trade agreement	Singapore, Australia
Japan–Singapore	30-Nov-02	Services agreement	Japan, Singapore
Japan–Singapore	30-Nov-02	Free trade agreement	Japan, Singapore
India–Sri Lanka	15-Dec-01	Free trade agreement	India, Sri Lanka
New Zealand–Singapore	1-Jan-01	Free trade agreement	New Zealand, Singapore
New Zealand–Singapore	1-Jan-01	Services agreement	New Zealand, Singapore
Chile–Mexico	1-Aug-99	Services agreement	Chile, Mexico
Chile–Mexico	1-Aug-99	Free trade agreement	Chile, Mexico
Canada–Chile	5-Jul-97	Services agreement	Canada, Chile
Canada–Chile	5-Jul-97	Services agreement	Canada, Chile
Canada–Israel	1-Jan-97	Free trade agreement	Canada, Israel
CER	1-Jan-89	Services agreement	Australia, New Zealand
NAFTA	1-Apr-94	Services agreement	US, Canada, Mexico
NAFTA	1-Jan-94	Free trade agreement	US, Canada, Mexico
CER	1-Jan-83	Free trade agreement	Australia, New Zealand
PATCRA	1-Feb-77	Free trade agreement	Australia, Papua New Guinea

Source: WTO (2006a) and APEC (2006c).

Table A1.2   RTAs between Asia-Pacific countries and other countries

Agreement	Date of entry	Type of Agreement	Countries Involved
EC–Chile	1-Mar-05	Services agreement	European Community, Chile
EFTA–Chile	1-Dec-04	Free trade agreement	Iceland, Liechtenstein, Norway, Swiss Confederation, Chile
EFTA–Chile	1-Dec-04	Services agreement	Iceland, Liechtenstein, Norway, Swiss Confederation, Chile
China–Macao, China	1-Jan-04	Free trade agreement	China, Macao, China
China–Macao, China	1-Jan-04	Services agreement	China, Macao, China
ASEAN–China	1-Jul-03	Preferential arrangement	ASEAN, China
EC–Chile	1-Feb-03	Free trade agreement	European Community, Chile
EFTA–Singapore	1-Jan-03	Services agreement	Iceland, Liechtenstein, Norway, Swiss Confederation, Singapore
EFTA–Singapore	1-Jan-03	Free trade agreement	Iceland, Liechtenstein, Norway, Swiss Confederation, Singapore
Canada–Costa Rica	1-Nov-02	Free trade agreement	Canada, Costa Rica
Chile–El Salvador	1-Jun-02	Free trade agreement	Chile, El Salvador
Chile–El Salvador	1-Jun-02	Services agreement	Chile, El Salvador
Bangkok Agreement–Accession of China	1-Jan-02	Preferential arrangement	Bangladesh, India, Lao PDR, Korea, Sri Lanka, China
United States–Jordan	17-Dec-01	Services agreement	US, Jordan
EC–Mexico	1-Mar-01	Services agreement	European Community, Mexico
Chile–Costa Rica	15-Feb-02	Services agreement	Chile, Costa Rica
Chile–Costa Rica	15-Feb-02	Free trade agreement	Chile, Costa Rica
United States–Jordan	17-Dec-01	Free trade agreement	US, Jordan
EFTA–Mexico	1-Jul-01	Free trade agreement	Iceland, Liechtenstein, Norway, Swiss Confederation, Mexico
EFTA–Mexico	1-Jul-01	Services agreement	Iceland, Liechtenstein, Norway, Swiss Confederation, Mexico
Israel–Mexico	1-Jul-00	Free trade agreement	Israel, Mexico

Table A1.2   (continued)

Agreement	Date of entry	Type of Agreement	Countries Involved
EC–Mexico	1-Jul-00	Free trade agreement	European Community, Mexico
Mexico–Nicaragua	1-Jul-98	Services agreement	Mexico, Nicaragua
Mexico–Nicaragua	1-Jul-98	Free trade agreement	Mexico, Nicaragua
MSG	22-Jul-93	Preferential arrangement	Fiji, Papua New Guinea, Solomon Islands, Vanuatu
AFTA	28-Jan-92	Preferential arrangement	Brunei Darussalam, Cambodia, Indonesia, Laos, Malaysia, Myanmar, Philippines, Singapore, Thailand, Vietnam. (ASEAN)
Laos–Thailand	20-Jun-91	Preferential arrangement	Laos, Thailand
GSTP	19-Apr-89	Preferential arrangement	Algeria, Argentina, Bangladesh, Benin, Bolivia, Brazil, Cameroon, Chile, Colombia, Cuba, Democratic People's Republic of Korea, Ecuador, Egypt, Ghana, Guinea, Guyana, India, Indonesia, Iran, Iraq, Libya, Malaysia, Mexico, Morocco, Mozambique, Myanmar, Nicaragua, Nigeria, Pakistan, Peru, Philippines, Republic of Korea, Romania, Singapore, Sri Lanka, Sudan, Thailand, Trinidad and Tobago, Tunisia, Tanzania, Venezuela, Vietnam, Yugoslavia, Zimbabwe.
CAN	25-May-88	Preferential arrangement	Bolivia, Columbia, Ecuador, Peru, Venezuela
United States–Israel	19-Aug-85	Free trade agreement	US, Israel
LAIA	18-Mar-81	Preferential arrangement	Argentina, Bolivia, Brazil, Chile, Columbia, Cuba, Ecuador, Mexico, Paraguay, Peru, Uruguay, Venezuela

Table A1.2 (continued)

Agreement	Date of entry	Type of Agreement	Countries Involved
SPARTECA	1-Jan-81	Preferential arrangement	Cook Islands, the Federated States of Micronesia, Fiji, Kiribati, Marshall Islands, Nauru, Niue, Papua New Guinea, Solomon Islands, Tonga, Tuvalu, Vanuatu, Western Samoa, Australia, New Zealand
Bangkok Agreement	17-Jun-76	Preferential arrangement	Bangladesh, India, Korea, Lao PDR, Sri Lanka
PTN	11-Feb-73	Preferential arrangement	Bangladesh, Brazil, Chile, Egypt, Israel, Mexico, Pakistan, Paraguay, Peru, Philippines, Korea, Romania, Tunisia, Turkey, Uruguay, Yugoslavia

Source: WTO (2006a) and APEC (2006c).

PART II

Regionalism: the World Trade Organization and the exchange rate

2. Preferential trade agreements and the role and goals of the World Trade Organization

Andrew L. Stoler

INTRODUCTION

Notwithstanding an ongoing multilateral trade negotiation in the World Trade Organization's (WTO) Doha Round, the world in 2006 is witnessing an unprecedented degree of activity related to the negotiation and implementation of Preferential Trade Agreements (PTAs).[1] In the time since the launch of the Doha Round, Australia – long seen as one of the most ardent backers of the General Agreement on Tariffs and Trade (GATT) and WTO – has negotiated and agreed on PTAs with Singapore, Thailand and the United States. Canberra has embarked on PTA negotiations with China, Malaysia and the UAE and, together with New Zealand, is negotiating a PTA with ASEAN's AFTA group. And Australia's pace of PTA activity, while impressive, pales in comparison with that of the United States. As of mid-2006, Washington is simultaneously negotiating PTA's with member countries of the Andean Group, Southern Africa Customs Union (SACU), Malaysia, Korea, Panama and the UAE (negotiations with Thailand started but are now suspended). In the past two years, the American Congress has approved PTAs with Australia, Morocco, Bahrain, the Central American Common Market and the Dominican Republic. And the United States has not given up in its now-stalled effort to negotiate a PTA encompassing nearly all of the countries of the Western Hemisphere. Japan and Mexico have concluded a PTA, as have Korea and Chile. Singapore and Panama are exploring a deal. The European Union is in active negotiations on a PTA with Mercosur. Little wonder why, in the face of this activity, a number of commentators have speculated that at least some of the blame for the WTO Round's slow progress should be ascribed to the enthusiasm key WTO Members are showing for PTA negotiations.

This chapter will examine aspects of both the economic and political interface between the WTO and PTAs. It will try to answer the questions of why PTAs are negotiated, what benefits they might produce relative to the WTO's multilateral system and whether PTAs complement or undermine the WTO trading system.

RECENT HISTORY OF PTAs

Notwithstanding the fact that the GATT included rules governing the establishment of PTAs for decades, only a very limited number of PTAs were actually negotiated and implemented prior to 1990. Many of the earlier PTAs were connected in some way with the European Communities, although Australia and New Zealand had Closer Economic Relations (CER) and the United States had entered into PTAs with Israel and with Canada. Putting the USA–Israel agreement to one side, most of the early PTAs were agreements involving neighbouring countries.

The number of PTAs notified to the WTO jumped importantly in the 1990–4 period, when 29 new PTAs were recorded (WTO 2003a, p. 47). Recalling that the Uruguay Round of WTO negotiations fell onto hard times following the disastrous 1990 Brussels ministerial meeting, it is possible that this surge in PTAs reflected to some degree a dissatisfaction with the GATT Round. Certainly, Washington's decision to pursue North American Free Trade Agreement (NAFTA) negotiations with Canada and Mexico and the United States' emphasis on APEC as a forum for trade liberalization were motivated to some degree by the feeling that GATT had slowed and that the 'bicycle of trade liberalization'[2] had to move forward by alternative means. The break-up of the former Soviet Union and the demise of the COMECON system also helps to explain the rise in PTAs in the 1990s as many of the newly independent transition economies sought to re-establish their trade links with former trade partners.

The successful conclusion of the Uruguay Round in 1993 and the entry into force of the new WTO system in 1995 were widely (and correctly) seen as a triumph of multilateralism and a vindication of the international trading system. The year 1996 saw agreement on the Informational Technology Agreement and the launch at Singapore of an impressive WTO work programme on some cutting edge issues. The following year, WTO Members concluded two new high visibility multilateral services agreements dealing with basic telecommunications services and financial services. Notwithstanding all of this successful multilateral activity, the number of PTA's recorded in the 1995–9 period grew by an additional 64 agreements, although 28 of these new PTAs were between the transition economies (WTO 2003a, p. 47).

More recently, South–South agreements have accounted for a much larger percentage of the new PTAs notified to the WTO, particularly in the period after 2000. In just three years (2000 through 2002), the world witnessed a 55 per cent growth in the number of PTAs between developing countries (WTO 2003a, p. 47). In its World Trade Report 2003, the WTO Secretariat estimated that, in addition to the 176 PTAs notified and in force, 70 PTAs were in force but not notified to the WTO and an equal number were under active negotiation (WTO 2003a, p. 46).

EXPLANATIONS FOR THE PROLIFERATION OF PTAs

Characteristics of the WTO System

There are a number of political and economic explanations that can be developed for the growth in the number of PTAs in recent years. Some of these explanations are more convincing than others. Because many of the explanations for PTAs relate in some way to actual or perceived failings of the multilateral system of the WTO, we can usefully spend some time here examining the institutional and other difficulties inherent in the WTO system.

Without any doubt, decision-making in WTO can be problematic, but WTO decision-making was purposefully made difficult by those who negotiated the Uruguay Round Agreement Establishing the World Trade Organization because they did not want to see decisions taken easily or lightly that might undercut the results of the Round or undermine the sovereignty of important trading nations. While the WTO Agreement contains many provisions addressed to decision-making by voting, it enshrines consensus[3] as the practice to be followed in all cases and permits recourse to voting only where a consensus cannot be achieved. Relying on consensus means important decisions, such as the initiation of trade liberalizing negotiations, are often problematic. If it is prepared to block consensus, tiny St Lucia has a power equivalent to the United States.

So decision-making to progress trade liberalization in the WTO requires arriving at a point where none of the WTO's members will oppose the negotiation. This is where we encounter another problem endemic to today's WTO – the very nature of its membership. The WTO of today includes scores of members that taken together cannot account for even 1 per cent of global trade. If trade is not yet an important element in these countries' international relations, it is much harder for trade-minded countries to persuade or cajole them into cooperating with a forward-looking trade agenda. The problem is, of course, aggravated by these WTO members' low capacity to participate actively in either the negotiations or in subsequent implementation of negotiated results.

A final aspect of the WTO system that is worth touching on at this point in this chapter is the WTO approach to regulating departures from the global non-discrimination rules through PTAs. Ideally, participants in a global system based on non-discrimination should not be able to introduce discrimination through a PTA unless they have some fairly good reasons to do so. On the face of it, the WTO Agreement supposes that a fairly good reason to depart from non-discrimination is the objective of setting up broader and deeper liberalization than is possible under the GATT and GATS. In order to make sure that the PTA partners are being honest about their stated objectives, GATT requires elimination of duties on substantially all of the trade between the partners and GATS mandates' substantial sectoral coverage. If two or more countries notifying a PTA to the WTO cannot satisfy these thresholds, then they don't have a legitimate PTA justifying the introduction of discriminatory treatment against other WTO Members. The problem is, the WTO system – which is supposed to operate through review and analysis of notified PTAs in the Committee on Regional Trade Agreements (CRTA) – doesn't work. No examination reports have been finalized or adopted for any PTA negotiated and notified to the WTO since the WTO was established in 1995. We will return to this issue later in this chapter. For now, and as a practical matter, this means that countries negotiating PTAs need not concern themselves with the possibility that their arrangement might not pass muster under WTO. If you don't have to be particularly worried about satisfying WTO criteria, why not negotiate a PTA?[4]

'THIRD WAVE'[5] PTAs

A fourth characteristic of WTO is its more limited scope and coverage. The original GATT rules for PTAs were written at a time when the system focused on tariffs and where non-tariff measures that were covered by the rules were nearly always measures that kicked in at the border. The Uruguay Round changed this focus rather importantly as many of the agreements in the new WTO system amounted to a 'second wave' in the system's scope – moving to behind the border regulatory issues addressed to health and safety standards, prudential regulation, conformity assessment procedures, government procurement and a host of other trade-related measures not covered by the GATT.

Probably a majority of recent PTAs – at least those involving at least one developed country partner – are 'third wave' PTAs, the scope of which extends not only to GATT and WTO-era disciplines but also to areas not yet covered in the WTO system. Typically, the agreements include chapters on investment protection and right of establishment, competition policy (with competition policy in some cases replacing recourse to antidumping between the parties), government procurement (today still only a plurilateral agreement in the WTO), environmental protection and, in the case of agreements involving the USA, a chapter on respect for labour standards. Intellectual property provisions in the agreements tend to be more extensive and updated relative to the WTO Trade-Related Aspects of Intellectual Property Rights (TRIPS) Agreement. It is often also the case that the trade in services chapters of these third wave PTAs are based on a top-down negative list approach that can be far more extensive in its liberalizing effect than the bottom-up approach of the GATS.

Some PTAs included 'third wave' provisions before the WTO even included 'second wave' rules. NAFTA addressed intellectual property rights, investment, labour and the environment. The Australia–New Zealand CER broke important new ground with its competition policy provisions. Investment, competition policy, government procurement and intellectual property are all important issues for many in the business community and if the business community is pressing government to secure improved access or rules in these areas in overseas markets, that improvement is not going to be possible – at least in the near-term – through the WTO. Today's limited scope of the WTO's coverage is another important incentive driving the negotiation of PTAs.

POLITICAL PTAs

Naturally enough, economic considerations are not the only factors that come into play when PTAs are negotiated. If the motivation for an agreement is essentially political, then the WTO's multilateral route is never a feasible alternative. Economic considerations certainly did not drive the negotiation of the USA–Israel, USA–Jordan or USA–Morocco PTAs. The Mercosur agreement linking Brazil, Argentina, Uruguay and Paraguay is another example of a politically motivated agreement (Pena 1997, p. 163).[6] The fact that an agreement has its origins in political considerations does not, of course, mean that it will not have important economic effects. Reciprocal trade between Argentina and Brazil increased eight-fold between 1985 and 1995 and intra-Mercosur trade tripled in the 1990–95 period (Pena 1997, p. 167).

It is evident that there are many reasons why governments today would find it expedient to negotiate trade liberalization through a PTA either:

(a) in place of; (b) prior to; or, (c) in tandem with trade liberalization at the multilateral level of the WTO. The underlying economic and political reasons unique to each PTA would most likely instruct us as to whether the PTA is likely to complement or undermine the multilateral system from an economic standpoint.

ENSURING COMPATIBILITY OF PTAs WITH THE WTO

Apart from considerations of whether the economic effects of PTAs are welfare enhancing and whether the motivations of PTA participants are likely to complement multilateral liberalization efforts in the WTO, there remains the important consideration of ensuring the legal and political compatibility of PTAs with the WTO system.

In 1997, the Carnegie Endowment for International Peace sponsored a report by a study group of eminent persons focused on the interaction of PTAs and the multilateral system (Carnegie Endowment for International Peace 1997).[7] In their report, Study Group members – many of whom had extensive experience in both bilateral and multilateral negotiations – warned that PTAs could have undesirable trade diversion and/or investment diverting effects and that it was therefore desirable for the WTO system to be better equipped to face the challenge of managing compatibility of PTAs with the goals and objectives of the WTO. The Group finished its report with five policy recommendations, most of which contain elements with continued validity today. It can also be seen that many of the concerns expressed by the Study Group and reflected in their 1997 recommendations have found their way into the proposals submitted in the current Doha Round negotiations on the rules governing regional trade arrangements (PTAs). The policy recommendations of the Study Group were the following:

- The WTO should strengthen Article XXIV to provide precise compliance criteria for RTAs, specifically on the following three topics: (a) Most Favoured Nation (MFN) tariffs; (b) rules of origin; and (c) transparency of enforcement.
- As a RTA matures, the trade rules employed by the member countries should be required to converge to a common set of rules. In addition, non-preferential rules of origin should not become more restrictive during the transition period to harmonization.
- The WTO should require that the architecture and accession conditions of RTAs not have the effect of preventing other countries from becoming members.

- The WTO should develop rules to ensure that RTA investment provisions and other investment treaties do not divert investment.
- The WTO should use its institutional structure and procedures to actively promote compatibility between RTAs and the WTO itself.

Although many of the Study Group's recommendations have continued validity, in some cases, the ground has moved under the Group's initial arguments. For example, the Study Group probably had no idea in 1997 just how long the 'transition period to harmonization' would last for the purpose of the rules of origin exercise. In addition, the Group suggested that the WTO should deal with its fourth recommendation by developing an 'Investment Rules Policy Roadmap' that should build on the (ill-fated) OECD Multilateral Agreement on Investment (MAI). The 'Roadmap' would have been complemented by an Investment Policy Review Mechanism as part of the WTO Trade Policy Review Mechanism that would serve two purposes: (1) monitoring actual investment performance; and (2) promoting accession to the MAI (Carnegie Endowment for International Peace 1997, p. 52). It is likely to be some time before the WTO gets around to acting on this recommendation. Not only is the OECD MAI long dead and buried, but it now appears that any negotiation in the WTO on anything like an 'Investment Rules Policy Roadmap' is no longer a potential objective of the current round of negotiations.

The remainder of this paper will focus on current aspects of three of the 1997 Study Group's policy recommendations: the need to strengthen compliance criteria in order to ensure that PTAs are consistent with the rules of the WTO; architecture and accession conditions of PTAs; and, how the WTO might use its institutional structure to promote compatibility between PTAs and the WTO.

STRENGTHENING COMPLIANCE CRITERIA

Although the Rules Group negotiations of the Doha Round are best known for work on provisions bearing on antidumping and countervailing duty laws' operations, the Rules Group is also charged with a mandate to strengthen, clarify and improve the WTO's rules on PTAs and also to make the Committee on Regional Trade Agreements (CRTA) more effective. While a considerable number of proposals have been tabled by a wide range of countries on a large number of substantive and procedural issues, we can illustrate the difficulties associated with the current negotiations by reference to one of the central issues: how to define for the purposes of judging a PTA's legal compatibility with the WTO, the requirement that trade barriers be eliminated on 'substantially all the trade' between the parties. One might be tempted at this stage to say that this should be an intuitive concept – you know it when you see it – but things are far from simple in the CRTA. A note prepared by the WTO Secretariat in August 2002 lays out the complicated debate rather succinctly (WTO Secretariat 2002a, p. 18):

> Despite the inclusion of the fourth paragraph in the Preamble to the 1994 Understanding,[8] the interpretation of that expression ['substantially all the trade'] has remained contentious. Two approaches, not mutually exclusive, are typical in that respect:
>
> - A quantitative approach favours the definition of a statistical benchmark, such as a certain percentage of the trade between RTA parties, to indicate that the coverage of a given RTA fulfils the requirement.
> - A qualitative approach sees the requirement as meaning that no sector (or at least no major sector) is to be kept out of intra-RTA trade liberalization; this approach aims at preventing the exclusion from RTA liberalization of any sector where the restrictive policies in place before the formation of the RTA hindered trade, which could well be the case if a quantitative approach was used.
>
> Apart from calls aimed at defining RTA's coverage as meaning that all sectors should be included, it has been suggested that the above two approaches could be bridged or complemented by:
>
> - Characterizing an RTA's product coverage not only in terms of trade flows but also in terms of a certain percentage of tariff lines:[9]
> - As a refinement to the quantitative approach, calculating the percentage of trade between the parties carried out under RTA rules of origin; and/or
> - Exploring whether footnote 1 to GATS Article V provides a basis for some clarification of the 'substantially all the trade' concept.[10]

Not surprisingly, this core issue of the RTA part of the rules negotiations in the Doha Round has benefited from a number of delegation proposals. Also not surprisingly, negotiators are still some distance from an eventual agreement on this issue as illustrated by a sampling of the proposals received in the Negotiating Group. In its proposal, tabled in document TN/RL/W/15, Australia argues that '"substantially all the trade" should be defined in terms of coverage by a free trade agreement or an agreement establishing a customs union of a defined percentage of all six-digit tariff lines listed in the Harmonized System (HS)' (WTO 2002b, p. 2). Australia further elaborates that 'such a percentage criterion should be established at a sufficiently high level to prevent the carving out of any major sector' (WTO 2002b, p. 2). In document TN/RL/W/32, Turkey argues that 'the qualitative approach which does not permit the exclusion of any sectors, or at least no major sector from the liberalization, is not considered to be in conformity with economic realities' (WTO 2002c, p. 3). India (document TN/RL/W/114) takes the position that 'Members may like to define "substantially all the trade" for the purpose of GATT Article XXIV in terms of both (i) a threshold limit of the HS tariff lines at the six-digit level; and (ii) the trade flows at various stages of implementation of the RTA' (WTO 2003b, p. 2).

If there is anything clear from all of this it is the fact that until such central issues are resolved – in the WTO and through negotiations – the regular machinery of the WTO will remain incapable of addressing the basic legal compatibility of PTAs with the rules of the WTO. There should be a certain urgency to this exercise because – as noted above – if prospective PTA participants start from a presumption (as they would be currently entitled to have) that the consistency of their agreement with the WTO is unlikely to be judged, they will be free to pursue PTAs for the objective of pure discrimination against other members of the WTO – and this could be a very negative thing, both for the health of the WTO and for economic welfare more globally.

PTA ARCHITECTURE AND ACCESSION CONDITIONS

The WTO rules permitting departure from the multilateral non-discrimination framework are essentially justified by the idea that a maximum amount of trade liberalization is good for members and the system and that as a result, the system should not prevent its members from going these extra steps where governments are willing and able to move to 'WTO Plus' levels of liberalization. A consequence of this is reflected in the 1997 Study Group's observations in their third policy recommendation. In essence, a good PTA should permit others to join on the same conditions. This is actually an important point.

Although not couched in exactly the same terms, this point is picked up in the WTO World Trade Report 2003, wherein the WTO Secretariat authors suggest two questions we might ask about any PTA to determine its policy compatibility with the WTO (WTO 2003a, p. 66). The first question we might ask is whether the participants in a particular PTA negotiation have refrained from engaging in regional commitments which they would be unwilling, sooner or later to extend to a multilateral setting. The second question turns on whether the PTA participants would be willing – eventually – to extend the commitments made in the PTA to non-discriminatory multilateral application. If one gets the correct answers to these two questions, then it is a pretty good bet that the PTA at issue will be complementary to the WTO and multilateral trade liberalization.

COMPLEMENTARITY AND COMPATIBILITY BETWEEN PTAs AND WTO

Resolving the issues undermining the current operations of the CRTA is important as a way of ensuring that PTAs are complementary to the WTO. In addition, there is much that can be done outside the strict context of the rules to promote the compatibility of the WTO and PTAs.

We cannot ignore two areas where there is real potential risk of some incompatibility arising out of possible conflict in dispute settlement and distortions associated with treating the same problem in a given market under two different sets of rules, depending on the origin of the product or service. To take the second problem first, if Chile and Canada agree in their PTA not to use antidumping measures against 'dumped' imports from the other party (using competition policy instead) but continue to employ antidumping measures against non-parties to the PTA, it is possible that the government might be pressured to employ the antidumping instrument with anticompetitive effect through a form of discrimination not envisaged by the drafters of the WTO rules governing PTA operations.

The other issue concerns dispute settlement and the unavoidable accumulation over time of jurisprudence on trade disputes. Most modern PTAs have their own internal dispute settlement provisions. Most often, parties to the PTA are able to choose between bilateral and WTO dispute settlement routes where a problem is susceptible to adjudication under either the WTO or the PTA. This is a potentially risky business. While compliance with a WTO obligation can clearly only be judged definitively through the WTO Dispute Settlement Understanding (DSU) and a PTA-only obligation must necessarily go through the agreement's dispute settlement provisions, there is a risk in the overlapping areas that dispute settlement under the WTO or the PTA could produce two different results on the same issue and that could be both politically and economically problematic. Ideally, PTAs should be written so as to exclude adjudication of questions that are clearly in the province of the WTO.

CONCLUSIONS

The world is unlikely to come to a consensus anytime soon on the question of whether or not PTAs assist, complement or undermine the multilateral system of the WTO. Probably no two PTAs are motivated by identical considerations and it is equally likely that no two WTO members would have the same political and economic policy reactions to what might appear to be identical chapters in a modern PTA.

Clearly, we need to do everything that we can to create an effective WTO review of PTA consistency with the multilateral system. The fact that the CRTA process has broken down so completely is a major systemic loophole that needs to be closed – or at a minimum significantly narrowed. Governments should not add to the potential difficulties arising out of the PTA-WTO interface by continuing to be in a position of not being able to say conclusively whether or not a PTA is consistent or not with the rules of the multilateral system.

Finally, motivation and outlook are important in assessing the interaction of PTAs and the multilateral system of the WTO. Here, the two ground rules of policy behaviour suggested by the WTO Secretariat in the 2003 World Trade Report should be seen as particularly helpful in ascertaining whether a particular PTA is likely to complement or undermine the multilateral system. In addition, the policy underlying the doctrine of 'competitive liberalization' can be a valid justification for pursuing PTAs only where the government does not lose sight of what should always be the ultimate objective in trade policy: multilateral liberalization effected through the World Trade Organization.

NOTES

1. The term 'Preferential Trade Agreement' will be used to refer to customs unions, regional trade and economic integration arrangements and bilateral free trade agreements.
2. Fred Bergsten is credited by some with popularization of the bicycle analogy, wherein a failure to keep moving forward with trade liberalization would likely lead to the bicycle falling over and reintroduction of protectionist measures.
3. In the WTO system, consensus should not be interpreted to mean positive unanimity. Rather a consensus is considered to exist where no WTO Member present at the time a decision is taken objects to the proposed decision.
4. There is, of course, still the risk that the PTA, or elements of it, might be judged as to consistency with WTO as a consequence of a dispute settlement action.
5. The term 'Third Wave' PTAs has been used by the Australian Productivity Commission to describe those modern agreements that include provisions addressed to measures and practices not yet addressed in the GATT (first wave) or post-Uruguay Round WTO (second wave).
6. In his chapter 'Some lessons from the MERCOSUR initial experience', Felix Pena (1997, p. 163) writes:

    The strategic objective of this political and economic process between nations of South America has been to create a common regional space in order to strengthen their own domestic efforts towards democracy consolidation, productivity transformation and competitive insertion in the global economy. . . . Therefore it [MERCOSUR] cannot be conceived solely from an economic point of view. On the contrary, although it is a process with economic foundations and contents, it also has a clear political nature and consequences.

7. Members of the Study Group included Jaime Serra, Guillermo Aguilar, Jose Cordoba, Gene Grossman, Carla Hills, John Jackson, Julius Katz, Pedro Noyola and Michael Wilson.
8. 'Recognizing also that such contribution . . . if any major sector of trade is excluded.'
9. A threshold has also been proposed at 95 per cent of all HS tariff lines at the 6-digit level, to be complemented by an assessment of prospective trade flows at various stages of implementation of the RTA, thereby allowing the incorporation of cases where trade is initially concentrated in relatively few products.
10. In referring to the need for Economic Integration Agreements (EIAs) to have substantial sectoral coverage, this footnote reads: 'This condition is understood in terms of number of sectors, volume of trade affected and modes of supply. In order to meet this condition, agreements should not provide for the *a priori* exclusion of any mode of supply.'

REFERENCES

Carnegie Endowment for International Peace (1997), *Reflections on Regionalism – Report of the Study Group on International Trade*, Washington DC: Carnegie Endowment for International Peace.

Pena, F. (1997), 'Some lessons from the MERCOSUR initial experience', in J.-F. Bellis, P. Demaret and G. Garcia Jiménez (eds), *Regionalism and Multilateralism after the Uruguay Round*, Brussels: European Interuniversity Press.

WTO (2002a), 'Negotiating group on rules – compendium of issues related to regional trade agreements – background note by the Secretariat', *WTO Document TN/RL/W/8/Rev1*. Available from: http://docsonline.wto.org/ DDFDocuments/t/tn/rl/W8R1.doc.

WTO (2002b), 'Negotiating group on rules – submission on regional trade agreements by Australia', *WTO Document TN/RL/W/15*. Available from: http://docsonline.wto.org/DDFDocuments/t/tn/rl/W15.doc.

WTO (2002c), 'Negotiating group on rules – paper by Turkey', *WTO Document TN/RL/W/32*. Available from: http://docsonline.wto.org/DDFDocuments/t/tn/rl/W32.doc.

WTO (2003a), *World Trade Report 2003*, Geneva: WTO.

WTO (2003b), 'Negotiating group on rules – discussion paper on regional trading arrangements – communication from India', *WTO Document TN/RL/W/114*. Available from: http://docsonline.wto.org/DDFDocuments/t/tn/rl/W114.doc.

3. Preferential trade agreements and exchange rate regimes

Larry A. Sjaastad

INTRODUCTION

In the written version of a lecture that Robert Mundell (Mundell 2000) delivered at the Universidad del CEMA in Buenos Aires, Argentina, on 17 April 2000, he declares in Part 6 of his lecture:

> What is the relation between free trade areas or customs unions and the exchange rate system? Put somewhat differently, is it possible to achieve the full benefits of a free trade area and at the same time have exchange rates that fluctuate? I will make the argument that free trade areas and currency areas (zones of fixed exchange rates) reinforce one another. [He goes on to say that] uncertainty over exchange rates affects trade directly because it affects profit margins and indirectly because it misdirects investment. Small changes in exchange rates can completely wipe out expected profits.[1]

In this chapter I intend to make points somewhat similar to those of Mundell, but in a rather different context.[2] My main point is that free (or preferential) trading arrangements are best undertaken among economies that constitute an optimum currency area. Mundell's analysis in his seminal article on optimum currency areas in 1961 was in the context of the Bretton Woods international monetary system, in which exchange rates among major (and many minor) currencies were fixed. His conclusion was that an optimum currency area is one in which there was free mobility of factors. Accordingly, the USA and Australia are optimum currency areas, but the euro zone may not be an optimum currency area for an obvious reason; a recent study indicates that 98 per cent of the euro zone members of the labour force are employed in the country of their birth. But would some collection of Asian countries entering into a free trade area constitute an 'optimum' currency area if they chose to have fixed exchange rates among them or even adopted a common currency? The answer is probably no. Even if the member countries have fixed exchange rates *vis à vis* one another or adopt a common currency, they can still experience large changes in their purchasing power parity (PPP) real exchange rates *vis à vis* one another.

The international monetary 'system' that came into being in 1973 has resulted in three major currency areas (North America, Europe and Japan) whose floating currencies have exhibited a great deal of volatility reflected in day-to-day fluctuations as well as in sustained real appreciations and depreciations, particularly during the 1973 to 1985 period. The US dollar has been highly unstable *vis à vis* the yen and the European currencies and, more recently, against the euro. When the euro was introduced in January 1999, the exchange rate was US$1.17 per euro; the euro then depreciated to a rate of US$0.82 and has since appreciated to US$1.30 and, in May 2006, the rate was US$1.28. Many of the minor currency countries of the world continue to peg their currencies in some fashion to a major currency or, in a substantial number of cases, to an existing basket of currencies such as the Special Drawing Right (SDC). That tendency was strengthened in Europe with the creation of the European Exchange Rate Mechanism in the late 1970s and, more recently, with the introduction of the euro. In the western hemisphere, the recent interest in 'dollarization' may lead to an arrangement with effects similar to those in the euro zone.

But in a fundamental sense even the minor currencies that are pegged to a major currency are floating. To attach one currency to another by means of an exchange rate rule is not the same thing when the major currencies are floating as it was under the Bretton Woods fixed exchange rate system. Under the current 'system', with the enormous fluctuations in the major currency exchange rates, fixing one's exchange rate with respect to a single currency (or currency basket) is to float against the rest. Thus one would not expect an exchange rate rule to produce the same results in the post-1973 period as under the Bretton Woods system.

The main emphasis of this chapter will be on the real effects arising from fluctuations in major currency exchange rates; as these real effects are manifested in markets for goods and services, even the minor currency countries experience real shocks as a consequence of fluctuations in the major currency exchange rates, shocks that are transmitted through the prices of internationally traded goods. To the extent that the law of one price holds for internationally traded goods, a change in an exchange rate means that the prices of those goods also must change in at least one currency, and if the major currency countries have significant market power over the international prices of their traded goods, a change in the exchange rate between two major currencies implies that those prices will change in both currencies. The resultant price fluctuations can impart inflationary or deflationary pressures to minor currency countries that have adopted an exchange rate rule, and these pressures can have strong effects over the domestic real interest rates of those countries. As inflationary and deflationary impulses are not necessarily identical for imports and exports, there can be significant changes in the terms of trade facing the minor currency countries as a result of a real appreciation or depreciation of a major currency.

A real appreciation (depreciation) of the US dollar tends to depress (increase) dollar prices of internationally traded goods, which became quite evident during the intense real appreciation of the dollar from 1980 to mid-1985. During that period the US dollar based IMF commodity price index fell by 30 per cent and both import export unit values (also dollar based) for the developing countries as a group fell by about 14 per cent. All of this occurred despite a 30 per cent rise in the US consumer price index and a 15 per cent increase in the US producer price index. Obviously, had the currency of a small open economy been fixed to the dollar at that time, that country would have experienced a deflation rate, on average, of about 3 per cent per annum. As the average US inflation rate from 1980 to 1985 was over 5 per cent per annum, the inflation rate differential was over 8 per cent per annum – and even greater for countries whose exports are heavily dominated by commodities.

This chapter examines the manner in which these effects are transmitted across the world economy and the extent to which exchange rate policy can be used to combat them. We assume that there are basically two types of countries or currency blocs: those that are 'large' in the sense that they can influence the world prices of traded goods, and the 'smaller' ones that cannot. The large countries will be designated as 'major currency' countries, quite independent of the actual status of their currencies, and the small countries will be referred to as 'minor currency' countries, even though their currencies may be quite important (for example the Swiss franc).

The remainder of the chapter consists of five sections. The first section contains the basic pricing model to be used throughout the analysis. In that model, we explore how changes in PPP real exchange rates among the major currencies are reflected in the relative prices of internationally traded goods. The following section deals with the effects of major currency exchange rate fluctuations. The third section concerns exchange rate rules and the important differences between the workings of a rule based on a single currency and one based on a basket of currencies. The fourth section examines the effects on minor country real interest rates of real appreciations or depreciations of major currencies, and how those effects might be attenuated by an appropriate exchange rate rule. The final section presents a summary and some conclusions.

THE FORMAL MODEL OF PRICE DETERMINATION

Appendix 3.1 contains a derivation of the determinants of the price level of goods traded internationally with up to $M - 1$ other countries by any arbitrarily chosen country X; the key result is Equation (A3.1.5)

$$PTF_X = \sum_{j}^{M} \theta_X^j \cdot PF_j + G(Z_X) \tag{3.1}$$

where PTF_X and PF_j are, respectively, natural logarithms of price indexes expressed in a foreign currency for goods traded internationally by country X and the price level of country j; the θ_X^j are non-negative fractions whose sum is unity and which measure the relative power possessed by country j in the world market over the goods traded internationally by country X; finally, $G(Z_X)$ is a function of a vector of variables, Z_X, that reflect the 'global fundamentals' for the set of goods traded internationally by country X.[3] In most of what follows, the variables contained in the vector Z_X will be suppressed so as to focus attention on the role of the exchange rate variables.

The classic 'small country' assumption corresponds to $\theta_X^j = 0$; that is, country j is a price taker in the world market as any changes in its exchange rate and/or its price level will have no effect on the prices of its traded goods in currencies other than its own. At the other extreme, if $\theta_X^j = 1$, country j is a price maker: any change in its own price level and/or exchange rate will be reflected in an equi-proportionate change in the prices of its traded goods in all other currencies. In short, the θ_X^j summarize the structure of the world market for country X's traded goods; with the appropriate time series data, one can estimate those coefficients.[4]

How 'External' Inflation Differs from 'Reference' Country Inflation

Assuming that country X has adopted a credible exchange rate rule *vis à vis* the currency of country k, both PTF_X and PF_j will be denominated in currency k. In that case, Equation (3.1) is readily manipulated into the following form;

$$PT_X^k = E_X^k + P_k + \sum_{j}^{M} \theta_X^j \cdot R_k^j \tag{3.2}$$

where PT_X^k and P_k are, respectively, natural logarithms of price indexes for country X's traded goods in its own currency and the price level of country k, also in its own currency, E_X^k is the natural logarithm of the price of currency k in terms of currency X, and $R_k^j = P_j + E_k^j - P_k$ is the PPP bilateral real exchange rate of country k *vis à vis* country j. The term $G(Z_X)$ has been suppressed. Equation (3.2) decomposes PT_X^k into three components: E_X^k, its own exchange rate rule; P_k, the price level of country k; and a third component reflecting the behaviour of the PPP bilateral real exchange rates between reference country k and all other countries.

Assuming now that country X has adopted a credible fixed exchange rate *vis à vis* the currency of country k, a dynamic version of Equation (3.2) can be written to indicate the inflation rate in country X's traded goods sector:

$$\Pi_X^{T,k} = \Pi_k + \sum_j^M \theta_X^j \cdot \dot{R}_k^j \qquad (3.2')$$

where $\Pi_X^{T,k}$ is the rate of inflation in the traded goods sector of country X, Π_k is the inflation rate in the reference country k; and $\dot{R}_k^j$ is the time rate of change of the PPP real exchange rate of country k *vis à vis* country j. In the usual treatment of sources of inflation in a small open economy operating under a fixed exchange rate, the second source of 'external' inflation in Equation $(3.2')$, $\sum_j^M \theta_X^j \dot{R}_k^j$, is ignored, even though it may be quite volatile and very important quantitatively. This neglect was unimportant during the period of the Bretton Woods system when PPP real exchange rates between the major currency countries were quite stable, but under the arrangement that has prevailed since 1973, the extreme volatility of those real exchange rates has been an important source of external inflation (and deflation) in countries that have adopted exchange rate rules linking their currencies to the US dollar.

The distinction between external inflation being defined as Π_k versus $\Pi_k + \sum_j^M \theta_X^j \cdot \dot{R}_k^j$ became apparent during 1975–85. In the first half of that period, the IMF commodity price index (a dollar based wholesale price index that does not explicitly include petroleum) rose 35 per cent relative to the US Consumer Price Index, only to fall by 42 per cent with respect to that index during the second half of that period; despite the intensity of US inflation, the IMF index actually fell by about 30 per cent from 1980 to 1985. It is no coincidence that the 1975–80 subperiod was one of intense real depreciation of the US dollar (that is, $\dot{R}_{US}^j > 0$), whereas the 1980–85 subperiod was one of an even more intense real appreciation of the dollar (that is $\dot{R}_{US}^j \ll 0$).

The foregoing analysis can be extended to the overall price level of a country pursuing a credible exchange rate rule against currency k. The price level of country X will be written as a geometrically weighted average of the domestic prices of her nontraded goods and services and traded goods:

$$\begin{aligned} P_X &= \alpha_X \cdot PNT_X + (1 - \alpha_X) \cdot PT_X^k \\ &= PT_X^k - \alpha_X \cdot (PT_X^k - PNT_X) \end{aligned} \qquad (3.3)$$

where PNT_X is a price index country X's nontraded goods and services, and $(PT_X^k - PNT_X)$ is the true real exchange rate, which is a function of real variables.[5]

Combining Equations (3.2) and (3.3) results in an expression for the price level of country X:

$$P_X = \alpha_X \cdot (PNT_X - PT_X^k) + (E_X^k + P_k) + \sum_j^M \theta_X^j \cdot R_k^j \qquad (3.4)$$

in which the first term reflects that country's internal relative price structure, the second term is a purchasing power parity component $(E_X^k + P_k)$, and the third term captures the structure of real exchange rates among all third countries.[6] A dynamic version of Equation (3.4), in which the term $\alpha_X \cdot (PNT_X - PT_X^k)$ is ignored but which takes into account the possibility that country X may have some market power over its own traded goods (which will be useful in the next section), is the following:

$$
\begin{aligned}
\Pi_X &= (\dot{E}_X^k + \Pi_k) + \sum_j^M \theta_X^j \cdot \dot{R}_k^j \\
&= (\dot{E}_X^k + \Pi_k) + \sum_{j \neq X}^M \theta_X^j \cdot \dot{R}_k^j + \theta_X^X \cdot (\Pi_X - \dot{E}_X^k - \Pi_k) \\
&= (\dot{E}_X^k + \Pi_k) + \sum_{j \neq X}^M \Theta_X^j \cdot \dot{R}_k^j \qquad (3.4')
\end{aligned}
$$

where the new 'thetas' are defined as $\Theta_X^j \equiv \theta_X^j / (1 - \theta_X^X)$; as $\sum_{j \neq X}^M \Theta_X^j = 1$, they measure country j's share of power in the world market for country X's traded goods, excluding country X. The inflation rate in the reference country k is $\Pi_k = \dot{P}_k$, and $\dot{E}_X^k$ is the exchange rate rule of country X. Note that the right hand side of Equation (3.4') remains the same if we substitute Π_X^T for Π_X on the left hand side.

As is evident from Equation (3.4'), country X can choose an exchange rate rule to provide any desired rate of inflation. For example, if country X preferred to have the same rate of inflation as country $k (\Pi_X = \Pi_k)$, it could insulate itself from shocks arising from fluctuations in major currency exchange rates by adopting the following rule:

$$
\begin{aligned}
\dot{E}_X^k &= -\sum_{j \neq X}^M \Theta_X^j \cdot \dot{R}_k^j \\
&= \sum_{j \neq X}^M \Theta_X^j \cdot \dot{R}_j^k \qquad (3.5)
\end{aligned}
$$

This rule, however, could be implemented only with a substantial lag as changes in PPP real exchange rates can be observed only well after the fact.

An alternative rule that would also insulate country X from deflationary and inflationary shocks and which could be implemented without a lag is one that sets the equilibrium inflation rate in country X equal to the world rate of inflation defined as the following weighted average:

$$\Pi_W^X = \sum_{j \neq X}^M \Theta_X^j \cdot \Pi_j \qquad (3.6)$$

and where the superscript x indicates that 'thetas' are defined for country X. Setting Equation (3.4′) equal to Equation (3.6) produces the following exchange rate rule:

$$\dot{E}_X^k = \sum_{j \neq X}^M \Theta_X^j \cdot \dot{E}_j^k \qquad (3.7)$$

that is, the exchange rate rule reacts immediately to changes in the nominal exchange rates among the major currencies. Obviously, one can readily define many other exchange rate rules to serve any specific purpose that might be desired.

An important implication of Equation (3.4) is that, while a credible exchange rate rule may result in interest rate parity, it is not sufficient to assure equality of real rates of interest. Even if the nominal interest rate in country X were to be governed by the nominal interest rate in country k and the exchange rate rule (E_X^k), the (short run) inflation rate in country X will be influenced by changes in real exchange rates among third countries, which can give rise to potentially large real interest rate differentials.

EFFECTS OF FLUCTUATIONS IN MAJOR CURRENCY EXCHANGE RATES

Assume now that two small open economies, X and Y, have entered into a free trade arrangement, and that both have a fixed exchange rate *vis à vis* the currency of country k, which implies that they also have fixed exchange rates *vis à vis* each another. Returning to Equation (3.2), changes in the price levels in the traded goods sectors of the two countries, X and Y, holding P_k, E_X^k and E_Y^k constant, are as follows:

$$\Delta PT_X^k = \sum_{j}^M \theta_X^j \cdot \Delta R_k^j \qquad (3.9)$$

$$\Delta PT_Y^k = \sum_j^M \theta_Y^j \cdot \Delta R_k^j \qquad (3.10)$$

As countries X and Y must have quite different sets of traded goods (otherwise the free trade arrangement would be pointless), the parameters θ_X^j and θ_Y^j must be quite different. As a result, when, say, the US dollar depreciates against the euro and the yen, the traded goods sectors of the two countries might experience quite different rates of inflation, giving credence to Mundell's argument that 'Small changes in exchange rates can completely wipe out expected profits', in this context, however, the relevant changes are in the major currency exchange rates.

Several empirical studies concerning estimates of the 'thetas' indicate that only two or three currency blocs have significant market power, those being the US dollar and euro blocs and, to a lesser extent, the yen bloc. Consider the case where only the US dollar and the euro blocs are relevant. In that case, $\theta_X^{EU} + \theta_X^{US} = \theta_Y^{US} + \theta_Y^{US} = 1.0$ and $\Delta R_{US}^{US} \equiv 0.0$. Suppose further that the euro bloc dominates the world markets of country X's traded goods (for example $\theta_X^{EU} = 0.8$), but that the US dollar bloc dominates those markets for country Y's traded goods (for example, $\theta_Y^{US} = 0.8$ so $\theta_Y^{US} = 0.2$), and that over a certain period of time the US dollar has depreciated against the euro such that $\Delta R_{US}^{EU} = 0.3$ (30 per cent), as we have recently seen. The result is $\Delta PT_X^{US} = 24$ per cent and $\Delta PT_Y^{US} = 6$ per cent! That is, the US dollar prices of country Y's traded goods will have risen very little, and the euro prices of country X's traded goods also will have fallen very little, meaning that the US dollar prices of that country's traded goods will have risen a lot. The upshot is that the price level of country X's traded goods, in US dollars, has risen by 18 per cent relative the price level of country Y's traded goods, as is readily seen by subtracting Equation (3.10) from Equation (3.9):

$$\Delta(PT_X^k - PT_Y^k) = \sum_j^M (\theta_X^j - \theta_Y^j) \cdot \Delta R_k^j \qquad (3.11)$$

which, in the above example, simplifies to:

$$\Delta(PT_X^{US} - PT_Y^{US}) = (\theta_X^{EU} - \theta_Y^{EU}) \cdot \Delta R_{US}^{EU} \qquad (3.12)$$

Since both countries have fixed their exchange rates against the US dollar, and they trade freely with each another, their trading relations would be severely disrupted. Moreover, if the fixed exchange rate regime in both countries is credible, they should have quite similar nominal interest rates, indicating that the real interest rates in the traded goods sectors of the two countries would be very different. The above scenario is, of course, an extreme one, but it illustrates the nature of the problem, a problem that cannot be solved by fixed exchange rates among the members of a preferential trading group, or even by the creation of a common currency for the member countries.

Since the euro bloc dominates the world market for country X's traded goods, a somewhat better outcome would be achieved if that country were to fix her exchange rate against the euro instead of the US dollar. In that case ΔPT_Y^{US} remains positive at 6 per cent, but $\Delta PT_X^{EU} = -6$ per cent, so the effect on the real interest rate in country X's traded good sector is much reduced; note, however, that ΔPT_X^{US} remains at 24 per cent.

BASKET BASED EXCHANGE RATES

A better solution to this problem lies in the adoption of an exchange rate rule defined against a basket of currencies rather than just a single currency. An exchange rate rule against a single currency admits but a single instrument – the rule itself. But as we know from a basic economic policy theorem (Tinbergen 1952), the number of policy instruments has to be at least as large as the number of targets. If countries wish to stabilize the real interest rates in their traded goods sectors, they must have two instruments, one for the nominal interest rate and another for the inflation rate. The advantage of a currency basket is that it allows two degrees of freedom – the composition of the basket and the rule itself. As will be seen, the additional degree of freedom permits targeting the real interest rate in the domestic traded goods sector, which involves two nominal variables. An exchange rate rule that is defined on a single currency, a special case of a currency basket, expends one degree of freedom inefficiently in that all of the weight is given to one currency, whereas defining that rule on a basket of currencies offers a richer choice of weights. Although in practice the number of 'large' countries seems unlikely to exceed two or three, at this stage the basket will be defined on all relevant currencies.

The Definition of the Basket

The basket rule for country X is developed in terms of its exchange rate with the currency of reference country 1. The basket is labelled 'B' and its value in terms of currency of country 1 is designated e_1^B:

$$e_1^B = \sum_{j=1}^{M} e_1^j \cdot X_j \qquad (3.13)$$

where X_j, the number of units of each major currency in the basket, defines its composition. The price of the basket in terms of currency X is:

$$e_X^B = e_X^i \cdot e_1^B$$
$$= e_X^1 \cdot \sum_{j=1}^{M} e_1^j \cdot X_j \qquad (3.14)$$

which also defines the exchange rate rule adopted by country X. It is quite straightforward to show, where $E_1^B = \ln e_1^B$, that:

$$\dot{E}_X^1 = \dot{E}_X^B - \sum_{j=2}^{M} \gamma_j \cdot \dot{E}_1^j \qquad (3.15)$$

and where $\gamma_j \equiv (e_1^j \cdot X_j)/e_1^B$ is the share of the jth currency in that basket.

As Equation (3.15) defines an implicit exchange rate rule on the reference currency (that is country 1's currency), we can replace $\dot{E}_X^k$ in Equation (3.4′) (with Π_X replaced with Π_X^T on the left hand side of that equation) with Equation (3.15) to obtain a general expression for the inflation rate in country X (or more precisely, the inflation rate in that country's traded goods sector) when that country pursues an exchange rate rule defined on a basket:

$$\Pi_X^b = \Pi_W^X = \dot{E}_X^B = \sum_{j \neq X}^{M} (\Theta_X^j - \gamma_j) \cdot \dot{E}_1^j \qquad (3.16)$$

By choosing the weights of the basket such that $\gamma_j = \Theta_X^j$, Equation (3.16) becomes:[7]

$$\Pi_X^b = \Pi_W^X = \dot{E}_X^B \qquad (3.16′)$$

and hence $\dot{E}_X^B$, the exchange rate rule *vis à vis* the currency basket, can be chosen to create whatever rate of inflation country X may desire.[8] Note that, despite the fact that the World Bank and the IMF continue to compute 'trade weighted' effective exchange rates, there is no relationship between the magnitudes of the Θ_X^j's and trade weights.

REAL RATES OF INTEREST IN SMALL COUNTRIES

Fluctuations in PPP real exchange rates among the major currency countries have a direct impact on real interest rates in small countries. If the exchange rate rule on major currency k is credible, we expect strong interest rate parity to hold, albeit with a spread:

$$i_X^k = i_k = \dot{E}_X^k = \text{spread} \qquad (3.17)$$

where the k superscript on i_X^k indicates that the exchange rate rule is defined on currency k.[9] We now turn to the factors that influence real interest rates in small countries and, in particular, the role of exchange rate rules.

The Case of a Single Currency Exchange Rate Rule

It is clear from Equation (3.4) that if a country adopts a single currency exchange rate rule with a constant rate of devaluation (including zero), it will be subject to inflationary and deflationary shocks arising from fluctuations in the PPP real exchange rates among the major currencies. Indeed, during the rapid real depreciation of the US dollar that occurred during the second half of the 1970s, several Latin American countries experienced inflation rates far higher and real interest rates far lower than could be explained by their exchange rate rules (the infamous *tablitas*, which were defined on the US dollar) and the US inflation rate. This behaviour was sharply reversed during the first half of the 1980s when the rapid appreciation of the US dollar, particularly during 1981–2, imposed strong deflationary pressures and very high real interest rates on those countries.

Equation (3.17) indicates that a single currency exchange rate rule can prevent changes in major currency exchange rates from impacting on domestic nominal interest rates but the domestic real rate of interest will still be affected by the gyrations in their inflation rates. On the other hand, if a country adopts a more complex rule, such as described by Equations (3.5) and (3.7), to insulate itself from inflationary or deflationary impulses due to fluctuations in the major currency real exchange rates, the rule itself will create disturbances in the domestic nominal interest rate. Insofar as single currency exchange rate rules are concerned, then, the choice is only with respect to the mechanism by which real interest rates are pummelled by the instability of the major currency exchange rates. To illustrate this, consider the (*ex post*) real rate of interest in the traded goods sector of country X, which we write in the usual Fisherian manner:

$$r_X^T = i_X - \Pi_X^T \tag{3.18}$$

where the values of i_X and Π_X depend upon the exchange rate rule and reference currency (usually taken to be currency k in the case of a single currency exchange rate rule). Substituting Equation (3.17) for i_X and Equation (3.4′) (with Π_X replaced with Π_X^T on the left hand side of that equation) for Π_X^T, we obtain the important result that:

$$r_X^{T,k} = r_k - \sum_{j \neq X}^{M} \Theta_X^j \cdot \dot{R}_j^k + \text{spread} \tag{3.19}$$

where the k superscript on $r_X^{T,k}$ indicates that the exchange rate rule has been defined on currency k, and r_k is the real interest rate in country k. What is important to note from Equation (3.19) is that, while the currency against which that rule is defined still matters, the exchange rate rule itself, $\dot{E}_X^k$, cancels out. As far as the real interest rate is concerned, one rule is as good as any other – as long as it is credible.

The explanation for the 'irrelevance' of the exchange rate rule is very simple: the rule determines only the channel by which external disturbances are transmitted to the domestic real rate of interest. A rule that eliminates those disturbances to the inflation rate may well introduce them into the nominal rate of interest; at worst, such a rule might exacerbate exchange rate risk to the extent that the country's access the international capital market is adversely affected. A rule that avoids the latter (for example, a fixed exchange rate) cannot neutralize external disturbances to the domestic inflation rate.

The Case of a Basket Based Exchange Rate Rule

It was argued earlier that an exchange rate rule defined on a currency basket provides greater scope for reducing the variance in real interest rates in a small country. To develop this theme, we begin with the nominal rate of interest in that country, assuming a credible exchange rate rule defined on a basket of M currencies. As the domestic currency is now convertible into a fixed basket of the M currencies, the domestic nominal interest rate will be a weighted average of the interest rates in all countries whose currencies are included in the basket, plus the rule itself and a spread:

$$ i_X^b = \sum_{j\neq X}^{M} \gamma_j \cdot i_j + \dot{E}_X^B + \text{spread} \tag{3.20} $$

where the b superscript on i_X^b indicates a basket based exchange rate rule. The real interest rate is again given by Equation (3.18), so by substituting Equations (3.16) and (3.20) for the inflation and the nominal interest rates into Equation (3.18), we obtain an expression for the real rate of interest in the traded goods sector that is similar to the result obtained for a single currency exchange rate rule:

$$ r_X^{T,b} = i_X^b - \prod_X^b + \text{spread} $$
$$ = r_W^b - \sum_{j\neq X}^{M} (\Theta_X^j - \gamma_j) \cdot \dot{E}_1^j + \text{spread} \tag{3.21} $$

in which $r_W^b \equiv \Sigma_{j \neq X}^M \gamma_j \cdot r_j$ is the 'world' real interest rate. As was argued previously, the summation term on the right hand side of Equation (3.21) can be eliminated by defining the basket in such a way that the γ_j weights are equal to the Θ_X^j coefficients; in that case:

$$r_X^{T,b} = r_W^b$$

which contrasts sharply with the single currency exchange rate rule result presented in Equation (3.19). In principle, then, the basket approach to the exchange rate rule permits a small country to completely insulate its domestic real interest rate from fluctuations in third country exchange rates so that its own real rate of interest is equal to the 'world' real interest rate.

SUMMARY AND CONCLUSIONS

Fluctuations in nominal exchange rates among the major currencies (the US dollar, the euro and the yen) can have profound effects on the external prices of goods traded internationally by small open economies. Small countries entering into preferential trading arrangements will generally have different compositions of their imports and exports (otherwise, the preferential trading arrangement would be pointless), and hence they will tend to be affected asymmetrically by changes in, for example, the US dollar/euro exchange rate. As a result, the prices of traded goods of the various member countries can diverge substantially when the major currency exchange rates fluctuate, leading to a disruption of trade among those countries. In addition, the real rate of interest in the traded goods sectors of the member countries can be strongly affected, both positively and negatively, by fluctuations in the major currency exchange rates. These unfortunate consequences will prevail even if all members of the preferential trading group peg their currencies to the same major currency or even create a common currency.

There do exist, of course, single currency exchange rate rules that can neutralize the effects of major currency fluctuations on the domestic prices of traded goods, but adoption of such rules will either introduce movements in the nominal (and hence real) interest rates in the country in question, or exacerbate exchange rate risk, undermining that country's access to the international capital market. Moreover, there exists no exchange rate rule defined on a single major currency that can neutralize the effects of fluctuations of the major currency exchange rates on both domestic interest rates and the domestic prices of a country's traded goods. The reason is straightforward: an exchange rate rule defined on a single currency admits but one instrument – the exchange rate rule itself, and a single instrument cannot target both the nominal interest rate and the inflation rate.

One solution might be to adopt two exchange rates, one for commercial operations and a second one for financial transactions. In the past this approach has been employed (for other reasons) by several Latin American and some European countries but with little success as it is difficult to eliminate the leakage between two markets with different prices for the same item.

The only other solution is to define the exchange rate rule on a basket of currencies. This approach, while inconvenient in some aspects, admits two instruments – the exchange rate rule and the composition of the basket itself, so both the inflation rate in the traded goods sector and the nominal interest rate can be targeted. Small countries contemplating the creation of a preferential trading arrangement would do well to examine the advantages of exchange rate rules defined on a basket of currencies.

NOTES

1. I am grateful to Ken Clements for bringing Mundell's paper to my attention.
2. Portions of this chapter draw on Sjaastad (2000), which uses the same basic pricing model; some errors in that paper have been corrected.
3. Upper case Latin letters refer to the natural logarithm of variables whose arithmetic value appears in lower case letters. Exceptions will be obvious.
4. In estimating Equation (3.1), one must assume that exchange rates are exogenous with respect to the nominal prices of traded goods; that is, there is no feedback from the prices of entire sets of traded goods to exchange rates.
5. As is well known, the Salter (1959) effect argues that the equilibrium value of $(PT_X^k - PNT_X)$ depends upon expenditure relative to income, Michaely (1981), for example, finds broad empirical support for the Salter effect, but the magnitude is highly variable, particularly in the short run. It is equally well known that an improvement in the external terms of trade also leads, under fairly general conditions, to an increase in PNT_X relative to PT_X. For a neat and succinct treatment of this point, see Neary (1988); for a more verbose treatment, but one that takes into account inter-temporal substitution as well, see Ostry (1988).
6. It is worth noting that, as $R_k^j = P_j + E_k^j - P_k$ and $\Sigma_j^M \theta_X^j = 1$, Equation (3.4) can be rewritten as:

$$\alpha_X \cdot (PT_X^k - PNT_X) = \sum_j^M \theta_X^j \cdot (P_j + E_X^k + E_k^j - P_X)$$
$$= \sum_j^M \theta_X^j \cdot (P_j + E_X^j - P_X)$$
$$= \sum_j^M \theta_X^j \cdot R_X^j,$$

So the true real exchange rate $(PT_X^k - PNT_X)$, is proportional to a weighted average of the PPP real exchange rates between country X and all other countries. The correct weights, however, are the θ_X^k which have little if anything to do with directions and volumes of trade.

7. Since γ_X must be zero (the basket cannot contain country X's currency), but θ_X^X need not be zero, it is evident why the Θs had to be replaced with the Θs.

8. There is a practical problem associated with fixed basket weights; if the γ_j are fixed, then the X_j must be adjusted continuously in response to fluctuations in major-currency exchange rates. See Appendix II of Sjaastad (2000) for a fixed-composition compromise.

9. Interest rates may not be exactly arbitraged as transaction taxes, country risk, and so on, introduce systematic spreads which we assume to be uncorrelated with the exchange rate movements among the major currencies. Moreover, since the nominal rate of interest in country X cannot be negative, the maximum rate of appreciation of that country's currency *vis à vis* currency k is i_k plus the spread. Were the exchange rate rule to require an appreciation at a rate greater than i_k, presumably the spread would have to increase.

10. To the best of the author's knowledge, this approach was first developed by Ridler and Yandle (1972) to analyse the effect of exchange rates on commodity prices. The actual model presented in this appendix first appeared Sjaastad (1985). A somewhat similar approach was developed by Dornbusch (1987).

11. The excess demand in country j is $D^j \equiv D^j - S^j$, where D^j and S^j are domestic demand and supply, respectively. The slope of the excess demand function is $(D^j/P_q^{j,R}) \cdot \eta_j - (S^j/P_q^{j,R})$, ε_j, where $\eta_j \leq 0$ and $\varepsilon_j \geq 0$ are the elasticities of domestic demand and supply, respectively, with respect to the real price of the commodity in country j. It is clearly evident that the slope is non-positive.

REFERENCES

Dornbusch, R. (1987), 'Exchange rate economics: 1986', *The Economic Journal*, **97** (385), 1–18.

Michaely, M. (1981), 'Foreign aid, economic structure and dependence', *Journal of Development Economics*, **9** (3), 313–30.

Mundell, R.A. (1961), 'A theory of optimum currency areas', *American Economic Review*, **51**, 507–17.

Mundell, R.A. (2000), 'Currency areas, exchange rate systems, and international monetary reform', (unpublished). Part 6 is titled 'Monetary arrangements in free trade areas and customs unions'. Available from: www.columbia.edu/~ram15/cema2000.html 30 January.

Neary, P. (1988), 'The determinants of the equilibrium real exchange rate,' *American Economic Review*, **78** (1), 210–15.

Ostry, J.D. (1988), 'The balance of trade, terms of trade, and real exchange rate', *IMF Staff Papers*, **35** (4), 541–73.

Ridler, D. and C.A. Yandle (1972), 'A simplified method for analysing the effects of exchange rate changes on exports of a primary commodity', *IMF Staff Papers*, **19**.

Salter, W.E.G. (1959), 'International and external balance: the role of price and expenditure effects', *Economic Record*, **35** (71), 226–38.

Sjaastad, L.A. (1985), 'Exchange rate regimes and the real rate of interest', in M. Connolly and J. McDermott (eds), *The Economics of the Caribbean Basin*, New York: Praeger, pp. 135–64.

Sjaastad, L.A. (2000), 'Exchange rate strategies for small countries', *Zagreb Journal of Economics*, **4** (2), 3–33.

Tinbergen, J. (1952), *On the Theory of Economic Policy*, Amsterdam: North Holland.

APPENDIX 3.1:   EXCHANGE RATES AND PRICES OF TRADED GOODS

Ignoring transport costs, tariffs and other barriers to trade, the 'law of one price' for internationally traded good q states that:

$$P_q^i = P_q^j = E_i^j \tag{A3.1.1}$$

where P_q^i is the (natural logarithm of the) price of currency j in terms of currency i.[10] With no loss of generality, set $i = X$; that is, the currency of country (or currency bloc) X will be the reference currency. The excess demand for good q in country j, $D^{j,q}$, will be written as function of its real price and a vector Z_q^j of all other relevant variables (that is, the market 'fundamentals' for country j):

$$
\begin{aligned}
D^{q,j} &= D^{q,j}[(P_q^j - P_j), Z_q^j] \\
&= D^{q,j}[(P_q^X - E_X^j - P_j), Z_q^j]
\end{aligned}
\tag{A3.1.2}
$$

where P_j is the (natural logarithm of the) price level in country j. Since $P_q^X - E_X^j - P_j = (P_q^X - P_X) - (E_X^j + P_j - P_X) \equiv P_q^{X,R} - R_X^j$, where R_X^j is the PPP bilateral real exchange rate between countries X and j, country j's excess demand for good q is a function of the natural logarithm of the ratio of its real price in country X to the PPP bilateral real exchange rate between countries X and j:

$$D^{q,j} = D^{q,j}[(P_q^{X,R} - R_X^j), Z_q^j].$$

In a world of M countries, market clearing requires that the M excess demands sum to zero:

$$\sum_j^M D^{q,j}[(P_q^{X,R} - R_X^j), Z_q^j] = 0$$

The summation is then differentiated totally and rearranged:

$$dP_q^{X,R} = \sum_j^M (D_1^{q,j}/D_1^q)dR_X^j - (D_2^{q,j}/D_1^q)dZ_q^j$$

where $D_1^{q,j} \equiv \partial(D^{q,j})/\partial(P^{X,R} - R_X^j)$, $D_2^{q,j} = \partial(D^{q,j})/\partial Z_q^j$, and $D_1^q \equiv \Sigma_j^M D_1^{q,j}$.[11] A local linear approximation relating the real price of good q to PPP bilateral real exchange rates is obtained by integration:

$$P_q^{X,R} = \sum_j^M \vartheta_j^q \cdot R_X^j + F(Z_q) \tag{A3.1.3}$$

where $\vartheta_j^q \equiv D_1^{q,j}/D_1^q$ and $F(Z_q)$ is the integral of $-\Sigma_{j=1}^M (D_2^{q,j}/D_1^q)dZ_q^j$. The excess demand (Equation (A3.1.2)) may be either positive or negative but, as all $D_1^{q,j}$ are non-positive, the ϑ_j^q are non-negative fractions that sum to unity. $F(Z_q)$ captures the Z_q^j vectors (the global fundamentals) and that term is explicitly assumed to be orthogonal to the RER_X^j. The fundamentals include all factors (including expectations) that influence the global demand for and supply of good q other than exchange rates.

The structure of the world market for good q is summarized by the ϑ_j^q in Equation (A3.1.3), as those parameters measure the relative market power possessed by each participating country. In the limiting case of $\vartheta_j^q = 0$, country j is a price taker in the world market for good q as any change in its real exchange rate *vis à vis* reference currency X will have no effect on the real price of good q in currency X. At the other extreme, if $\vartheta_j^q = 1$, country j is a price maker in that market as any change in its real exchange rate will be fully reflected in an equi-proportionate change in the real price of good q country X. Moreover, the magnitudes of the ϑ_j^q have no logical relation to existing patterns of international trade.

The expression for the price of good q can be generalized to an index of the real prices of any set of N traded goods (for example, imports and/or exports) denominated in currency X; that is defined as $PT_X^R \equiv \Sigma_q^M w_q P_q^{X,R}$, where the w_q are non-negative weights that sum to unity. Combining that index with the above expression for $P_q^{X,R}$ results in:

$$PT_X^R \equiv \sum_q^N w_q \left[\sum_j^M \vartheta_j^q \cdot R_X^j + F(Z_q) \right]$$
$$= \sum_q^N \left[\sum_j^M (w_q \cdot \vartheta_j^q) \cdot R_X^j \right] + G(Z_X)$$

where $G(Z_X) \equiv \Sigma_q^N w_q F(Z_q)$ captures the global fundamentals for the set N of traded goods. Moreover, as the $\Sigma_q^N w_q \cdot \vartheta_j^q$ terms are non-negative and sum to unity, PT_X^R can be written as a weighted average of the R_X^j:

$$PT_X^R = \sum_j^M \theta_X^j \cdot R_X^j + G(Z_X) \qquad (A3.1.4)$$

where $\theta_X^j \equiv \Sigma_q^N w_q \cdot \vartheta_q^j$. The θ_X^j have the same interpretation as the ϑ_j^q; they measure the relative market power possessed by country j over the prices of the set N of goods traded internationally by country X. The θ_X^j will not be the same for different sets of goods (for example, imports versus exports), but the PT_X^R index can be tailored to refer to any subset of tradables for any country by choosing the w_q to correspond to that subset.

Equation (A3.1.4) can be converted into an index defined on nominal prices simply by adding P_X to both sides of equation (A3.1.4):

$$PT_X = \sum_j^M \theta_X^j \cdot (E_X^j + P_j) + G(Z_X)$$

Moreover, PT_X can be expressed in the currency of, say, country Y by using the identity $E_X^j \equiv E_X^i + E_i^j$ and the property that $\sum_j^M \theta_X^j = 1$:

$$PTF_X = \sum_j^M \theta_X^j \cdot PF_j + G(Z_X) \tag{A3.1.5}$$

where the appended 'F' indicates that both PT_X and P_j are expressed in a foreign currency (that is, $PTF_X = PT_X - E_X^i$ and $PF_j = P_j + E_i^j$). It is this expression that appears as Equation (3.1) in the text.

4. Major trade trends in APEC economies: implications for regional free trade agreements

Yanrui Wu

INTRODUCTION

The concept of bilateral free trade agreement (FTA) has recently attracted a lot of attention in the Asia-Pacific region.[1] Several countries are leading the race by successfully signing free trade agreements (FTAs) with each other. For example, Australia recently completed FTAs with Singapore, Thailand and the United States; Singapore had an FTA with Chile, New Zealand and the United States, respectively. Other members of the Asia-Pacific Economic Cooperation (APEC) group are also in the process of negotiation towards an FTA such as Australia and China, and Japan and ASEAN. There is, however, little empirical research which would provide economic rationales for the completion of those FTAs and potentially more to be signed. This chapter attempts to make a contribution towards the understanding of bilateral trade among APEC economies by examining the changing trends in trade among APEC members, and between members and non-members, and to use the findings to draw implications for regional free trade agreements. This chapter is not aimed at presenting a comprehensive survey of the field. Instead it focuses on several key issues associated with bilateral trade between APEC economies and sheds some light on the development of FTAs in the Asia-Pacific region.

The rest of the chapter begins with a description of the trend in growth of trade among APEC members. This is followed by an examination of intra-regional trade and then an exploration of comparative advantages of APEC members in selected commodity groups. The chapter continues with an analysis of intra-industry trade and finishes with a conclusion and comments.

GROWTH IN TRADE

APEC group was established in 1989. The original 12 members include Australia, Brunei Darussalam, Canada, Indonesia, Japan, Republic of Korea, Malaysia, New Zealand, the Republic of the Philippines, Singapore, Thailand and the United States of America. Its current members also include Chile, People's Republic of China, Hong Kong Special Economic Region (henceforth Hong Kong), Mexico, Papua New Guinea, Peru, the Russian Federation, Chinese Taipei and Vietnam. Due to missing data, this study covers 16 APEC members (excluding Brunei Darussalam, Papua New Guinea, Peru, the Russian Federation and Vietnam). This section describes briefly the growth trend, composition and direction of trade among APEC members, and between member and non-member economies.

Growth Trends

Most APEC members have adopted a pro-trade economic policy. As a result, APEC as a group has played an important role in international trade. Table 4.1 shows that the share of exports from APEC over the world total has increased from 31.6 per cent in 1980 to 43.9 per cent in 2002. A similar pattern of growth for imports is also recorded (but not shown in the table). In particular, APEC members' shares over the world total exports and imports increased substantially during the 1980s and the first half of the 1990s. However, APEC shares over the world totals hardly changed during the period of 1996–2002, reflecting the negative impact of the 1997 Asian financial crisis. In fact, after 1996, the export and import shares of most members fell. Mainland China (henceforth China-M) and the USA are two exceptions. Both China-M's export and import shares have increased since 1996. The USA imported relatively more in 2002 than in 1996. It is clear that China-M and the USA may have been the key contributors to the recovery of the Asian economies after the 1997 crisis. It has been argued that the increasing competitiveness of Chinese products may have a crowding-out effect on exports from other Asian economies in particular ASEAN members (Weiss and Gao 2003). However, empirical evidence has shown that, while China-M's neighbours have lost their market shares in the USA and Japan, their loss has been compensated by the rapid growth of their exports to China-M (Weiss 2004). Table 4.1 also demonstrates that in terms of gaining export shares, China-M and Hong Kong have been the star performers, followed by Korea, Mexico and Thailand. Developed members' shares are relatively stable over time. Indonesia is an exception among the developing members. Table 4.1 demonstrates that

Table 4.1   Values and shares of APEC exports in selected years

	Total exports (US$Billion, f.o.b.)				World share of exports (%)			
	1980	1989	1996	2002	1980	1989	1996	2002
Australia	21.9	37.1	60.3	64.1	1.1	1.2	1.1	1.0
Canada	67.7	121.8	201.6	252.4	3.5	4.0	3.8	4.0
Chile	4.7	8.1	15.7	18.3	0.2	0.3	0.3	0.3
China-M	18.1	52.5	151.0	325.6	0.9	1.7	2.8	5.1
Hong Kong	19.8	73.1	180.8	200.1	1.0	2.4	3.4	3.1
Indonesia	21.9	22.2	49.8	38.4	1.1	0.7	0.9	0.6
Japan	130.4	273.9	410.9	416.7	6.7	9.1	7.7	6.5
Korea	17.5	62.4	129.7	162.5	0.9	2.1	2.4	2.5
Malaysia	12.9	25.0	78.3	93.3	0.7	0.8	1.5	1.5
Mexico	18.0	35.2	96.0	160.7	0.9	1.2	1.8	2.5
New Zealand	5.4	8.9	14.4	14.4	0.3	0.3	0.3	0.2
Philippines	5.7	7.8	20.4	36.3	0.3	0.3	0.4	0.6
Singapore	19.4	44.7	125.0	125.2	1.0	1.5	2.3	2.0
Taiwan	19.8	66.2	115.7	130.5	1.0	2.2	2.2	2.0
Thailand	6.5	20.1	55.7	68.9	0.3	0.7	1.0	1.1
United States	225.6	363.8	625.1	693.9	11.6	12.0	11.7	10.9
APEC 16	615.5	1197.8	2330.5	2801.0	31.6	39.6	43.6	43.9
World	1945.9	3024.1	5350.9	6384.5	100	100	100	100

Source: Calculated by the author using data from the International Monetary Fund (2002 and 2003).

Indonesia suffered the most from the 1997 crisis, and Indonesian trade shares have actually declined over time.

Composition of Trade

According to the Standard International Trade Classification (SITC) system, APEC as a whole has exported mainly three categories of commodities: manufactured goods (SITC 6), machines and transport equipment (SITC 7) and miscellaneous manufactured articles (SITC 8). The value of exports of those three categories of goods accounted for 76 per cent of APEC total exports in 2002 (see Table 4.2). Associated with this pattern of exports is the dominance of mineral fuels, lubricants and related materials (SITC 3), manufactured items (SITCs 6 and 8) and machinery and transport equipment (SITC 6) in the list of APEC imports. This pattern of trade has remained very much the same in the past decade.

Table 4.2   Commodity shares (%) in selected years

SITC code	Description	Exports			Imports		
		1989	1996	2002	1989	1996	2002
0	Food and live animals	6.8	5.6	4.3	6.6	5.6	4.6
1	Beverages and tobacco	0.8	0.8	0.5	0.9	0.8	0.8
2	Crude materials, inedible, except fuels	7.2	4.5	3.3	6.4	4.4	3.3
3	Mineral fuels, lubricants and related materials	5.4	4.6	4.6	11.0	9.2	10.1
4	Animal and vegetable oils, fats and waxes	0.5	0.5	0.4	0.3	0.3	0.2
5	Chemicals and related products, n.e.s.	6.5	6.9	7.7	7.0	7.5	8.5
6	Manufactured goods classified chiefly by material	13.0	12.5	11.6	15.4	13.6	12.1
7	Machinery and transport equipment	43.1	47.7	50.2	36.7	42.2	43.5
8	Miscellaneous manufactured articles	12.4	14.0	14.2	13.1	13.9	14.5
9	Not classified elsewhere	4.3	2.9	3.1	2.6	2.6	2.5
	Total	100	100	100	100	100	100

Source: Author's own calculation using data from UN Comtrade database SITC Revision III (UN Statistics Division 2005).

Direction of Trade

In terms of direction of trade, Table 4.3 shows that, during 1980–2002, members traded more with other members and most members increased their trade with other APEC members. In particular, by 2002, Canada and Mexico imported more than 80 per cent of their products from other APEC members (mainly the USA, to be discussed later) and exported more than 90 per cent of their products to other member economies. In 2002, all members but Chile exported (imported) more than 50 per cent to (from) other APEC members (see Table 4.3).

In summary, trade by APEC as a bloc has expanded substantially in the past two decades. Growth has however been uneven among individual members and during different time periods. The 1997 Asian financial crisis did have a negative impact on members' trade, in particular trade by Indonesia. Members' trade tends to focus on certain groups of commodities. This pattern has remained the same in recent decades. APEC members also tend to trade more with other members.

Table 4.3   Shares of trade with APEC members over total trade in 2002 (%)

	Exports				Imports			
	1980	1989	1996	2002	1980	1989	1996	2002
Australia	52.2	57.5	59.1	56.4	56.1	61.2	60.9	62.7
Canada	74.0	85.2	88.4	92.8	78.2	79.3	81.0	79.8
Chile	28.4	39.6	46.6	50.5	38.7	41.2	48.2	37.8
China-M	n.a.	74.5	73.5	69.5	n.a.	64.3	59.9	55.1
Hong Kong	54.6	70.9	73.5	77.3	70.6	73.5	75.6	78.5
Indonesia	85.7	80.7	71.7	70.0	67.4	64.0	62.1	64.0
Japan	52.5	63.5	68.2	69.3	48.2	59.1	62.8	62.8
Korea	57.9	74.6	64.6	65.0	60.6	71.5	64.6	64.1
Malaysia	69.5	73.4	73.3	72.7	67.4	73.0	74.1	73.2
Mexico	71.9	78.7	89.3	92.2	75.4	76.6	86.6	82.3
New Zealand	52.8	65.3	65.8	68.6	59.7	66.3	69.6	68.6
Philippines	71.4	75.4	75.8	72.5	61.5	65.2	69.0	75.2
Singapore	59.2	67.9	70.1	69.5	57.1	66.7	68.7	68.4
Taiwan	n.a.	76.5	76.8	77.4	n.a.	73.1	71.2	74.6
Thailand	53.2	61.9	67.4	n.a.	57.9	64.5	64.4	n.a.
United States	43.8	55.1	59.4	61.4	45.6	59.0	63.1	62.0

Source: Author's own calculation using data from UN Comtrade database SITC Revision III (UN Statistics Division 2005).

INTRA-REGIONAL TRADE

An increasingly important part of trade by APEC members is intra-regional trade or trade among members. To measure this type of trade, several statistical indices have been developed. One such index is the trade intensity index (Brown 1949 and Kojima 1964). The latter appears in two forms; the export intensity index (XII) and import intensity index (MII). They can be defined as follows:

$$XII_i = \frac{x_{ij}/X_{iw}}{M_{jw}/(M_w - M_{iw})} \tag{4.1}$$

and

$$MII_i = \frac{m_{ij}/M_{iw}}{X_{jw}/(X_w - X_{iw})} \tag{4.2}$$

where

XII_i = country i's export intensity index
MII_i = country i's import intensity index
x_{ij} = country i's exports to country j
X_{iw} = country i's total exports to the world
M_{jw} = country j's total imports from the world
M_w = world total imports
M_{iw} = country i's total imports from the world
m_{ij} = country i's exports to country j
X_{jw} = country j's total exports to the world
X_w = world total exports

Export and import intensity indices reflect the ratio of the share of country i's trade with country j relative to the share of world trade destined for country j. An index of greater (less) than unity has been interpreted as an indication of larger (smaller) than expected trade flow between two parties concerned. Table 4.4 demonstrates that all members' export intensity indices with APEC are greater than one (with the exception of Chile's import intensity index which is not shown in the table) on the basis of 2002 trade data, implying a strong link between individual members and APEC as a bloc. As for bilateral trade, Table 4.4 also shows strong trade flows among most members. Trade flow is particularly strong among members in several sub-groups as highlighted in bold. Those sub-groups are associated with three free trade areas: North American Free Trade Area (NAFTA), Australia–New Zealand Close Economic Relationship (ANZCER) and ASEAN Free Trade Area (AFTA). Thus, it may be concluded that bilateral FTAs or regional free trade arrangements may actually promote trade. In addition, Table 4.4 also shows that geographic location or distance does play an important role in regional trade flow. According to these tables, the intensity indices are generally low for Canada, Mexico and Chile reflecting their relative isolation from most APEC Asian members. In the meantime, the intensity indices between close neighbours are generally high, for example, USA and Canada, and Singapore and Malaysia.

COMPARATIVE ADVANTAGES

While distance plays an important role in international trade, the extent of trade by a country is largely determined by the competitiveness of that country. To compare the competitiveness of each country in trade of a

Table 4.4 Export intensity indexes

With:	Australia	NZ	Taiwan	PRC	HK	Japan	Korea	Malaysia	Indonesia	Thailand	Philippines	Singapore	Canada	Mexico	US	Chile
Australia		**16.34**	1.08	1.21	1.05	1.70	1.27	2.01	4.51	1.24	0.88	2.38	0.26	0.05	1.39	0.29
NZ	**27.11**		0.70	0.76	0.60	1.42	0.84	1.50	1.69	0.65	0.25	1.41	0.22	0.02	0.93	0.22
Taiwan	n.a.	n.a.		n.a.	n.a.	n.a.	n.a.	n.a.	n.a.	n.a.	n.a.	n.a.	n.a.	n.a.	n.a.	n.a.
China-M	1.25	1.02	**1.66**	n.a.	**8.48**	**2.01**	**3.17**	1.24	1.67	1.30	0.83	1.19	0.22	0.06	0.58	1.48
HK	0.88	0.62	**7.34**	**5.41**		**1.83**	**1.93**	1.77	1.02	1.58	2.04	2.84	0.09	0.04	0.47	n.a.
Japan	3.02	2.22	**1.75**	**2.76**	**1.02**		**1.77**	2.16	6.08	2.17	2.82	1.36	0.40	0.06	1.18	2.04
Korea	3.12	1.89	**1.26**	**1.96**	**0.88**	**2.80**		1.42	4.60	2.59	1.58	1.76	0.21	0.05	1.15	1.67
Malaysia	1.26	1.54	1.94	1.20	0.83	2.06	1.59		**4.32**	**2.48**	**3.72**	**14.04**	0.10	0.04	1.00	0.10
Indonesia	4.98	3.58	2.84	2.59	1.08	3.66	4.88	n.a.		**2.17**	**1.45**	n.a.	0.31	0.01	0.78	0.90
Thailand	1.92	1.14	1.75	0.88	1.08	3.04	1.42	**4.26**	**3.23**		**3.01**	**4.54**	0.13	0.03	0.58	0.28
Philippines	1.62	2.64	2.62	1.06	1.96	3.39	3.13	**2.49**	**3.56**	**1.79**		**4.20**	0.13	0.01	1.51	0.37
Singapore	2.30	0.61	1.86	1.15	1.13	1.82	1.43	**9.52**	**7.82**	**4.97**	**3.82**		0.07	0.10	1.07	0.11
Canada	0.28	0.58	0.33	0.36	0.42	0.48	0.41	0.17	0.28	0.33	0.30	0.08		**0.49**	**5.45**	0.41
Mexico	0.12	0.55	0.26	0.31	0.30	0.32	0.50	0.22	0.25	0.07	0.31	0.22	**0.22**		**4.26**	1.84
US	0.46	0.81	1.10	1.12	1.13	1.49	1.08	1.09	1.07	1.18	1.30	0.82	**4.59**	**4.73**		1.03
Chile	0.48	0.41	0.49	1.12	0.57	0.43	1.05	0.18	0.66	0.22	0.12	0.09	0.26	0.60	1.18	
APEC 16	1.21	1.38	1.59	1.39	1.58	1.37	1.32	1.50	2.17	1.66	1.46	1.43	1.87	1.87	1.05	1.00

Note: Thailand's figures are based on 1996 statistics; n.a. = not available.

Source: Author's own calculations using data from UN Comtrade database SITC Revision III (UN Statistics Division 2005).

particular commodity group, the revealed comparative advantage (*RCA*)
index is often computed using the following formulae:

$$RCA_{ic} = \frac{x_{ic}/X_{iw}}{x_{cw}/X_w}$$
(4.3)

where

RCA_{ic} = revealed comparative advantage index of commodity group *c* for
            country *i*
x_{ic} = value of exports of commodity group *c* by country *i*
X_{iw} = value of total exports by country *i*
x_{cw} = value of world exports of commodity group *c*
X_w = value of total world exports

Country *i* has comparative advantage in exporting commodity group *c*
when RCA_{ic} has a value greater than unity, that is, when country *i*'s export
share of commodity group *c* is larger than the world export share of the
same commodity group.[2] On the contrary, if RCA_{ic} is less than unity,
country *i* has comparative disadvantage.

According to Table 4.5, APEC economies as a bloc have comparative
advantages in five product groups – SITCs 2, 4, 7, 8 and 9. For individual
members, lower income members tend to have a comparative advantage in
the production of goods in groups SITCs 6, 7 and 8 and more developed
members in groups SITCs 0, 2, 7 and 9. There are however exceptions. For
example, Japan's comparative advantage seems to be different from other
developed economies, while Chile and Indonesia are outliers among the
developing APEC economies. At the two digital level, APEC has shown
comparative advantage in product groups such as SITCs 63, 65, 71, 75–79,
83–85 and 87–89.

It is interesting to note that China-M has shown comparative advantage in commodity groups SITCs 6, 7 and 8. In the meantime, the four
ASEAN economies (Indonesia, Malaysia, the Philippines and Singapore)
tend to have comparative advantage in groups such as SITCs 3, 4 and 7.
SITC 7 is the only group in which both China-M and ASEAN countries
have comparative advantages. Thus, the findings implied in Table 4.5 do
not support the view that China-M is a direct competitor of ASEAN
economies as postulated by some authors (see, Lall and Albaldejo 2004;
Weiss and Gao 2003).

At the more disaggregate level (three digits), Ng and Yeats (2003)
considered 60 groups (mostly SITCs 7 and 8) and 12 APEC economies
(see Table 4.6). They showed that most APEC economies have strong

Table 4.5   Revealed comparative advantage indices in 2002

SITC Code:	0	1	2	3	4	5	6	7	8	9
China-M	0.85	0.33	0.48	0.37	0.08	0.46	1.26	1.01	2.64	0.09
Hong Kong	0.20	0.46	0.37	0.03	0.14	0.48	1.06	1.13	2.95	0.47
Chile	4.27	3.75	7.96	0.16	0.25	0.58	2.44	0.06	0.12	1.88
Mexico	0.71	1.35	0.35	1.26	0.07	0.35	0.63	1.52	1.22	0.05
Indonesia	1.78	0.76	4.21	5.12	18.17	0.76	2.20	0.66	1.82	0.38
Malaysia	0.40	0.40	0.85	1.22	13.27	0.46	0.54	1.55	0.73	0.57
Philippines	0.72	0.19	0.40	0.16	2.72	0.10	0.24	1.91	0.97	0.11
Singapore	0.25	0.87	0.24	1.10	0.47	0.91	0.30	1.64	0.72	1.84
Korea	0.25	0.26	0.36	0.57	0.03	0.83	1.28	1.58	0.55	0.26
Japan	0.08	0.10	0.30	0.05	0.05	0.78	0.81	1.74	0.72	1.93
Australia	3.40	2.44	6.68	2.96	0.71	0.42	0.88	0.31	0.32	5.35
NZ	8.47	1.44	4.74	0.25	1.20	0.64	0.95	0.19	0.32	2.06
Canada	1.22	0.44	2.62	1.78	0.44	0.59	1.16	0.98	0.58	3.21
USA	1.10	0.74	1.45	0.24	0.72	1.18	0.72	1.30	1.01	1.70
APEC 16	0.77	0.55	1.09	0.61	1.02	0.70	0.84	1.21	1.13	1.31

Note: Taiwan and Thailand are excluded due to missing data.

Source: Author's own calculation using data from UN Comtrade database SITC
Revision III (UN Statistics Division 2005).

comparative advantages in assembly operations, and Japan and the USA,
the most developed members, have a comparative advantage in the production of parts and components. China-M has shown catch-up in both
areas. The newly industrialized economies, Taiwan, Mexico, Hong Kong,
Korea and Singapore, have performed strongly in both fields. It is interesting to note that Japan's comparative advantage in assembly operations actually increased in the 1990s. This may be the result of the
withdrawal of many Japanese companies from overseas operations since
the early 1990s.

INTRA-INDUSTRY TRADE

Another important feature associated with trade among the APEC region
is the dramatic increase in intra-industry trade (IIT). To provide an assessment, the following conventional IIT index proposed by Grubel and Lloyd
(1975) is computed:

$$IIT_{ic} = \frac{x_{ic} + m_{ic} - |x_{ic} - m_{ic}|}{x_{ic} - m_{ic}} \qquad (4.4)$$

Table 4.6   Percentage of products in which APEC members have a comparative advantage

APEC Economies	Production operations			Assembly operations		
	1985	1995	2001	1985	1995	2001
China-M	6.7	11.7	20.0	41.7	55.0	53.3
Hong Kong	18.3	23.3	23.3	36.7	23.3	31.7
Korea	6.7	13.3	15.0	25.0	41.7	33.3
Taiwan	20.0	31.7	28.3	13.3	35.0	31.7
Indonesia	n.a.	5.0	10.0	65.0	55.0	63.3
Thailand	8.3	11.7	15.0	33.3	55.0	58.3
Malaysia	8.3	15.0	18.3	53.3	45.0	43.3
Philippines	6.7	10.0	10.0	38.3	50.0	31.7
Singapore	20.0	23.3	20.0	36.7	40.0	38.3
Mexico	n.a.	20.0	33.3	45.0	46.7	53.3
Japan	43.3	58.3	56.7	3.3	8.3	21.7
USA	61.7	63.3	66.7	30.0	33.3	31.7

Note: The numbers are a percentage of products in which APEC member economies have a comparative advantage. They are based on SITC revision 2 classification and do not include all APEC member economies (Ng and Yeats 2003, Table 19.1).

where

IIT_{ic} = index of intra-industry trade in commodity group c for country i
x_{ic} = value of exports of commodity group c by country i
m_{ic} = value of imports of commodity group c by country i

IIT index defined in Equation (4.4) has a value range between zero and one or zero and 100 in percentage form.[3] A large value implies great trade between firms in the same industry. As illustrated in Table 4.7, generally more intra-industry trade occurred in commodity groups such as SITCs 5, 6 and 7. This pattern is consistent with the comparative advantage of APEC economies illustrated in Table 4.5. Table 4.7 also shows that members such as Canada, China-M, Hong Kong, Malaysia, Mexico, the Philippines, Korea and Singapore have been more engaged in intra-industry trade than others.

CONCLUDING REMARKS

This chapter examined the major trends in trade among APEC members, and between APEC members and the rest of the world. It has shown that

Table 4.7   Intra-industry trade industries, 2002

	0	1	2	3	4	5	6	7	8	9	Total
Australia	0.37	0.48	0.21	0.47	0.86	0.73	0.98	0.34	0.40	0.54	0.47
Canada	0.79	0.77	0.50	0.16	0.72	0.93	0.81	0.98	0.85	0.29	0.80
Chile	0.11	0.06	0.07	0.42	0.80	0.73	0.40	0.12	0.22	0.55	0.24
China-M	0.42	0.16	0.34	0.94	0.12	0.54	0.83	0.94	0.28	0.16	0.70
HK	0.54	0.75	0.89	0.16	0.45	0.91	0.98	0.96	0.97	0.54	0.94
Indonesia	0.87	1.00	0.75	0.40	0.11	0.75	0.58	0.91	0.22	0.05	0.62
Japan	0.09	0.13	0.28	0.10	0.25	0.72	0.73	0.53	0.75	0.55	0.53
Malaysia	0.71	0.99	0.98	0.54	0.26	0.91	0.87	0.93	0.79	0.67	0.87
Mexico	0.83	0.17	0.50	0.49	0.12	0.39	0.70	0.87	0.86	0.23	0.79
NZ	0.35	1.00	0.33	0.49	0.86	0.78	0.98	0.32	0.43	0.14	0.49
Philippines	0.83	0.44	0.59	0.55	0.33	0.23	0.57	0.98	0.43	0.92	0.85
Korea	0.48	0.94	0.29	0.80	0.09	1.00	0.86	0.81	0.88	0.58	0.81
Singapore	0.65	0.87	0.96	0.71	0.48	0.67	0.74	0.98	0.98	0.78	0.91
Thailand	0.29	0.93	0.86	0.44	0.32	0.43	0.66	0.74	0.66	0.88	0.65
USA	0.98	0.79	0.92	0.29	0.93	0.78	0.75	0.73	0.51	0.59	0.69
Total	0.64	0.58	0.56	0.39	0.41	0.76	0.79	0.80	0.65	0.52	

Source: Author's own calculation using data from UN Comtrade database SITC Revision III (UN Statistics Division 2005).

APEC as a group has become an important player in international trade, accounting for more than 40 per cent of world exports and imports in 2002. Substantial growth in trade has been recorded over the past decades though the rate of growth varies between members and over time. In particular, China-M, Hong Kong, Korea, Malaysia, Thailand and Mexico have successfully expanded their shares in international trade since 1980.

Commodities of SITC 7 group (machines and transport equipment) still dominate APEC countries' export products. APEC members also tend to trade more with each other. Especially, members associated with subgroups within APEC, such as ASEAN, NAFTA and ANZCER are more likely to trade with members within the same sub-group. It is also shown that developed and less developed members of APEC have comparative advantages in different areas with the exception of machines and transport equipment (SITC 7). Japan, Indonesia and the Philippines tend to be outliers among the members. This study also demonstrates that the pattern of intra-industry trade among members is consistent with their comparative advantages.

Though descriptive in nature, this chapter does reveal some important findings. These findings show that bilateral or multilateral free trade agreements do promote trade among members. It can be anticipated that there is still scope for the further expansion of trade among APEC members should a free trade area be formed in the near future.[4] However, geographical location or distance between trading partners does matter. Neighbouring nations tend to trade more and benefit more from a free trade agreement. Good examples include trade between Mexico and the USA and between Australia and New Zealand. Should an APEC free trade area be formed, trade between countries such as China-M and Russia, and Japan and Korea would increase substantially.

NOTES

1. See, for example, Chirathiva (2002) and Kathie and Kharas (2004).
2. It should be pointed out that this RCA index is asymmetric in the sense that it ranges from one to infinity for products in which a country has comparative advantage but only zero to one for the case of comparative disadvantage. To correct this skewed distribution, several symmetric RCA indices have been proposed (see, for example, Dalum *et al.* 1998 and Laursen 1998).
3. It is noted that alternative forms of IIT index have been proposed by Hamilton and Kniest (1991), Greenaway *et al.* (1994) and Brulhart (1994).
4. According to APEC plan, an APEC free trade area would be formed by 2010.

REFERENCES

Brown, A.J. (1949), *Applied Economics: Aspects of World Economy in War and Peace*, London: George Allen and Unwin.
Brulhart, M. (1994), 'Marginal intra-industry trade: measurement and the relevance for the pattern of industrial adjustment', *Weltwirtschaftliches Archiv*, **130** (3), 600–13.
Chirathiva, S. (2002), 'ASEAN-China free trade area: background, implications and future development', *Journal of Asian Economics*, **13** (5), 671–86.
Dalum, B., K. Laursen and G. Villumsen (1998), 'Structural change in OECD export specialization patterns: de-specialization and "stickiness"', *International Review of Applied Economics*, **12** (3), 423–44.
Greenaway, D., R.C. Hine, C. Milner and R. Elliott (1994), 'Adjustment and the measurement of marginal intra-industry trade', *Weltwirtschaftliches Archiv*, **130** (2), 418–27.
Grubel, H. and P.J. Lloyd (1975), *Intra-Industry Trade*, London: Macmillan.
Hamilton, C. and P. Kniest (1991), 'Trade liberalization, structural adjustment and intra-industry trade', *Weltwirtschaftliches Archiv*, **127** (2), 356–67.
International Monetary Fund (2002), *International Financial Statistics Yearbook 2002*, Washington, DC: IMF.
International Monetary Fund (2003), *International Financial Statistics Yearbook 2003*, Washington, DC: IMF.
Kathie, K. and H. Kharas (eds) (2004), *East Asia Integrates: A Trade Policy Agenda for Shared Growth*, Washington, DC: Oxford University Press and World Bank.

Kojima, K. (1964), 'The pattern of international trade among advanced countries', *Hitotsubashi Journal of Economics*, **5** (1), 16–36.

Lall, S. and M. Albaldejo (2004), 'China's competitive performance: a threat to East Asian manufactured exports', *World Development*, **32** (9), 1441–66.

Laursen, K. (1998), 'Revealed comparative advantage and the alternatives as measures of international specialization', *DRUID Working Paper No. 98–30*, Danish Research Unit for Industrial Dynamics, Denmark. Available from: http://ideas.repec.org/p/aal/abbswp/98-30.html.

Ng, F. and A. Yeats (2003), 'Major trade trends in East Asia: what are their implications for regional cooperation and growth?', *World Bank Policy Research Paper 3084*, Washington, DC: World Bank.

United Nations Statistics Division (2005), 'Commodity Trade Statistics Database (UN Comtrade)', unstats.un.org/unsd/comtrade, 31 January.

Weiss, J. (2004), 'People's Republic of China and its neighbours: partners or competitors for trade and investment?', *ADB Institute Discussion Paper No.13*, Tokyo. Available from: www.adbi.org/articles/547.prc.and.neighbors/default.php, September 2004.

Weiss, J and S. Gao (2003), 'China's export threat to ASEAN: competition in the US and Japanese markets', *ADB Institute Discussion Paper No.2*, Tokyo. Available from: http://www.adbi.org/articles/86.prc.export.threat/default.php, September 2004.

PART III

East Asia and the Pacific

5. Australia–United States free trade agreement and its implications for Japan

Ippei Yamazawa

INTRODUCTION

Since both the United States and Australia are major trading partners of Japan, it is natural for Japan to be concerned about any possible negative impacts of the recently concluded Australia–United States free trade agreement (AUSFTA). The main focus of this chapter is on various implications of AUSFTA for the economy of Japan. It is divided into five sections. Impacts of AUSFTA on the Japanese economy are discussed in the next section which is followed by an analysis of Japan's economic relationship with Australia and the USA in the context of AUSFTA. Possible implications of AUSFTA for Japan's FTA strategy with regards to its major regional trading partners such as East Asia, ASEAN and China are discussed in the fourth section. The chapter concludes with an analysis of the possibility of greater Asia-Pacific regional integration in light of AUSFTA.

IMPACTS OF AUSFTA ON THE JAPANESE ECONOMY

Australia, Japan and the United States are all major trading nations in the Asia-Pacific region and bilateral trade between any pair of the three countries is important for all of the parties. Both the USA and Australia are important trading partners of Japan. The USA is the largest trading partner of Japan. Its export to and imports from the USA amounted to US$126 839 million and US$62 435 million respectively during 2004 (JETRO 2004a, pp. 25–6). It was the USA's third largest export destination and fourth largest source for imports in 2004 (US Bureau of Economic Analysis 2004).

Australia is another important source of imports for Japan, ranking at number four with US$19 430 million in 2004 (JETRO 2004b). The main contributors to this amount were coal, iron ore and bovine meat (DFAT 2005a). Australia ranked twelfth in Japan's export destinations, with US$11 796 million in 2004, in which passenger motor vehicles made up a large proportion (JETRO 2004b and DFAT 2005a). Japan's importance to Australia as a trading partner is unquestionable. Japan is Australia's largest receiver of exports and the third largest supplier of imports, making this country Australia's largest trading partner. Historically, Australia enjoys a healthy trade surplus with Japan. During 2004, this surplus was to the tune of US$7633 million.

On the contrary, Australia incurs a large trade deficit with the USA. During 2004, it was the largest supplier of Australia's imports and the fourth largest export destination (DFAT 2005b). For the USA, Australia was its 30th source of imports and 14th receiver of exports (US Bureau of Economic Analysis 2004).

However, judging from the commodity list of Japan's exports to Australia and the USA, it is unlikely that the AUSFTA will affect significantly Japan's exports to Australia and the USA. In particular, Japanese main exports items to these two countries such as transport, electric, and precision machineries do not compete directly with Australian or American products. Tariffs on these products have already been reduced in these two countries. Consequently, few of these Japanese products will be replaced by American or Australian products in each other's market when the AUSFTA is implemented. However, the impact of Japan–USA FTA, if it happens, on Australia products or that of Japan–Australia FTA on American products is expected to be much bigger. Australia and the United States have been competing with each other in their exports of agricultural and mineral products to Japan since the 1970s. In recent years, the Japanese Government stopped importation of beef from the United States because of the manifestation of the BSE among American cows and substituted it by Australian beef.

AUSFTA AND JAPAN'S RELATIONSHIPS WITH AUSTRALIA AND THE UNITED STATES

Historically, Australia has pursued a multi-dimensional RTA approach, which includes multilateral, regional and bilateral approaches to ensure the best possible trading environment for Australian exporters. Australia's longstanding commitment to an open and transparent world trading system remains the bedrock of its trade policy. In addition to the multilateral agenda, Australia is keen to broaden and deepen its economic relationship with all of its major trading partners and its policy is to consider those FTAs which can deliver substantial benefits to the Australian economy in a faster timeframe than can be achieved under WTO negotiations. FTAs can, in fact, complement its wider trade objectives in the WTO. Any FTA concluded by Australia will be fully consistent with its WTO commitments (APEC 2003).

The AUSFTA was negotiated along this strategy and was finalized in February 2004 after 11 months of negotiations. It was agreed to abolish tariffs on all manufactures except for textile and clothing at once, which, according to United States Trade Representative (USTR), will bring forth a large benefit to the US manufacturers. However, sensitive items remained much less liberalized or even excluded. In the United States textile and clothing will be liberalized over 15 years. Beef and dairy products will be liberalized only marginally, and sugar has been completely excluded from the FTA. Australia postpones medicines and investment. The AUSFTA seems to have been highly influenced by political and economic considerations. Australia seems to have been concerned about being left out from the NAFTA and ongoing Free Trade Agreement of the Americas (FTAA), while the USA accommodated Australia's wishes in exchange for their support to the war in Iraq. However, being constrained by farmers' resistance at home before the Presidential election, the USTR implemented only a small liberalization package.[1] No strong criticism has been heard against AUSFTA in Japan because of the reasons stated in the previous section.[2]

What about Japan's approach to Australia and the United States? Japan has maintained strong trade ties with Australia since the 1960s when the rapid growth of Japanese steel and machinery industries was supported by the rapidly expanded imports of iron ore, coal, and other minerals from Australia. This honeymoon period ended with the oil crisis in the 1970s but the complementary trade ties have continued. Tariffs and non-tariff measures have remained only in a few sensitive areas and the two countries have not resorted to a FTA to eliminate them.[3] In May 2003 Prime Minister Koizumi visited Australia and agreed with Prime Minister Howard to continue a regular consultation at the deputy minister level on how to enhance mutual cooperation in the areas of trade and investment further. Few Japanese insist that Japan should start an FTA negotiation with Australia which would include different types of agricultural products and would demand substantial liberalization of the agricultural sector (JETRO 2003).

On the other hand, an FTA between Japan and the United States has been proposed occasionally by both countries. In the early 1990s, the US Ambassador Mansfield proposed a USA–Japan FTA in order to mitigate trade frictions between the two countries. Japan's Ministry of Industry and

International Trade commissioned a study team to respond to it with a Japanese proposal (Matsushita and Kuroda 1990). Although titled 'Japan–US FTA', it focused on policy dialogue between the two countries and partly implemented the Structural Impediment Initiative (SII) in 1992.

Fred Bergsten, Director of the Institute of International Economics (USA), proposed a new USA–Japan FTA in his paper presented at the Foreign Correspondents' Club of Japan in Tokyo in May 2004. After appraising the recent resurgence of the Japanese economy which experienced a lost decade of economic growth since 1992, he suggested the need to introduce a new policy initiative to take advantage of the revival. Further, he recommended that the USA–Japan relationship be further strengthened, referring to dispute settlement and geo-political benefit that would be realized.

There has neither emerged a strong economic rationale for the Japan–Australia FTA nor the Japan–USA FTA. If either goes ahead of other agreements, it will lead to serious concern about trade diversion from other members of the Asia-Pacific region.

JAPAN'S FTA STRATEGY IN EAST ASIA

After 1997–8 Japan adjusted its commercial policy stance to a pragmatic one allowing a wider choice of policy tools, including various forms of RTAs. Japan, more than many other countries, used to show strong attachment to the traditional multilateral approach to trade relations. But with the regionalist trend gaining ground around the world and the increased pressure of competitive liberalization, it had to leave its options open. Without a flexible approach to regionalism, Japan could well end up tying its own hands in the diplomatic sphere.

In 1997, the Japan External Trade Organization (JETRO), a public corporation subordinate to the Ministry of Economy, Trade and Industry, started a joint study with the Mexican Ministry of Commerce on the feasibility of a Japan–Mexico FTA. It responded to Japanese firms' concern about being discriminated against in Mexico compared with American and European firms as a result of the NAFTA and the EU–Mexico FTA. In 1999–2000, the JETRO Institute of Developing Economies conducted a joint study with KIEP, the Korean Institute of International Economic Policy, on a Japan–Korea FTA (Yamazawa 2001). The IDE-KIEP reports highlighted the dynamic effects to be achieved through the integration of the two markets.[4]

In 2000, Japan and Singapore conducted a joint official study on an FTA between the two countries, which was followed by intergovernmental negotiations in 2001. The Japan–Singapore Economic Partnership Agreement was concluded by the two nations' prime ministers in January 2002. It conforms to Prime Minister Goh Chok Tong's 'new age FTA' concept and incorporates facilitation and ecotech elements as well as the elimination of tariffs and non-tariff measures. Singapore is to eliminate all tariffs, while Japan is to eliminate 98 per cent of its tariffs on manufactured products but exclude some sensitive agricultural products. Services trade is to be liberalized 90 per cent by Singapore and 86 per cent by Japan. Agreements on investment, mutual recognition of procedures, the movement of professionals and intellectual property rights are also included. The scope for economic partnership is extended to cover information technology (IT), human resource development, trade and investment promotion, small and medium enterprises, tourism, electronic trade and document exchange. Prime Minister Koizumi made it clear in his 14 January 2002 speech in Singapore that Japan was willing to conclude similar economic partnership agreements with other ASEAN members whilst working out a Japan–ASEAN FTA.

Japan–China Rivalry in their Approach to ASEAN

China and Japan are now negotiating FTAs with ASEAN. When the ASEAN + 3 summit was held in Phnom Penh in November 2002, China signed a comprehensive economic cooperation framework agreement with ASEAN, concluding a year-long round of negotiations. China also announced that it would sign an FTA with ASEAN between 2010 and 2015. Moreover, when China joined the WTO in 2002, it promised ASEAN that it would open its domestic markets in eight agricultural product categories, such as fresh vegetables, fruit and ornamental plants, before such an FTA was reached.

Japan has already had close economic ties with ASEAN for more than 30 years. Trade intensity between Japan and ASEAN has already risen to as high as 2.5, while China–ASEAN trade intensity was still at around 1.1. Unlike traditional bilateral economic cooperation between Japan and ASEAN members, the Japan–ASEAN Comprehensive Economic Partnership Agreement aims at economic integration between Japan and the unified ASEAN market. If AFTA is successful, the ASEAN economies will form a single market. If Japan signs an FTA with a unified ASEAN, Japanese firms and ASEAN corporations will both benefit from newly emerging business opportunities. Expecting AFTA to be implemented this year, many firms, mainly Japanese corporations, are working to establish ASEAN-wide business networks. However, such networks will require smooth distribution and telecommunications services between ASEAN countries. For this to be possible, the ASEAN countries need to ease customs procedures, liberalize transportation and telecommunications services, and create more coherent rules of origins and certification standards. The comprehensive economic partnership is a new type of FTA that will address these challenges. At the time of the ASEAN + 3 Summit in October 2003 Japan and ASEAN agreed to negotiate a FTA within a ten-year framework.[5]

FTAs Help Revitalize Japan

Japan's change in its policy stance also responds to the need to utilize East Asian dynamism in order to sustain the growth of its matured economy. The relationship between Japan and East Asia has undergone fundamental changes in the last ten years. A decade ago, Japan stood out as the leader of the 'flying geese' in Asian development (industrial transformation). It provided assistance for development in other East Asian countries much as a father would treat his sons. Now the sons have grown strong and the father has matured and entered old age. Japan still has money and technology, but it has lost its vigour for new growth and has little stomach for bold reforms. Not only must it live in harmony with its sons, it must also survive in a globalized world.

The East Asian region is the home base for the Japanese economy. Ever since the appreciation of the yen since 1985, Japanese companies have been moving out of Japan and establishing business networks throughout the region. This continued even during the prolonged domestic slump of the 1990s. It is important for Japanese companies and the Japanese economy that East Asian countries and regions move forward with structural reforms and return to the path of steady economic growth. The keys to this are the promotion of trade and investment liberalization, the reinforcement of market competition functions, and the resolution of remaining structural problems. This requires support for capacity building, and economic cooperation will be vital in this.

Japan's Changing Industrial Structure

Japan is now implementing a variety of reforms in public institutions and regulations and its industrial and firm structures are undergoing drastic changes. This reform is partly being stimulated by dynamic changes in China and ASEAN, but also by feedback to the changes in those two areas in the form of accelerated and adjusted performance of Japanese firms. The Japan–ASEAN Comprehensive Economic Partnership has to be designed so that the dynamic interaction of these changes can be taken into consideration.

Industrial adjustment should not be overwhelmed by short-term conflict over interest. On the Japanese side, agriculture is currently seen as the biggest barrier. Rather than worrying about how to exclude it from FTA talks, the nation should be working on this issue positively. For example, in 1993 production of Japan's rice crop decreased by 26 per cent compared with normal years due to cold weather, and emergency imports of 263 000 tonnes of rice were conducted for 1993–4. Of this amount, 42 per cent was from China, 30 per cent was from Thailand and 21 per cent was from the United States. After that, the crop returned to the normal harvest amount and rice imports were reduced to minimum-access levels. However, according to agricultural experts, there is a big probability that Japan will need to rely on imports of substantial amounts of rice every year in the next five to ten years. This is because the farmers, many of whom are already ageing, are facing difficulty in passing on their jobs to such a degree that regular crops will decrease. In this case, from where would Japan import?

Would it be fine to rely on the United States or Australia, which have problems relating to water shortages? Would it not be natural to rely on East Asian countries that are close, in the same monsoon area, and manage rice cropping through small, family-run farms? If this is the case, then Japan should actively advise East Asian countries on agricultural management by promoting such issues as the non-use of excessive agricultural chemicals and genetically modified seeds, offering solutions to water shortages, and securing safe agricultural imports, rather than simply saying that 'importing rice should not be permitted'. A comprehensive FTA is the framework that could make this type of industrial cooperation possible. Rather than leaving agricultural imports as a taboo and obstructing an FTA, we should make use of an FTA and seek ways of sustainable reliance on agricultural imports in the longer term. Securing safe and stable food imports should be the essential goal of the East Asian economic community.

Obstacles to integration also exist in Japan's domestic markets. Liberalization of agricultural product markets takes time because Japanese farmers possess disproportionate political power and seek to use that power to oppose liberalization. However, many Japanese economists understand that Japan and ASEAN will both benefit from opening up agricultural product markets.[6]

Japan's move towards regionalism has been accelerated since late 2003. Both Japanese and Korean Government started the FTA negotiation in December 2003. Bilateral FTA negotiations with Thailand, Malaysia and Philippines started in January to March 2004. Although the Japanese Government planned to conclude negotiations with three ASEAN members by 2004 and with Korea by 2005, this is yet to happen. The Japanese Government finally agreed to establish a FTA with Mexico in

March 2004, under which Japan conceded a large increase of import quota for pork and orange juice, the first occasion of meaningful liberalization of agricultural products by Japan.

Towards East Asian Community

Although both Japan and China are seeking FTAs with ASEAN, neither Tokyo nor Beijing has proposed a Japan–China FTA. Top political leaders agree that trilateral cooperation among Japan, China and Korea would be desirable, but only scholars have explored this issue. In forming an East Asian economic community, it will be essential to involve the ASEAN + 3 countries, Hong Kong and Taiwan in the future. Only by doing so can the East Asian economies form an economic zone comparable to North America and the European Union. Though an East Asian economic zone would be viable in my belief, economic disparities among Japan, Korea and China, differences in economic systems, a lack of experience in regional economic integration and residual distrust from events of the past century have prevented the successful formation of a regional economic community. However, success in the era of globalization will require that the countries of East Asia make every reasonable effort to achieve successful economic integration, such as bilateral and multilateral integration schemes. However, East Asia should attempt to avoid a situation in which the region has only a China–ASEAN FTA, because in such a situation, the region will suffer adversely from trade-diversion effects. For this reason as well, all of East Asia should aim at an East Asian Economic Community as its ultimate goal, while making efforts to form bilateral and multilateral FTAs in the intermediate process.

AUSFTA AND THE ASIA-PACIFIC ECONOMIC COOPERATION

In the Asia-Pacific region we have another common action agenda for liberalization and integration, the Bogor Goal of APEC. In 1994, the APEC leaders committed themselves to 'achieving free and open trade in the region by 2010 and 2020' (Yamazawa and Urata 2000). It has played a locomotive role of APEC but the literal realization of the Bogor Goal is difficult due to the voluntarism of APEC and the lack of an enforcement mechanism. However, APEC conducts a peer review of its members' Individual Action Plans for liberalization and facilitation.[7]

APEC can at best play a catalyst or cheer leader role in the WTO liberalization. However, APEC can also help liberalization by coordinating regional trading arrangements between its members. Open regionalism has been an important asset of APEC. Pacific Economic Cooperation Council (PECC) (2003) strongly recommends it and encouraged all APEC members to apply their liberalization on an unconditional MFN basis to members and non-members alike. However, it would be too strict if we defined open regionalism as the unconditional MFN application of liberalization by individual members. Its more practical definition will be delivered by rephrasing it as 'open regional cooperation', that is, promoting regional cooperation consistently with the multilateral rules such as WTO, World Bank and IMF. The catalyst role of APEC suggested above fit this concept of open regionalism well.

The Bogor Declaration called on the Eminent Persons Group (EPG) 'to review the interrelationships between APEC and the existing sub-regional trading arrangements (Sub-Regional Trading Arrangements (SRTA), such as NAFTA, ANZCERTA and AFTA then) and to examine possible options to prevent obstacles to each other and to promote consistency in their relations'. The Third EPG Report (APEC 1995) emphasizes that any SRTA acceleration or linkage must be fully consistent with the WTO. It recommended that any new RTA initiatives within APEC be promptly submitted to the WTO for confirmation that they meet this test and for surveillance of their performance in practice.

It also recommends that any SRTA acceleration or linkage be extended to other APEC economies under the non-mutually exclusive four-part formula already proposed by the EPG for the extension of APEC liberalization itself to non-members of the broader grouping:

- SRTA members should implement their acceleration or linkage via unilateral (and hence MFN) liberalization to the maximum possible extent;
- each SRTA acceleration or linkage should be accompanied by a clear policy statement by the member economies that they intend to continue reducing their trade barriers to other APEC members as well as to other members of their SRTA;
- each SRTA acceleration or linkage should be accompanied by the respective group's indication of a willingness to extend its new liberalization to other APEC members on a reciprocal basis;
- any individual SRTA member can unilaterally extend its SRTA acceleration or linkage to other APEC economies on a conditional or unconditional basis. It would have to do so to all non-APEC members as well if it were to proceed on an unconditional basis, however, because the WTO does not permit selective extension of preferences to non-members of an SRTA.

The proposal for an FTA for APEC (FTAAP) made recently by some economists and businessmen seems to be along this line. In order to strengthen the weakened momentum in APEC for achieving the Bogor goal and to prevent the bi- and sub-regional FTAs prevalent among APEC members from distorting trade and investment and dividing the Asia-Pacific, they argue APEC should tackle a new attempt, negotiation for FTAAP, departing from traditional non-binding and open regionalism approach. They detail the design of FTAAP.

It seems to me that FTAAP is beyond the capacity of APEC at the moment. I share with them the need for strengthening momentum for achieving the Bogor Goal and the concern about possible trade and investment distortion by the FTA moves among APEC members. But we witness severe conflicts of interest between APEC members. APEC trade ministers support the Doha Development Agenda (DDA) in general but have not been able to resolve the conflicts in individual areas. I cannot see why APEC ministers can agree on major DDA issues within the FTAAP framework before they do in Geneva. I would like to see more efforts to resolve these conflicts within APEC in order to support the feasibility of FTAAP.

After all, the FTAAP proposal seems to be a hasty approach and it may endanger the APEC framework itself. Rather I would like to take advantage of current momentum for bi- and sub-regional FTA moves among APEC members and cleverly guide them in the direction consistent with multilateral rules; that is along the line of Trade Forum Proposal for an APEC Common Understanding on FTAs (PECC 2003). APEC should remain a catalyst rather than playing a negotiator role itself.[8]

NOTES

1. *American New Policy*, JETRO New York Center, No. 3556 and 3579, both February 2004 (in Japanese).
2. It is often argued that Japanese financial institutions will complain about Australian discrimination in favour of US competitors under the AUSFTA. However, they are now not so much engaged in external operations as in domestic restructuring and it will take some time for them to pay attention to possible discrimination in Australia. Nevertheless it is Australia that will lose from her limiting foreign financial institutions other than American to come into Australia.
3. The author belonged to a study group on Japan–Australia's relationship under Dr Sabro Okita and Sir John Crawford in the 1970s and 1980s when we discussed not the feasibility of an FTA between the two but such measures as alternative forms of long term contract and better access to international capital markets for mineral resources exports. Although a FTA was proposed to strengthen Australia's ties with China and other East Asian countries at our symposium on AUSFTA, various facilitation measures will work well for two countries with complementary trade patterns.
4. The Japanese and Korean governments took the additional step of following up the initial study with a joint business forum in 2001, in order to observe the public acceptance

of this proposal in both countries. They finally started official negotiations in December 2003.

5. The underlying logic for the Japan–ASEAN Comprehensive Economic Partnership agreement was proposed jointly by JARIM, a group of the JETRO Institute of Developing Economies and ten ASEAN research institutes (IDE 2003).

6. In 2003 Japan suffered again from a cold summer in northern areas and rice production decreased by 20 per cent. However, the reduced production was offset by declining rice consumption and accumulated reserves for the past years so that Japan did not have to resort to emergency imports of rice.

7. I participated in this peer review process of APEC as a consultant and helped to draft the IAP Study Report on Australia (APEC 2003). APEC senior officials completed this peer review for most of the APEC members within 2005.

8. I would like to update my discussion presented two years ago. AUSFTA has been implemented so that US investment to Australia can increase due to no examination requirements, but no complaints of discrimination have been heard from Japanese competitors. The momentum for East Asian Community increased in Kuala Lumpur in December 2005, when both the ASEAN plus Three Summit and the East Asian Summit (involving ASEAN plus Three and Australia, New Zealand and India) were held, However, trade and investment liberalization and facilitation will be handled within the ASEAN plus Three framework, while the latter mainly aims to discuss a wider regional cooperation such as anti-terrorist measures, epidemics and natural disasters. Both the Leaders Declaration and Ministerial Statement of APEC Busan in November 2005 focused on the promotion of the WTO's DDA negotiation and open regionalism but did not mention the FTAAP in the APEC region. The developments of the past two years have been consistent with my arguments in this chapter.

REFERENCES

APEC (1995), 'Implementing the APEC vision, third report of the Eminent Persons Group', in *Selected APEC Documents 1995*, Singapore: APEC Secretariat, pp. 151–7.

APEC (2003), *IAP Study Report on Australia*, Singapore: APEC Secretariat.

Bergsten, F. (2004), *The Resurgent Japanese Economy and a Japan–United States Free Trade Agreement*, presented to the Foreign Correspondents' Club of Tokyo, 12 May 2004, Tokyo.

DFAT (2005a), 'Country, economy and regional information – Japan', www.dfat.gov.au/geo/japan/index.html, 1 February.

DFAT (2005b), 'Country, economy and regional information – USA', www.dfat.gov.au/geo/us/index.html, 1 February.

Institute of Developing Economies (IDE) (2003), *Toward Japan–ASEAN Comprehensive Economic Partnership*, Joint research program among Japanese and ASEAN economic institutes (JARIM), Tokyo: Japan External Trade Organization.

JETRO (2003), 'White Paper on Trade and Investment for 2003', www.jetro.go.jp/en/stats/white_paper/, 3 February.

JETRO (2004a), 'Japanese Trade in 2004', www.jetro.go.jp/en/stats/statistics/, 3 February.

JETRO (2004b), 'Japanese Trade and Investment Statistics', www.jetro.go.jp/en/stats/statistics/gaikyo_200412.xls, 1 February.

Matsushita, M. and M. Kuroda (1990), *Japan–US Economic Cooperation Charter: Constructing a Framework for a Japan–US Global Partnership in the 21st Century (in Japanese)*, Tokyo: PHP Research Institute.

Pacific Economic Cooperation Council (PECC) Trade Forum (2003), *Asia-Pacific RTAs: an Avenue s for Achieving APEC's Bogor Goals*, PECC.

US Bureau of Economic Analysis (2004), 'US International Trade in Goods and Services', www.bea.gov/bea/newsrelarchive/2005/trad1305.xls, 1 February.

Yamazawa, I. (2001), 'Assessing the Japan–Korea FTA', *The Developing Economies*, **39** (1), 3–48.

Yamazawa, I. (2003), 'East Asian economic cooperation', in Zhang Yunling (ed.), *East Asian Cooperation: Progress and Future*, Beijing: World Affairs Press.

Yamazawa, I. and S. Urata (2000), 'APEC's progress in trade and investment liberalization and facilitation', in Yamazawa, I. (ed.), *Challenges and Tasks for the Twenty-First Century*, London: Routledge.

6. Free trade areas and economic integration in East Asia: the view from China

Christopher Howe

INTRODUCTION

This chapter is divided into four parts. The first discusses major issues thrown up by past experience and analyses of regional economic integration and the light they throw on contemporary enthusiasms to establish Free Trade Areas (FTAs) in Asia. Second, we examine the major trends in China's external sector and, in the third section, consider how these relate to Chinese approaches to trade policy. Finally we pull these strands together to examine what the FTA drive actually means in the Chinese context and what priorities Chinese trade policy is likely to adopt.

Understanding Chinese thinking is by no means easy. These issues are open and debated so that there is no commanding official view on the subject and good material in English is rather limited.[1] However, the Chinese trade literature is quite rich and combined with an examination of actions as well as words, at least the main outlines of what is happening can be identified.

FREE TRADE AREAS: EXPERIENCE AND POLICY ISSUES

Free Trade Areas are one of the simplest arrangements of all systems of regional integration. A brief listing of this hierarchy is shown in Figure 6.1, with the most advanced forms at the bottom of the chart.

Before considering this sequence further, it is important to bear in mind that international economic integration requires as prerequisites a reasonable degree of economic institutional sophistication and a successful internal process by which barriers to trade and resource movement have been eliminated. On the basis of internal resource flexibility and competitively

Type of cooperation	Key features
Sectoral Cooperation Arrangements	Lowering of national frontiers restricted to limited sectors/commodities
Free Trade Area (FTA)	Removal of tariff barriers between members with variable external barriers against outsiders
Customs Union (CU)	Above, with a common external tariff
Common Market (CM)	Above, with free movements of labour and capital
Economic Union (EU)	Above, with policy and further institutional harmonization to ensure the rationality of specialization, trade and factor flows
Total Economic Integration	Above, with complete harmonization of macro-economic, social policies and common currency system

Figure 6.1　The typology of regional integration agreement

based specialization, gains can be made through international integration of varying types. The overall history whereby a country achieves a successful interlock between internal and external market development may therefore often be a lengthy one, involving as it must the dissolution of traditional forms of economic organization and new attitudes to international relationships.

Once an economy moves to a point on the hierarchy of international arrangements outlined above, economic logic will pull the economy towards further integration. Comparative advantage in trade, for example, can only work properly if price formation mechanisms in the trading partners are similar in character and this requires institutional arrangements that ensure the functioning of competitive mechanisms. Further, since trade and factor movements substitute for each other, a 'level playing field' for movements of labour and capital will also be needed. This in turn will require coordination of fiscal, monetary, social and other policies.

These long run processes of national and international integration will be subject to conflicting pressures. For while on the one hand the gravity pull of economics will be reinforced by the self-interest of newly created bureaucracies and economic gainers, change will be hindered by vested interests – both of the narrow, sectional variety and those of the wider regional or nationalistic variety. The latter will focus particularly on the equity of the distribution of gains from new arrangements under the new order (Balassa 1969; Das 2004).

This last point reminds us that however interested we may be in the *economics* of Regional Integration Agreements (RIAs), their foundation and history are always going to rest heavily on *political* factors. If we think, for example, of three of the most important RIAs formed before the Second World War, these would be:

1. the Prussian Tariff Union (1818) leading to the pan-German Zollverein (1834);
2. the British system of Imperial Preference; and
3. the Japanese East Asian Co-Prosperity Sphere (EACPS).

In each case politics were basic. Thus the Prussian systems, supported by subsidized railway building, contributed significantly to the formation of a new German state; a state that then continued on a trajectory of state inspired, protected industrialization.[2] In the British case, while domestic vested economic interests supported Imperial Preference, anxieties about the overall political integrity of the Imperial system were also key factors – a point frequently emphasized by Churchill. Finally, in the Japanese case, the intra-regional specialization and stabilization called for by the Co-Prosperity Sphere incorporated elements of strong economic logic and was in part rationalized by early versions of the 'Flying Geese' theory of trade and development. However, pushed to extremes by politics and war, the lack of access to high technology and raw materials led ultimately to an economic, as well as a strategic demise.

In the post-war period two new regional integration systems appeared, both again built on political foundations. The first of these was the Soviet based Council for Mutual Economic Assistance (CMEA).

The CMEA was designed to rationalize resource allocation and facilitate trade between planned economies and to do so in ways that were to the Soviet advantage. The problem with the system was that by the time it got under way in the early 1960s, members had already created (through central planning) extremely similar domestic industrial structures, thus making the task of achieving inter- or intra-industry specialization very difficult. Planners understood from purely physical data that economies of scale could be improved by specialization, but there were no rational guidelines to advance this process which was in any case resisted on grounds of national interest and distrust in the capability of planned systems to deliver reliably across borders. Thus in the end, the limited criterion of raw material endowment tended to be the only consistent determinant of CMEA inter-country specialization.[3]

The other post-war system was the European Economic Community.

The EEC was an arrangement designed to cement a peace after 75 years of the Franco-German war and hostility. The economic basis of the Union

was market enlargement and a protected exchange between French agriculture and German industry. This proved to be an arrangement which,
with its congruent economic and political dimensions, achieved its core
objective over many decades.

It is important to note two important features common to many of these
experiences. First, in the first four cases there was a single political hegemon
with the power to dictate the terms of the arrangement, to put pressure on
short term losers and, naturally, to guide the allocation of longer term gains
to ensure benefits for itself. Also, in all of these cases, the RIA embraced a
mixture of advanced and relatively backward economies, with the hegemon
at the upper end of the spectrum and hence not concerned with trade diversion losses often suffered at the other end. The EEC, in contrast, has been
a system of economies at approximately similar levels of development.
Leadership in the EEC has not been the monopoly of a single hegemon,
but for long was the property of a Franco-German alliance. This was a
'core' strong enough to resolve most policy and distributional conflicts.

The 1960s and 1970s brought a new type of RIA. These were the FTAs
and 'Common Markets' established between developing countries (for
example the Latin American Free Trade Area and the East African
Common Market). These were, essentially, attempts to lower the cost of
protection and industrial import substitution policies.

In broad terms, therefore, post-war RIAs may be said to have had three
different economic objectives:

- improved static re-allocation of resources based on inter- and intra-
  industry specialization;
- improved dynamic performance to be achieved by market enlargement, economies of scale and a self-sustaining process of technical
  change; and
- improved stability based on a localized insulation from destabilizing
  elements in the world economy.

The important lessons to be drawn from the generally unsuccessful RIAs
created by developing countries are, first, that gains in the form of newly
created or expanded industries tend to be very unequally distributed and
tend to accrue to those economies that are initially more advanced and
larger in the scale of their domestic markets. Second, unless this economic
inequality is matched by political inequality in the form of a political
hegemon, this strain is likely to prove fatal. A third lesson is that successful
RIAs call for substantial bureaucratic skills both to ensure that feasible
arrangements are established in the first place, and then to monitor
progress and adjust the system as it evolves. Most of these probems have

been illustrated by the history of the Association of South East Asian Nations (ASEAN), an Asian RIA that also started from a primarily political base.

Finally, both pre- and post Second World War experience draws attention to a fundamental decision that has to be made by RIAs. Is the basic mechanism of resource allocation to be predominantly market forces, or is some form of administrative guidance and market management to be a central feature of the new arrangement? For example, the Japanese EACPS was clearly understood to require some form of supra-national 'industrial policy' to ensure that mutual adjustments took place expeditiously. In contrast, the EEC system has always been a predominantly market driven institution, operating it must be said within a rather weak regime of competition policy.

We shall find that the problems of the interplay between politics and economics, of distributional conflicts likely to arise as dynamic gains accrue, and of choice between market and state led adjustment systems, are all directly relevant to our understanding of China's current policy options in respect of FTAs. As we shall see, China's recent initiatives are extremely varied. They range from highly localized bilateral and cross-border arrangements, to big, long term visions that embrace the entire East Asia region. These options therefore embrace RIAs with every possible combination of country size, level of development, potential basis for specialization and number of partners. To speculate on the likely outcomes of Chinese initiatives and to form some view of why they have already formed priorities for immediate action, we need to take into account the experience and considerations outlined above. Further, while the past often has much still to tell us, old lessons have to be modified to take into account new features that have appeared in the East Asian economic landscape during the past decade or so.

THE RECENT EVOLUTION OF CHINA'S INTERNATIONAL ECONOMIC RELATIONS

Before exploring the institutional and policy issues, we need to sketch some of the recent developments in the evolution of China's international economic relations.

The basic data for visible trade are shown in Table 6.1 and these are converted into growth rates in Table 6.2. In these tables, 1980 represents the beginning of the Open Door policy and 1990, 1995 and 2000 are the last years of the Seventh, Eighth and Ninth Five Year Plans respectively. What is remarkable about these figures is the persistence and exuberance of this

Table 6.1   China's visible trade: selected years 1980–2003, US$ billion

Year	Exports	Imports	Total trade
1980	18.12	20.02	38.14
1990	62.09	53.35	115.44
1995	148.78	132.08	280.86
2000	249.2	225.09	474.29
2001	266.1	243.55	509.65
2002	325.57	295.2	620.77
2003	438.23	412.76	850.99

Source: National Bureau of Statistics China (2004), p. 158.

Table 6.2   Rates of growth of China exports, 1980–2003, per cent
             per annum

1980–1990	1990–1995	1995–2000	2000–2003
13.11	19.1	10.87	20.8

Source: National Bureau of Statistics China (2004), p. 158.

expansion. It might well have been expected that after a long period of constraint under a policy of autarchy and a system of planning biased against the foreign sector, a burst of activity would occur. But what is seen here, in fact, is trade expansion under what the Chinese analysts term the three regimes or 'models' of development. These are the 'Hong Kong-Guangdong' regime (the 1980s); the 'Jiangsu-(Taiwan)' regime (the late 1980s to mid-1990s); and, the Globalization era (mid-1990s to the present). Each of these regimes essentially reflects a new tide of inward investment and the emergence of new regional clusters of such investment in China.

Expansion has been accompanied by marked structural change in the trade sector. The data for 2002 are shown in Table 6.3. These data relate to the three broad phases of trade expansion referred to above. There was an early phase in which raw materials remained quite important, a second phase based on simple labour intensive products (especially textiles) and the current phase (shown above) in which China plays a central role in the global division of labour. The shares of machinery and transport equipment broadly indicate the intra-industry nature of current trade exchanges, and the high share of 'miscellaneous' products reflects the growth of components and semi-finished products to be expected in this 'globalization' phase.[4]

Table 6.3   Commodity composition of China's foreign trade, 2003, percentage shares

Commodity	Exports	Imports
Primary commodities	7.9	18
Of which: grains and food fuel products	(4)	(7)
Industrial products	92	82
Of which: machinery and transport equipment	(43)	(47)
Light industry, textile, footwear and similar chemicals	(16)	(12)
Miscellaneous products	(29)	(8)

Source: National Bureau of Statistics China (2004), p. 158.

One result of this expansion and transformation is that China's share of world trade has risen from below 1 per cent in 1975 to above 6 per cent by 2002, at which level China had become the world's fifth largest exporter. Domestically, in the same period, China has become the world's largest producer of steel, coal, cement, chemical fertilizers, televisions, of processed sugar and of six major agricultural products. China is also the second largest producer of cloth and electricity (*Tongji yanjiu* (*Statistical Research*) 2003). Looked at through the data on trade composition, the result is that China has a huge surplus on trade in finished goods, and a deficit in intermediate products and this is one of the reasons why China's trade has such different impacts on different economies (Gaulier *et al.* 2005).

This huge trade expansion is closely related both to FDI and to a variety of novel arrangements for processing trade, compensation trade and Original Equipment Manufacturer (OEM) contracting introduced into China after the Open Door policy was initiated in 1979. As a percentage of total exports, processing trade has risen to above 50 per cent and the current estimate is that approximately 60 per cent of exports are from foreign invested enterprises. Total foreign direct investment over the period 1979–2002 was US$446 billion. This investment took off in the early 1990s, peaked in 1998, dipped in the Asian crisis, but is now back to high levels which make China one the world's largest recipients of FDI.

The above sketch is, essentially, the global picture. However, to grasp the mechanics of China's development it is important to become much more spatially focused. For trade, the starting point is the East Asian region as a whole. In Table 6.4 we can inspect the changing shares of world trade in four significant regions.

We see here that, inclusive of Japan, the East Asian region has more than doubled its share of world trade to account for more than a quarter of

Table 6.4   Shares of world exports, four regions, 1975–2001

Country/region	1975	2001
NAFTA	18	19
EU	39.2	34.3
East Asia ex Japan	5.4	18.7
Japan	5.9	7
East Asia with Japan	11.3	25.7
ASEAN	2.7	6.3

Source: Ng and Yeats (2003), p. 3. This paper is an invaluable piece of research relevant to this topic.

Table 6.5   Intra-regional trade expansion, major blocs and ASEAN, 1975–2001

Intra-regional trade as a share of world exports	1975	2001	Rate of growth of intra-regional trade, 1975–2001
East-Asia (ex Japan)	1	6.5	16.4
NAFTA	6.7	10.1	9.9
EU	24.1	20.2	7.5
ASEAN	0.3	1.2	13.9

Source: Calculated from, Ng and Yeats (2003), pp. 3–4.

world exports by 2001. Even more spectacular, however, is the performance of East Asia ex Japan, where the growth is almost fourfold in the same period.

The additional element that can now be added to this is the contribution of the growth of intra-regional trade to these changes.

In Table 6.5 the exceptional performance of the East Asian region is shown clearly, with a growth rate more than 50 per cent higher than the NAFTA group. The EU is the weakest performer. ASEAN is also shown as having increased intra-regional trade very rapidly, but this is from a very low absolute base and ASEAN's share of world trade in 2001 was still only 1.2 per cent.

Where does China fit into this picture? During the period 1985–2001 China's global exports increased thirteenfold. In the same period, China's share of intra-East Asian trade (ex Japan) rose modestly from 24.7 per cent to 30.6 per cent. However, if we look at the world-wide destination of

Table 6.6   Destinations of China's exports

Year	Total exports billions US$	Share to: East Asia (ex Japan) (%)	Of which: ASEAN	Japan	EU	NAFTA
1985	31.356	34.7	10.7	20.8	10	14.7
1995	232.623	39	4.5	15.4	13.9	22.7
2001	415.879	30.7	5	13.9	15.3	29.5

Source: Ng and Yeats (2003), p. 6.

China's exports, it is the EU and above all NAFTA, that emerge as the key expanding destinations.

We see here that East Asia and Japan account for declining shares of the totals, the EU share rises by a half, and the NAFTA share doubles. Much of this trend is explained not simply by Chinese direct exports of labour intensive goods, but also by the relocation of Taiwanese, Hong Kong and Japanese production to China for the purposes of exporting to third country markets in the developed economies.

Moreover, in thinking about these figures one must bear in mind the huge absolute expansion in trade from China. Thus while the share of Chinese exports to the East Asian region may be declining, the volumes involved in absolute terms, notably for the smaller Asian economies, may be enormously significant. Further, if we turn now to look at China's imports during the 'globalization phase' 1995–2001, (that is, the growth of markets for regional exporters) we find that for ten out of 13 East Asian economies, China is the fastest growing market for their exports over this period, and the second fastest in two others. Indeed, the only Asian economy for whom China was not either the fastest or second fastest growing market was Lao PDR which, in 2001, held a share of intra-regional trade of one tenth of one per cent.

Finally, if we look at the individual commodity composition of this intra-regional trade we find that China's exports fall into distinct categories – as was suggested by data in Table 6.3. On the one hand are the labour intensive products: textiles, footwear, toys and so on. Then come the components and semi-finished goods (especially telecoms and office equipment), and, finally, a broad group of electrical goods ranging from motors to switchgears, relays, wires, cables and the like. Overall, of the 30 most important products at the four digit SITC level in East Asian intra-regional trade, China is the largest supplier of 17. Of these nine fall into the labour intensive category and eight into the components/electrical category.

PRELIMINARY STEPS TOWARDS REGIONAL FTA's AND CHINESE THINKING BEHIND THEM

Figure 6.2 lists the major events relevant to a discussion of China's exploration of regional integration agreements of all kinds.

How are we to understand the growing interest of China in regional FTAs indicated by participation in these events? The starting point for this must be a brief description of the main elements of the Chinese 'world view' and the way in which this has evolved, particularly since the Asian economic crisis of 1997 and China's WTO entry in 2002.

There are four important components of this view:

- the underlying 'real' trends in the world economy;
- the evolving strengths, weaknesses and relevance to China of the major trade-related international institutions;
- the 'Japan' problem; and
- issues and challenges around the frontier periphery of China.

'Real' Trends

The keyword in Chinese statements to describe these trends is without doubt 'globalization'. China's rapid economic development and increasing integration into the world economy is, it is argued, based on intensified inter- and intra-industry specialization. This specialization process has been propelled by a combination of trade and foreign direct investment. In the Chinese case, the principal external actors have been Multinational Corporations and overseas Chinese business networks. These are not necessarily alternatives, since they often act in consort, with the overseas Chinese providing the interface between MNCs and Chinese officials and businessmen at local and national levels. The resulting patterns are often complex, linking Chinese producers to a wide variety of companies and national economies (Zhao Jingxia 2002).

Within China, the authorities see and are increasingly concerned with the ways in which this partially market led process of development generates inequalities. These are of many kinds, but of particular concern are those created by the spatial and other advantages of the coastal regions because these have generated a serious East–West cleavage. In a society historically concerned with maintaining strong elements of centralization within its huge natural diversity, this is a serious matter. The 'West' here, it must be emphasized, includes both the Autonomous Regions of the semi-arid north west and the sub-tropical Provinces bordering on Laos, Cambodia and Thailand in the south west.

1989	Formation of APEC with its policy of 'open liberalization'
1990	Malaysian proposal for the 'East Asian Economic Caucus'
1992	ASEAN agrees on proposal to form an FTA
1997	Asian economic crisis breaks First meeting of ASEAN plus 3 (China, Korea and Japan) Proposals for an Asian Monetary Fund
1998	Establishment of the East Asian Vision Group (EAVG) Establishment of ASEAN Surveillance Process to monitor signs of financial distress (ASP)
1999	'Joint Statement on East Asian Cooperation'
2000	The Chiang Mai Initiative on currency cooperation agreed by 10 plus 3 to make bilateral swap arrangements, with the 3 as major contributors China–ASEAN leaders discuss Premier Zhu Rongji's FTA proposal
2001	China joins WTO The EAVG blueprint for the 10 plus 3 region set aside in favour of examining detailed proposals for a FTA, in particular with reference to agricultural issues and the Mekong River Development plans
2002	Singapore–Japan FTA formally signed The ASEAN–China FTA Framework Agreement signed Shanghai meeting of ASEAN plus 3 fails to improve significantly on the Chiang Mai initiative China, Korea and Japan establish machinery to begin research on the possibilities for enlarged cooperation in East Asia China–ASEAN 'South China Sea Code of Conduct' established to defuse tension
2003	China, Korea and Japan confirm intention to establish a North East Asian RIA China agrees Closer Economic Partnership (CEPA) agreements for Hong Kong and Macao
2004	CEPA implementation begins Premier Wen Jiabao emphasises the importance of 'the peaceful rim' Initiation of plans for Pan Pearl River Delta '9 plus 2', that is, Hong Kong/Macao and nine southern Chinese provinces November first meeting of China–ASEAN business summit
2005	October meeting of China–ASEAN Business Summit in Nanning confirms intentions to press ahead with FTA Framework Agreement

Figure 6.2 Major events for advancing the institutional economic integration in Asia, 1989–2004

The other major anxieties about the development process are problems of raw materials, above all, energy shortages. Beijing apart, the latter are now manifested in frequent and widespread power outages in the large Chinese cities. In Beijing, general cuts are replaced by summer factory closures that avoid the international embarrassment that would be caused by intermittent electricity supply to the international office and hotels sector.

The economic challenge to China, therefore, is to continue to maximize the growth, welfare and technological gains from globalization, but to do so on terms that increase raw material and energy security. The political imperatives are both internal and external. The internal necessity is to spread the gains more equitably; the external one is to minimize avoidable trade-related disruptions to the world economic order.

The Institutional Starting Point

China's entry into the WTO is seen as an event of great significance. However, in the short run the direct gains are expected to be slow after the initial effects work through, and certainly not trouble free. This is partly because, in spite of China's size and other eye-catching features, the country is not yet a major power broker inside the WTO. As in the case with UN entry, the Chinese style is to keep a low profile for many years, reserving interventions for crucial issues. Also, the recent record of the WTO is regarded as unimpressive in its delivery of major liberalizing events. For an economy with China's ambitions and track record, the WTO is too slow moving to be an important vehicle for further progress. The fact that regional integration movements are being embraced and deepened so enthusiastically in other parts of the world confirms this perception. It also adds to the urgency of China participating in new, counterbalancing Asian arrangements.

In one important way WTO membership is, nonetheless, seen as having made a big difference. This is because it has given China a new international status, a status that can serve as a powerful resource for leadership outside of the WTO arena. China's new role becomes clear when one examines the details of the many Asian economic meetings that have taken place since 1997. These include regular summits for heads of state and finance ministers, and meetings of expert committees of various kinds. The intensity of these interactions has already done much to create a new type of East Asian economic community, with a leading place for China, but without any strong formal organization.[5]

The two other institutions of concern to China in this context are APEC and ASEAN. In terms of trade creation, both are regarded as basically unsuccessful and of limited value to China in their current form. APEC, as is widely perceived everywhere, is now too geographically comprehensive and too politicized to be effective in the purely trade and economic arenas. In addition, its broad and somewhat vague formula of 'non-discriminatory liberalization' is seen as unlikely to deliver the objectives that China seeks from regional integration.

ASEAN's weakness in promoting trade liberalization is partly attributed to the smallness of the internal ASEAN market and, even more important, to what the Chinese see as a lack of political leadership.[6] This leadership, they believe, should have been supplied either by a single hegemon or, by a Franco-German style 'leadership core'. This latter concept is one now familiar and much favoured by the Chinese elite in their domestic politics (Li Da 2002).

The 'Japan Problem'

The 'Japan problem' links to the institutional problem in several ways. First, however, the Chinese see Japan as an economic model whose achievements have been impressive, but which has been revealed as having serious flaws during the relative stagnation of the past 15 years. Politically, the Chinese detect in Japan an incapacity to play a full Asian leadership role, in spite of the fact that it has the economic and financial resources to do so. This was a major problem in the early years of APEC when Japan was the unchallenged but basically passive leader of APEC in Asia, but was revealed most starkly in Japan's perceived lack of financial support and institutional leadership in the aftermath of the Asian crisis of 1997. The inability to handle the American veto on the project for a new Asian financial institution and the willingness of the Japanese to allow yen weakening (while the Chinese held the renminbi) are seen as especially significant.[7] Of course, in spite of the Chinese holding these negative views, Sino-Japanese trade has flourished to an extraordinary degree. The boom that began in 1992 and lasts to the present has turned out to be the third great 'China Boom' experienced by Japan in the twentieth century.[8]

The Periphery Challenge

The Chinese periphery presents two kinds of challenge to the central Government. First, for 30 years China had a centralized system of foreign trade control. This had advantages; important national priorities could be imposed and a fit between the planned internal sector and the workings of the external sector could be maintained. The disadvantages of the system were that it was inflexible and lacked the information, the degree of disaggregation and the planning criteria that were required to take advantage of the myriad trading opportunities available in direct, cross-border trade. Given the scale and variety of the Chinese periphery, this was a huge loss.

Gradually, since reform started, mechanisms have been brought into play to facilitate cross-border trade and these have already begun to transform the border economies. But this is a slow and difficult process. In the short run, simple relaxation of controls can lead to gains, but to maximize the potential of these remote and generally backward sub-regional economies calls for substantial investment. This is partly physical investment in roads, riverine ports and other communications, and partly institutional invest- ment including local customs posts and regulations, and currency, banking and business licensing arrangements. To be successful such investments often need the additional support of new mind sets in local populations that are still locked into the past, pre-reform era.

Economic problems are compounded by the fact that in each major sector of the border regions serious political and public order issues are to be found. In the north east is the Korean threat. In the north west China borders on Muslim central Asia which is alive with aspirations for political and cultural independence. While in the south west, drug trafficking, smug- gling and resource depredation are all endemic. In all three of the above, cross-border national minority populations are an added complication. Finally, in the south east are the challenges posed by the integration of Hong Kong and relations with Taiwan. Thus in each border quadrant eco- nomic, political and strategic issues are combined. Where choices have to be made the political and strategic factors are usually regarded as over-riding.

The Objectives of Current Trade Policy

To sum up, therefore, now that the globalization processes have gone through their initial stages, China seeks further access to foreign markets for its exports, opportunities for mutual foreign investment and, where pos- sible, secure access to long run raw material needs and solutions to local security and political problems.

In thinking about market access, we must bear in mind that China is moving up two different hierarchies of skill and comparative advantage. One is the hierarchy of comparative advantage determined by basic factor/skill endowment. In this, moving to the more capital and knowledge intensive activities has historically always been a difficult process since, in its early stages, it involves competition against existing suppliers who necessarily have the benefits of scale, knowledge and cumulative experience. Further, because China's expansion to large scale exporting in the lower level activities has been through the 'globalized' route of sub-contracting, component and OEM production, the Chinese also seek to move up the value chains in these activities, advancing to the design/distribution/marketing and 'own brand' segments where value added is much higher and the import components of production somewhat lower. Because new low wage economies continue to enter the lower reaches of the chains, returns are under great pressure and this is becoming an urgent concern. Economically what China needs, therefore, is rapid, specific access to markets where Chinese goods are likely to be competitive, where learning can be rapid and arrangements put in place that encourage desirable mutual foreign direct investment.

Enhanced trade with Asian partners willing to enter localized integration agreements meets many of the economic criteria suggested by these considerations. Further, such localized agreements offer China opportunities to combine economic with political advantages and to ensure that changes flowing from liberalization are controllable. In the short run, bilateral and smaller scale agreements are obviously the most feasible and attractive. But in the longer run, and in the wider strategic frame, the Chinese also see pan-Asian arrangements as a solution to what has sometimes been called the problem of the 'peaceful rise' (*hoping jueqi*) that is, the problem of how China can avoid its growing power causing serious conflict and disruption to the world system. The argument is that some of the individuality and perils of China's national rise can be disguised, so to speak, in the regional rise of the Asian economies. From the Chinese perspective this provides a broad political argument for Asian integration that transcends even the narrower political issues of the kind that are faced in the 'periphery' regions.

Let us now remind ourselves of the options opened to China by discussions to date. These include the following:

1. An agreed plan for an ASEAN FTA, which links China to a group of economies that have not hitherto played a large role in China's trade ('10 plus 1').[9]
2. A long term, multi-party, economically speculative plan involving large numbers of countries at very different levels of development. That is ASEAN plus China, Japan and Japan ('10 plus 3').
3. A plan to link China to Japan and Korea, both economies being considerably more mature and technologically advanced than China itself.
4. Local, bilateral agreements for immediate implementation such as the Closer Economic Partnership Agreements (CEPA) with Hong Kong and Macao and those that could be made with individual ASEAN members.
5. The more wide ranging Shanghai Cooperation Organization (SCO) which involves Russia, Kazakhstan, Kyrgyzstan, Tajikistan and Uzbekistan, where there is a particularly strong mixture of economic and security elements and finally,

6. Un-titled but detailed arrangements to promote cross-border trade in
    Yunnan Province that parallel those found in the north eastern and
    north western borders to integrate the SCO economies.

This list clearly reflects a very wide range of possibilities, greatly differing
in their feasibility, time frames and in the nature of likely ultimate benefits.
Basically, drawing on the discussion in the first section and the analysis of
Chinese views above, the most immediate, feasible gains are likely to be
those obtained by agreements that are small in scale, involve partners at
similar levels of economic development and where economic, political and
security issues are particularly pressing. Of the listing above, categories 4–6
are the ones that would most likely appear to be attractive.[10]

There is good evidence that this is indeed the case. A clear example has
been the steps to implement the Hong Kong/Macao CEPA arrangements
(Hong Kong Trade Development Council 2003). Moving on from the
formula of 'one country two systems' developed for Hong Kong and Macao,
the Chinese see CEPA as part of their new 'one country four regions'
formula. (The four regions being China, Hong Kong, Macao and 'Chinese
Taiwan' (*Jingji da cankao* (*Economic Reference Materials*) 2003)). Under
this concept, China seeks to bind the other three into a closely knit group in
which market driven economic partnerships are reinforced by special measures and investment in infrastructure. In the short run, the Hong Kong case
was seen as most important. Unlike Macao, the Hong Kong economy fared
badly during the transition years and was, in any case, not only of great
importance to the continuing expansion of the south China region but also
a gateway for foreign direct investment into the whole of the Chinese mainland. The CEPA therefore included a group of measures designed to accelerate Hong Kong's êntrepot role and to allow its service sector to flourish
and expand across the border. The FDI role in the agreement is summed up
in the slogan, 'first the office, then the factory' that is, encourage MNCs to
establish offices in Hong Kong and this will encourage them to invest across
the border in factories. Agreed in 2003 and progressively implemented in
2004 and 2005, the CEPA has clearly had some positive effects, although by
far the most important way in which the mainland's efforts have stimulated
the economy has been through the boom in mainland tourists. In the longer
run, the planned physical infrastructure projects will undoubtedly also play
a big role in realizing the objectives of CEPA.

Among the border trade arrangements, those in the north east with
Russia and those across the Yunnan border are the most interesting. The
Russo-Chinese trade differs from other border trades in that cross border
cultural and linguistic differences are greater than in other border regions.
Direct trades were renewed in 1982 and by 1987 trade agreements cover-

ing Heilungjiang, Jilin, Inner Mongolia and Xinjiang had been made. Although progress is made in fits and starts, by 2001 it was estimated that for Heilungjiang Province, border trade amounted to nearly half its total 'foreign' trade.[11] Nonetheless much further work needs to be done on the harmonization of the two reformed systems, and on regulation, financing and other aspects of these exchanges before the full effects of regional specialization can be reaped.

The Shanghai Cooperation Organization which embraces and goes further than simply the Russian borders is a more systematic attempt to do this. The SCO is currently focusing specifically on issues relating to tariffs and the facilitation of FDI and is attempting to standardize many aspects of the economic relationships in accordance with WTO regulations. With an intermediate landmark of 2009, the SCO has a long term goal of creating a Free Trade Area among the participants by 2015. Although this is a strictly trade objective, the political significance of the SCO system is never lost sight of (Liu Gang and Liu Huaqing 2003).

The south western provinces share the problems of long neglect, poor infrastructure and relative backwardness that obstruct the expansion of cross-border specialization in the north east and north west. In one important respect, however, they too have a unique feature in that the Province of Yunnan, in particular, borders directly on members of ASEAN. Plans to create comprehensive Free Trade Areas and Economic Partnership Agreements with ASEAN will be much weakened if the most direct and obvious forms of cross-border trade do not function.[12] For whereas China-ASEAN 'internal' trade is at present less than 10 per cent of total trade, for Yunnan Province, trade with Burma, Thailand and Vietnam in 2003 was approximately half of the province's total trade. Within total trade, *small scale* direct 'border trade' was about 15 per cent of the total (Statistical Bureau of Yunnan Province 2004).

Regulating and expanding legitimate trade in this region are, therefore, important stepping stones to the longer term vision. As in the north east, rivers are key arteries and national frontiers in Yunnan and the facilities for this need much improvement. These are planned under the slogan 'one river two countries'. Also, the border economy remains weak and relatively small. For the early stages, tourism has been designated as the key sector for expansion. Within the tourist sector, it is the growth in numbers of visitors from other Chinese provinces (rather than foreign and overseas Chinese) that has been the dynamic element (Yan Zhuang 2004).[13]

One policy adopted in both northern and south western border trade is that of extending the renminbi currency area. The Chinese currency tends to gain strongly against the border currencies, which suffer from instability as well as weakness against the renminbi. The Chinese believe that if they can regionalize renminbi use across some of the peripheral borders the impact on trade and investment flows will be a strong one (*Guoji Maoyi* (*International Trade*) 2003b).[14]

Of the other types of agreements that are contemplated ASEAN plus 1 (China) is the next most attractive. There are two quite different reasons for this. One is political. In ASEAN plus 1 China is clearly the dominant partner and would be able to control the shape of the group's development. Enlargements that include Japan, on the other hand, involve potential conflict not least because of the huge competitive superiority that Japan maintains over China in terms of technology and corporate skills which is obviously not synchronized with the Chinese view of their political import-ance and Asian leadership potential. These political complications would be compounded by the economic challenges if China faced competition in an FTA with the mature industrial economies of Korea and Japan. There is a strong logic, therefore, from the Chinese viewpoint, in a strategy that improves competitiveness in the ASEAN arena first, and then is better able to draw benefits from closer relationships with the advanced economies of Asia at a later date. These relationships could either be within an ASEAN plus 3, or the subject of separate arrangements.

ASEAN, on the other hand, might well prefer an FTA which includes other powerful members who can offset Chinese dominance. For while there are several clear potential areas for mutual specialization, there are a number of labour intensive industries and processing positions in the product chains where competition between China and ASEAN members may be acute.[15] The same economic and technological arguments would also apply to relationships with Taiwan. However in this case there is no doubt that should opportunities for closer integration across the Taiwan Straits open up, the political attractions would be judged to far outweigh any potential economic problems.

We argued in the introduction that, historically, RIAs were either market or state led. But as China moves towards enhanced FTA type relationships with groups of economies that go well beyond what is involved with peri-pheral and smaller scale agreements, the Chinese see the mechanisms of control as in need of change. Over the long term they see the past as forming three main phases.

Phase 1: 1980 to the early 1990s

These are regarded as the years of 'wu wei' and 'formlessness', that is, gov-ernment is basically passive and inactive and integration occurs without the benefit of any formal frameworks.[16] What this means is that having taken decisions to Open the Door and initiate domestic reforms, development was left to depend on new incentives provided for domestic enterprises, relocation FDI, processing/compensation trade and joint ventures of various kinds. Central Government played little or no role in the details of this unfolding outcome, largely lacking the bureaucratic capabilities to do so and not, at the time, really understanding what the impact of FDI inflows and Open Door policies would be. Under this *laissez faire* regime, a market driven concentration of development began to take place in the key seaboard regions, creating worrying inequalities and tensions in the process (Kung Pinmei 2003; Zhang Yunling 2003).

Phase 2: 1990s to 2001
This period is seen as the transition from 'formless' development to development within more formal frameworks. During this period Central Government initiatives reappear. Serious participation in APEC begins and the Central Government encourages the Tyumen River Project and cross border trade in all the major quadrants. In this phase the key to change was local Government behaviour. This used new incentives to induce successful clusters of development based on FDI and localized cross-border initiatives. In addition to provision of financial incentives and physical infrastructures, local governments also disseminated information and encouraged region to region and city to city links and exchanges of all kinds.

Phase 3: 2002 onwards
This is the current stage when Central Government leadership becomes vital. In this phase the transition to development with 'form' is being completed. There are several reasons why local government is no longer adequate to guide the economy in more complex integration schemes. One is that the big political factors come to the fore and require proper diplomatic input. Another is that the Centre does not wish for further integration to lead to further geographical concentration within China. The share of the Pearl and Yangzi River Deltas are already very high and they and the Dalian/north eastern concentrations would be likely beneficiaries from 'ASEAN plus' type FTAs if the results are left entirely to market forces.[17] Finally, in any ASEAN plus 1, the Chinese might need industrial guidance to find some basis for a pattern of industrial specialization that would not lead to the early demise of much industry in the existing ASEAN economies (see, Jun Xiangshuo 2004).

CONCLUSIONS

China's policy towards FTAs is still in its early stages. There is a clear hierarchy of possibilities that have been opened by Chinese and Asian initiatives, all representing alternatives to going down the WTO road of fully multilateral, consensus based agreements. In all of the possibilities opened, however, three points seem to be in common. First, proposals are all of the 'FTA plus' variety. That is to say they go beyond simple tariff reduction by including measures that specifically aim to increase FDI and trade simultaneously. Also, in the cases where geographically contiguous states are involved they usually also include plans for physical and institutional infrastructure designed to increase economic interaction. Third, economic and political factors mix in all these schemes. This is particularly the case in the peripheral arrangements, but also in the broader regional plans since these inevitably involve the 'Japan factor', still one of the most sensitive aspects of China's foreign relations.

The Chinese see the future as an evolving one in which, as regional integration enlarges, the role of central government becomes critical. In the early stages informal, market driven cross-border relations developed, later to be re-enforced by active local government initiatives. In the bigger schemes that the Chinese see as lying ahead, national foreign policy elements will have to be attended to, also central government steer will be needed to influence patterns of specialization and to at least moderate the tendencies towards regional inequality that have become so pronounced during the past 25 years.

Quite what the longer term relationship between current thinking and outcomes will be is hard to assess. Market forces, regional and sub-regional actors will continue to bring their influences to bear on trade, investment, environmental and other forms of cooperation. It may well be that these prove to be more powerful in shaping the future than the policies of the Chinese central government. Two particularly powerful forces lie behind the sub-regional initiatives. One of these is the rivalry between the Pearl River Delta and the Yangzi River Delta. In search of competitive advantage both press ahead with cross-boundary initiatives. The other factor is the Japan problem. Given the difficulties of national level relations, the Japanese encourage their regions and key cities to develop contacts and invest in transport and other relational infrastructure. Particularly impressive have been the achievements between the Osaka/Kansai and Shanghai/Jiangsu regions, and those between parties to the North East Asia Economic Conference (NEAC), which includes Korea. Both of these relationships have very firm historical bases and have been strongly active since the early 1990s.[18]

NOTES

1. For example, of the 15 contributors to an important recent book on South East Asia and China, only one was based in mainland China (Ho Khai Leong and Ku 2005).

2. Before the Tariff Union, Prussia alone had 67 distinct tariff districts and 3000 classes of traded goods. The union of the reformed Prussian system with the politically hostile and agriculturally oriented southern German states was difficult, but eventually accomplished. Interestingly, the simplification of the tariff system produced large rises in fiscal revenue (Lee 2001).

3. The system involved arbitrary specialization decisions requiring that different members produce or desist from producing different types of industrial goods, for example tractors, heavy lorries and so on. However, members were rarely willing to abandon production of products of critical significance to their economies, probably doubting the capability of the trading mechanism to provide delivery. These disputes in a sense also pre-echoed developing country disputes about dynamic gains from RIAs, see below. For the CMEA see Pryor (1963).

4. Between 1988–91 and 1996–2000, the intra-industry share of China's total trade rose from 23.1 per cent to 57 per cent. Easily the largest rise in a 30 country case study from OECD data (see, Song Quancheng 2003).

5. Among the expert groups, the East Asian Vision Group (EAVG) has been particularly interesting and important. Between 1998 and 2000 the EAVG worked to produce a comprehensive and ambitious scenario for the region's future. The Group proposed a region-wide FTA supplemented by coordinated macroeconomic policy, financial harmonization, capital market development and technological cooperation. This view was set aside by the regional leaders during 2000, and replaced by a more pragmatic, 10 plus 1 FTA Framework Agreement in 2002.

6. These negative views of ASEAN are well known inside ASEAN. See the valuable paper by Chia Siow Yue (2004).

7. The issue of the bank is a retrospective criticism. At the time the Chinese supported US doubts about the bank, but for their own reasons.

8. The Chinese attribute this less to positive government than to the new perception by Japanese businessmen that China is an 'opportunity' rather than a 'threat'. On the Japanese side, Chinese FTA initiatives are seen as a highly political response to the Asian economic scene (see, *Nichu keikyo journal* (*The Journal of the Japan-China Economic Association*) 2003 and Ma Chengsan 2003).

9. In 2004, the highest ranking ASEAN economy in China's trade by an ASEAN economy was Singapore which ranked seventh. Total trade with Singapore was only one-seventh of the top ranked (USA) economy, and was only half of China-Taiwan trade (US-China Business Council 2005).

10. Chinese priorities are discussed in a very comprehensive article, in *Guoji maoyi* (International Trade) (2003a).

11. Data on these trades is clearly of poor quality, with much trade under-reported or misdescribed. See details in, Chang Liangping (2003).

12. This policy has also been given a slogan by the Yunnan Party Committee: 'Gain a foothold in the Asia Pacific. Rejuvenate border [trade]. Open the Southern Gate. Go towards South East Asia.'

13. Statistical data from Statistical Bureau of Yunnan Province (2004) and The Editorial Committee of the China Commerce Yearbook (2004). Note that a great deal of tourism is still 'one night stop' tourism, which is why cross-border linkages with other destinations to make packages is so important.

14. Interestingly, with similar motivation, Japanese banks attempted to create a yen zone to encourage Russian–Manchurian border trade before the Second World War.

15. ASEAN doubts about 10 plus 1 are explained in Ba (2003). For a survey on some of the competitiveness issues, see Chia Siow Yue (2004). In addition to thinking about the individual sectors, estimation of dynamic effects of an FTA will depend heavily on the long run impact of FDI flows, and these are not easy to estimate quantitatively, since much depends on fluctuating business sentiment, especially in Japan.

16. The term 'wu wei' used in this literature may seem to hold a pejorative connotation from its literal translation. However, to the Chinese, the strategy of 'wu wei' which allows

others to make mistakes and creates occasions for opportunistic strikes, is seen as the best course available in certain situations.
17. In 2000 the Pearl River and Yangzi River Delta regions accounted for 57 per cent of all FDI inflows and 62 per cent of China's foreign trade.
18. The NEAEC group have plans to establish a development finance bank, and have been able to attract Japanese public and quasi-public money to support regional initiatives, particularly those relating to common environmental problems.

REFERENCES

Ba, A.D. (2003), 'China and ASEAN: renavigating relations for a 21st Century Asia', *Asian Survey*, **43** (4), 622–47.

Balassa, B. (1969), *The Theory of Economic Integration*, Homewood, IL: R.D. Irwin.

Chang Liangping (2003), 'Regulate and promote the development of China-Russia border trade', *Guoji maoyi (International Trade)*, **2**, 14–17.

Chia Siow Yue (2004), 'ASEAN–China Free Trade Area', Singapore Institute of International Affairs, paper for presentation at the AEP Conference, Hong Kong 2004.

Das, D.K. (2004), *Regionalism in Global Trade*, Cheltenham, UK and Northampton, MA, US: Edward Elgar.

The Editorial Committee of the China Commerce Yearbook (2004), *China Commerce Yearbook 2004*, Beijing: Ministry of Commerce, PR China.

Gaulier, G., F. Lemoine and D. Unal-Kesenci (2005), 'China's integration in East Asia: production sharing, FDI and high-tech trade', CEPII Working Paper, Brussels.

Guoji Maoyi (International Trade) (2003a), 'Develop from initiating FTAs', **6**, 4–8.

Guoji Maoyi (International Trade) (2003b), 'Speed up progress. Renminbi regionalisation and the development of border trade', **5**, 9–13.

Ho Khai Leong and Ku, S.C.Y. (2005), *China and Southeast Asia, Global Changes and Regional Challenges*, Singapore: Institute for South East Asian Studies.

Hong Kong Trade Development Council (2003), 'CEPA: Opportunities for Hong Kong Services Industries', www.tdctrade.com/econforum/tdc/tdc030901.htm, 1 February.

Jingji da cankao (*Economic Reference Materials*) (2003), 'CEPA expedites the Greater Pearl River Delta strategy', **19** (July), 18–20.

Jun Xiangshuo (2004), 'The change in the direction of China's trade policy and trade structure', *Shijie jingji* (World Economy), **3**, 62–3.

Kung Pinmei (2003), 'From no form to form', *Guoji maoyi* (International Trade), **12**, 14–17.

Lee, R. (2001), 'Relative backwardness and long run development', in Breuilly, J. (ed.), *19th Century Germany. Politics, Culture and Society 1780–1918*, London: Arnold.

Li Da (2002), 'The political economy of a China–ASEAN FTA', *Guoji maoyi wenti* (International Trade Problems), **9**, 16–20.

Liu Gang and Liu Huaqing (2003), 'Research into economic cooperation within the region [covered by] the Shanghai Cooperation Organisation', *Guoji maoyi* (International Trade), **8**, 28–32.

Ma Chengsan (2003), 'From menace to opportunity – an analysis of Japan's economic strategy towards China', *Guoji maoyi* (International Trade), **8**, 13–16.

National Bureau of Statistics China (2004), *Chinese Statistical Yearbook 2004*, Beijing: National Bureau of Statistics China.

Nichu keikyo journal (The Journal of the Japan–China Economic Association), (2003), ' "China and FTAs", Tokushu (Special Report)', **109**, February.

Ng, F. and A. Yeats (2003), 'Major trends in East Asia. What are their implications for regional cooperation and growth?', *World Bank Policy Research Paper 3084*, Washington, DC: The World Bank.

Pryor, F.L. (1963), *The Communist Foreign Trade System*, London: Allen and Unwin.

Song Quancheng (2003), 'A positive analysis of our country's intra-industry trade', *Guoji maoyi* (International Trade), **12**, 10–12.

Statistical Bureau of Yunnan Province (2004), *Yunnan Statistical Yearbook 2004*, China Statistics Press.

Tongji yanjiu (Statistical Research) (2003), 'International comparisons of our country's economic and social development, 1998–2002', No. 10.

US–China Business Council (2005), 'China's trade performance', www.uschina.org/statistics/2005tradeperformance.html, 1 February.

Yan Zhuang (2004), 'The advantages, opportunities, choices and policies for Xixuangbanna in the construction of a China-ASEAN Free Trade Area', *Zhongong zhongyang dangxiao baogao xuan* (Select Reports to the School of the Central Committee of the Chinese Communist Party), **5**, 37–43.

Zhang Yunling (2003), 'East Asian cooperation and integration: where to go?' in, *East Asian Cooperation: Progress and the Future*, Beijing: World Affairs Press.

Zhao Jingxia (2002), 'East Asia regional co-operation as a consequence of globalisation', *Guoji maoyi wenti* (International Trade Problems), **12**, 24–9.

7. Reflections on impacts and outcomes of regional trade liberalization in an Asia-Pacific context

Kenneth E. Jackson

INTRODUCTION

This chapter reflects on particular issues of trade liberalization and impacts, including individual food security as well as more general aspects of the topic of trade liberalization. World Trade Organization (WTO) requirements are the usual consideration for most researchers, but there has been a virtual plethora of regional and bilateral agreements since the mid-1990s, partially resulting from opposition and delays to the WTO process. Sub-global agreements are not an adequate replacement for global ones, but they need to be analysed fully in any consideration of recent trade liberalization. They are an increasing fact of life and appear likely to continue to be so, whether Doha is revived or not. They have important impacts on distributional issues, including food security, especially given the regional nature of much international food trade.

There are five sections to this chapter. The next section attempts to examine the issues relating to the impacts and outcomes of RTAs with special focus on Australia New Zealand Closer Economic Relations Trade Agreement (ANZCERTA). The third section sets out an approach to analysing the impacts of change in a disaggregated manner including food security. The fourth section is a brief reflection on some aspects of the liberalization experience in particular cases in the Asia-Pacific region. The final section deals with some concluding remarks.

IMPACTS AND OUTCOMES OF RTAs: BASIC ISSUES

Regional agreements are viewed as very much the less-preferred option compared with full global multilateral agreements. Changes resulting from any agreement need to be looked at in disaggregated form as well as the aggregated studies usually adopted. Issues of common currency and other degrees of integration need to be considered, as well as trading arrangements. In addition, the type of RTA is an important factor in considering its impact. Ghosh and Yamarik (2004, p. 215) distinguish five varieties in their study:

- preferential tariff agreements;
- free trade areas;
- customs union;
- common market; and
- monetary union.

Institutional background factors are also important. These can alter the impact of an RTA or can be affected by the RTA itself. Path dependency issues in a Douglass North sense are important. Australia/NZ relationships have been influenced by their previous experience and this in turn helped to decide the form of RTA adopted. Politics, culture and social factors are part of the context.

General Feature Contexts of RTAs

- The more integrated an agreement is, the more trade creation is likely to be an outcome, rather than diversion (Ghosh and Yamarik 2004, p. 218). Agreements, which include the agriculture sector within the bloc arrangement, carry high diversion risks, if support of high cost sectors results (Josling 1998, p. 68). To date many RTAs have been concluded between economies with relatively high cost agricultural sectors.
- RTAs can be incomplete, unequal or counterproductive, all of which hold the potential to bring such processes into disrepute and disfavour. For small countries the level of bargaining, transaction and compliance costs of multiple RTAs may make them undesirable, even if trade creation dominates diversion. Small agricultural producers may not feature in RTAs or find them attractive in consequence.

Where do RTAs Fit?

A global multilateral system of trade such as the WTO is worth supporting, not least to reduce some of the transaction costs. In a previous work (Jackson 1998) an attempt was made at the beginnings of a very simplistic taxonomy, or hierarchy, of decision-making as to what was the best choice for trade liberalization. Global, multilateral agreements (WTO) were placed at the top, open regional agreements of a WTO type, although the term appears slightly contradictory in nature, were placed second, less open regional agreements next and bilaterals last. This is far too simplistic an approach and neglects issues such as the way in which preferential RTAs develop, speed of openness for example, or rather the lack of it and the possibility of entrenchment of less competitive structures, which are subsequently difficult to dislodge. Preferential treatment of less efficient producers can lead to trade diversion and subsequent difficulty in moving to full multilateral benefits, especially if the less efficient become effectively 'institutionalized'. Others have found intranational impact and diversion issues in RTAs (see Coulombe 2004, for a discussion).

The multilateral (WTO) principle appears based on a belief in the virtues of freer trade rather than less free and of the workings of the market. This does not imply that all benefits will automatically follow or be well distributed. The extent of the agriculture and textile agreements and their implementation can be seen as particular problem areas. If such multilateral agreements are potentially problematical, the problems are compounded in regional and bilateral arrangements.

ANZCERTA in the Long Run

Australia and New Zealand's somewhat ambivalent regional trade relationship has a long history. Trans-Tasman aspects of Empire preference schemes of the early twentieth century were less than amicable. New Zealand preferences were not liberalizing, affording preference to partners by increasing the tariff on all non-partners, meeting neither the spirit, nor the rules, of the WTO and present-day preferential tariff agreements.

The Closer Economic Relationship (CER)'s precursor, dating from the 1960s,[1] was relatively ineffective, not least because items had to be positively included in the agreement, rather than needing specific exclusion, as per CER. The stronger CER still only accounts for some 10 per cent of all intra-regional exports (UN–ESCAP 2004, p. 53). Particular problems for CER, as with other trade agreements, include the issue of exchange rates. The year following CER's inception (1984), saw New Zealand devalue by 20 per cent, which almost certainly more than wiped out the impact of any tariff reductions to that point. Floating exchange rate regimes have reduced the issue's importance in recent times, but there is still the issue of monetary policy impacts through interest rates and capital movements. The CER experience points out the importance of the type of RTA and that the issues of common currency and other degrees of integration are as important as trading arrangements.

TOWARDS AN ANALYTICAL FRAMEWORK FOR IMPACTS AND OUTCOMES OF RTAs AT THE DISAGGREGATED LEVEL

Food Security Issues

This section starts with food security issues, which are claimed to form part of the reasoning behind the reluctance of countries, such as Japan, to fully commit to liberalization at the global level. Since, however, most food trade is intraregional not global, such objections apply at the RTA level as well. Such opposition is expressed by governments or the production industry rather than by individual consumers. The Japanese food consumer appears to be more concerned with taste and safety than with security of supply. Individual consumption differentiated by age from macro-data suggests that income and price are not the dominant factors they once were. Rice consumption on average has fallen from over 45 kilograms per year to just over 30 kilograms between 1979–81–1999–2001, with those aged 39 and under consuming only 16.5 kilograms each per year (Tanaka *et al.* 2004, pp. 20–1).

Any Japanese fears of greater price volatility from increased reliance on imported cereal supplies, does not appear to have been borne out by past experience under WTO measures. Food and Agriculture (FAO) studies, suggest that increasing globalization of production and greater trade, has not produced greater volatility (Sarris 1998) although WTO changes may differ from the RTA ones. RTAs have the potential for trade diversion effects as well as creation.

The degree of integration of the members of RTAs matters, as does the exchange rate. Aggregative approaches such as the gravity model approach and the use of CGE modelling can provide useful general information as to likely policy outcomes (see, Scollay and Gilbert 2001 and Gilbert *et al.* 2001), but there are other useful approaches for analysing issues such as food security. 'The difficulty with "general equilibrium" models is that they tend to assume away the problems which, in reality determine, the outcome' (UNCTAD 2002, p. 148). Identifying and quantifying these problems, however, is problematic.

The work of Amartya Sen, particularly (1981) is a useful adjunct to such studies. It is some time since the Sen entitlement studies were undertaken. The Pacific Islands, Thailand and Vietnam, all still have important agricultural sectors from an employment and food production entitlement perspective, which RTAs will affect.

The impact on the agricultural sectors and food security in developing countries from an entitlement (distributional) perspective is relatively neglected. A recent study by Stevens *et al.* (2003), explores linkages between these and trade reform. They suggest the need for situation and scenario analysis based on the situation pre- and post-reform. Trade, labour effort, transfers and production form the basis for gaining entitlements (Stevens *et al.* 2003, p. 1).

Food security analysis focuses on individual level approaches more than the aggregates. If more market solutions are generally to be favoured, the questions of the possibility of market failure or negative distributional outcomes are important, but neglected issues the aggregate approach considers. Economic studies of aggregate welfare outcomes are valid in their own terms, but merit further examination, especially where entitlement is gained extensively through non-market production. Other recent discussions on individual food security, as reviewed in Maxwell and Wiebe's (1999) paper in the *Journal of Development and Change*, use this type of approach although not necessarily using Sen's terminology. It has been applied to food markets and their impacts examined in normal and critical periods by Sen himself and by others including Martin Ravallion (1987). Entitlement is found to have a significant impact in the absence of any overall declines in food availability even, if not especially, in famine conditions.

Any work of this type is not necessarily straightforward. It needs to be considered within a property rights and institutional change framework. Some key points follow:

- It is linked to specific groups' ability to secure entitlement to the necessary levels of sustenance to avoid poverty.
- Apart from studies by the United Nations University – World Institute of Development Economics Research (UNU – WIDER) – there is very little in the way of trade studies utilizing such an approach.
- The approach emphasizes distributional outcomes complementing aggregative studies by conventional techniques and allowing examination of the negative outcomes produced by studies antagonistic to liberalization, which rely on rhetoric.
- Particular institutional, cultural, political and social structures are important factors in determining individual experiences, net welfare may increase, perhaps at the expense of, or slowing down of, poverty alleviation.
- For countries where agricultural and fishing activity is significant in terms of direct production entitlement and employment, such an approach is useful in analysing the impact of changes in trade policy. Individual and household food security issues are important aspects

of such outcomes at least in the first round of impacts, through trade, market, production and transfer entitlements.

- RTAs have often been of as much importance to individual trading nations, as have the global ones. The role of existing regional preferences and their erosion by liberalization should be considered.
- Implications of trading rule changes in the future involve not just the arena of agriculture, but the whole menu of negotiations: for example, fisheries rules and regulations, environmental standards and intellectual property rights issues including genetically modified crops, seed production and plant species.

These factors can have different effects. Generally liberalization and globalization might be thought likely to reduce price volatility. Ravallion's study of the operations of rice markets, however, finds otherwise (Ravallion 1987). Speculation can be destabilizing, as well as stabilizing. If current stocks of food and subsidies are removed or significantly reduced before full market reforms occur, prices could well increase significantly, at least in the short term. Institutional detail and path dependency issues are important in determining outcomes and the differences in those outcomes from case to case. Some brief reflections on country experience can illustrate these and other points.

REFLECTIONS ON SOME ASPECTS OF TRADE LIBERALIZATION EXPERIENCE IN THE ASIA-PACIFIC REGION

Asia

Path dependency and institutions matter in looking at China and other Asian economies. Similarly the arcane mechanisms of the WTO and GATT, no less than RTAs, are as important as economic analysis to developing an understanding of how things are decided. The slowness of negotiations in the succeeding rounds of WTO may reflect a lack of understanding of such matters by negotiators. Douglass North's stress on institutions (see North 1990 and 1991) and how markets evolve, is but another example of such issues, as is Dani Rodrik's work on the importance of institutional change (see Rodrik *et al.* 2004).

China has great influence within its own region, particularly as a food importer. Price rises for Vietnamese rice have an impact on the market entitlement of the Vietnamese labourer as well as the Chinese one. The Vietnamese subsistence producer may or may not be affected greatly, at least not until brought into the market sector by the Government's need to replace lost tariff revenue from liberalization, with other taxes.

Effects on the ASEAN countries of regional agreements whether plus one, two or three, may therefore be considerable. China, Korea or Japan can individually dominate the region.

For some South East Asian economies, such as Myanmar, the choices are limited. Global multilateralism is not an option. They are open to the danger of abusive power relationship agreements with those willing to trade with them, similar to the experience of South-Eastern Europe's reliance on German trade in the 1930s. Trade negotiations are neither dispassionate nor value free.

Vietnam appears to have been somewhat at a disadvantage in bilateral negotiations with the USA – wanting to join the International Club left it vulnerable. So far the impacts in terms of individual food security do not appear to have been that significant. Food production per capita increased by over 3 per cent per annum from 1991–9 according to UN–FAO statistics. This again is the average, rather than the entitlement situation, however.

The Pacific

Pacific Island countries appear to have experienced mixed fortunes in terms of their outcomes. Previous preferential arrangements with Australia and New Zealand, under their RTAs have been reduced as liberalization has become more global, although some safety valves in terms of migration possibilities have been available to them, to the USA, to Australia and to New Zealand in particular. European Union – countries of Africa The Caribbean and the Pacific Group (EU–ACP) agreements have similarly had a patchy history. In some cases 80 per cent of inhabitants rely on agriculture as a means of livelihood and commercial operations are limited. The outcome of reform and change requires study on a case-by-case basis. An examination of entitlement structures will contribute to the overall analysis of the outcomes of global and regional agreements.

New Zealand Expectations and Outcomes from Multilateral Agreements

The non-realization of expected gains from agreements is often due to a lack of implementation. This is particularly true in respect of both agriculture and textiles. The Uruguay Round and the appearance of the WTO itself re-introduced these areas to the trade negotiations, but there was some dissatisfaction with outcomes.

New Zealand producers' over expectation from the Uruguay Round can be seen from a study by Rae and Nixon (1994), using standard CGE modelling. The eventual outcomes were uniformly less than anticipated, partly because of a bias towards overestimation in the original assessments.

Reductions in the level of subsidized export volumes were seen as the source of most benefit from the disciplines associated with the Uruguay round. Increased market access was seen as the next most beneficial change. Budget constraints in the European Union may well have been as big a source of control over subsidization of exports as the agreement requirements themselves. Another and vague benefit was expected to come from the fact that trade reform was then firmly on the agenda.

Volume increases and increased returns from sales and higher prices were shown to be concentrated on a few products such as skimmed milk powder and to have limited volume effects, not least because of the high capital-output ratio of New Zealand farming and an inelastic output response to increased prices. The impact on National Income was also seen as restricted, approximately the equivalent of some six months' increase in real national income, or something like 1.25 per cent. The increase in agricultural export earnings was anticipated at 7 per cent of the 1991–2 level.

Compared with what might have been, the outcome of the Round was modest. To the extent that dilution of requirements and commitments occurred subsequently, this modesty was increased. In fact the 1.25 per cent gain in income was not achieved, whilst domestic price rises in New Zealand were substantial. Producers gained at domestic consumers expense.

Food security issues were not a factor in this case, there are not starving millions in New Zealand, but there was a fall in food entitlements for most of the population. In return consumers could expect to benefit from cheaper imports overall, with the net outcome for them depending upon welfare gains and losses. From a growth perspective the one off addition was welcome, but relatively small. Overstating the expectation of benefits can have a downside in that many people will not believe what they are told the next time round, thus undermining the argument for free trade. Assessments of potential benefits in advance, especially when used to argue in favour of agreements may have long-term downsides.

TRADE AND OPENNESS: SOME REFLECTIONS ON NZ[2]

New Zealand is claimed as an open economy, a great trading nation. Trade to income ratios have not moved greatly from the approximately 30–35 per cent mark over much of the European history of New Zealand, scarcely placing it amongst the top performers by current measures.

A freely floating exchange rate, liberal capital flow controls do, however, support its claim as an open economy.

With CER and external liberalization and 20 years of internal reform, there is little to suggest that growth rates were significantly different before or after the mid-1980s. If there was a structural change in growth rates it is around 1900, when the process of bringing easily utilizable natural resources into the production system was essentially complete. Since then growth has been essentially reliant upon productivity improvements rather than upon finding extra natural resources to bring into the system.

Multilateral global or regional agreements and adherence to precepts of comparative advantage does not automatically produce desired outcomes. What the counterfactual would have been, without reform, is unknowable, although modelling could provide some clues.

CONCLUSIONS

The intention was to demonstrate the drawbacks of conventional or typical methodologies in assessing the impacts of multilateral, global, regional or bilateral trade agreements, through their concentration on the aggregates and neglect of distributional impacts.

Attempts to use CGE modelling face many problems. It is felt that the entitlement approach of Sen can make for a richer process of investigation, particularly for food security issues. The actual experience of RTAs demonstrates that many outcomes are possible. A distributional and institutional perspective is seen as an important addition.

Bargaining power is part of the determinants of the outcomes of all trade negotiations. There are currently widely divergent views as to the likely benefits to Australia from its agreement with the USA as with all such agreements. Others will also be affected. Outcomes of past agreements have been different to expectations. Usually prior estimates of the benefits have been overestimated, based on full and speedy implementation.

Conventional methods tend to overstate expected gains. Institutional rigidities reduce the 'free market' estimate. Manipulation of exchange rate movements can outweigh liberalization effects. Trade Agreements tend to be producer/exporter orientated, partly because of the way in which negotiations are conducted. The real incomes of the majority may only rise with a time delay. Impacts such as food and nutritional security may be adversely affected for individuals although not apparently threatened at the aggregative level.

In the current multilateral structure, there is freer trade in both goods and services. We have freer movement of capital, what we do not have is freer movement of people. Paraphrasing Bhagwhati (1998) the most difficult trick is to be a free immigrationist. Remittances from migration have become significant for many economies and assist some individual's food security. Movement of labour is more likely to be part of the RTAs than of global agreements.

NOTES

1. The NZ-Australia Free Trade Agreement (NZAFTA) came into force 1 January 1966, originally for ten years. This was subsequently replaced with the ANZCERTA (CER) agreement of 1983.
2. This section is based on two studies (Jackson 2002 and 2003) relating to openness and growth performance.

REFERENCES

Bhagwhati, J. (1998), *A Stream of Windows: Unsettling Reflections on Trade, Immigration and Democracy*, Cambridge, MA: MIT Press.

Coulombe, S. (2004), 'Intranational trade diversion, the Canada–United States free trade agreement, and the L Curve', *Topics in Economic Analysis & Policy*, **4** (1), 1–21.

Ghosh, S. and S. Yamarik (2004), 'Does trade creation measure up? A re-examination of the effects of regional trading arrangements', *Economics Letters*, **82** (2), 213–19.

Gilbert, J., R. Scollay and B. Bora (2001), *Assessing Regional Trading Arrangements in the Asia-Pacific*, New York: United Nations.

Jackson, K.E. (1998), 'Sectoral Uruguay Round Agreement: the agricultural sector', in E. Toews (ed.), *International Trade Regulation: EDAP Joint Policy Studies Number 7*, Seoul UNDP: Korean Development Institute, pp. 11–29.

Jackson, K.E. (2002), 'Open and closed: some historical dimensions of New Zealand's participation in the world economy', Working paper No 232 of Dept. of Economics (University of Auckland Business School).

Jackson, K.E. (2003), 'Issues of food security in a WTO world', *Asia-Pacific Situation and China–New Zealand Relations Conference*, Shanghai Institute for International Studies, Shanghai, 9–10 December, 2003.

Josling, T. (1998), *Agricultural Trade Policy: Completing the Reform*, Policy Analyses in International Economics, No. 53, Washington DC: Institute for International Economics.

Maxwell, D. and K. Wiebe (1999), 'Land tenure and food security: exploring dynamic linkages', *Journal of Development and Change*, **30** (4), 825–49.

North, D.C. (1990), *Institutions, Institutional Change and Economic Performance*, New York: Cambridge University Press.

North, D.C. (1991), 'Institutions', *Journal of Economic Perspectives*, **5** (1), 97–112.

Rae, A. and C. Nixon (1994), *The GATT Settlement: Analysis of its Impact on New Zealand Agriculture*, Wellington, NZ: NZ Institute of Economic Research.

Ravallion, M. (1987), *Markets and Famines*, Oxford: Clarendon Press.

Rodrik, D., A. Subramaniam and F. Trebbi (2004), 'Institutions rule: the primacy of institutions over geography and integration in economic development', *Journal of Economic Growth*, **9** (2), 131–65.

Sarris, A. (1998), *The Evolving Nature of International Price Instability in Cereals Markets*, Commodity Policy and Projections Service, Commodities and Trade Division, ESCP/No. 4, Rome: UN–FAO.

Sen, A. (1981), 'Ingredients of famine analysis: availability and entitlements', *Quarterly Journal of Economics*, **96** (3), 433–64.

Scollay, R. and J. Gilbert (2001), *New Regional Trading Arrangements in the Asia Pacific?*, Policy Analyses in International Economics, No. 63, Washington DC: Institute for International Economics.

Stevens, C., S. Devereux and J. Kennan (2003), 'International trade and food security in developing countries', *IDS Working Paper 215*, Brighton, Sussex.

Tanaka, M., Hiroshi Mori and Toshio Inaba (2004), 'Re-estimating per capita individual consumption by age from household data', *The Japanese Journal of Rural Economics*, **6**, 20–30.

UNCTAD (2002), *Trade and Development Report 2002*, New York: United Nations.

UN-ESCAP (2004), *Meeting the Challenges in an Era of Globalization by Strengthening Regional Development Co-operation*, New York: United Nations.

8. Korea's approaches to regionalism

Inkyo Cheong

INTRODUCTION

The Asia-Pacific region including East Asia is the least developed region in terms of regionalism. However, many countries in East Asia began to be concerned with free trade agreements (FTAs) after the East Asian financial crisis. In 1998, Korea announced its plan to proceed with an FTA with Chile and also began a joint study with Japan.

The Korea–Chile FTA negotiations were launched in December 1999 and concluded in October 2002. In addition to the FTA with Chile, Korea is under negotiation for bilateral FTAs with Japan and Singapore. In addition to these FTAs, Korea is studying or discussing the feasibilities of FTAs with other countries such as ASEAN, Mexico, Canada, India and so on.

This chapter overviews Korea's FTA policies, focusing on major issues present in a Japan–Korea FTA. It starts with the general discussion on Korea's position towards FTAs.

KOREA'S POSITION TOWARDS FTAs

Korea concluded its first FTA with Chile in October 2002 and it was implemented in April 2004. The core issue for Korea's trade policy was the ratification of its FTA with Chile by the Korean National Assembly in early 2004. Farmers believed that the Korean Government's promotion of FTAs would prove a further blow to the agricultural sector and as a result, the agricultural sector opposed the FTA with Chile for fear of the consequences of other FTA promotion in general (rather than a specific objection to a partnership with Chile). Korea has opened the agricultural market with the Korea–Chile FTA ratification, and hereafter, Korea's FTA promotion is expected to progress to encompass other economies.

The successful conclusion of the first FTA will be especially important to Korea, as other potential FTAs will heavily depend on the first model. Prior to launching its long-term goal of establishing FTAs with larger trade partners such as the USA, Japan, China and the ASEAN Free Trade Area

(AFTA), Korea needs to pursue FTAs with smaller partners in the short term. The experience will help the Government to minimize risks and possible losses, as well as to be better prepared for the operation and negotiation of FTAs.

The ratification of the FTA with Chile is an epochal turning point for Korea's trade policy; herewith, Korea established a foothold to progressively cope with global proliferation and the deepening of regionalism. Moreover, it enables Korea to actively prepare for economic integration in the Asia-Pacific region through FTAs with major trade partners such as Japan, Mexico, ASEAN, USA and China. The agreement is the first trade policy pursued and concluded by Korea on its own after the decision to use a FTA as a strategic trade policy, and not by means of multilateral trade liberalization such as the Uruguay Round (UR) or the Doha Development Agenda (DDA).

Korea's Government (a participatory Government), which started in February 2003, has made a policy that it would promote FTAs. After the inauguration of the new Government, the new administration has set the goal of passing the Korea–Chile FTA and the FTA Implementation Act through the National Assembly at the earliest possible time. On 2 July, President Roh Moo-hyun requested that the National Assembly ratify the free trade agreement made between Korea and Chile and pass other pending economic bills in a letter to National Assembly Speaker Park Kwan-yong.

Several reasons why the new Government supports FTAs can be provided. Recently in Korea there has been a strong consensus that the Government must deal with the spread of economic regionalism in the world. Korean newspapers have treated FTAs as major economic issues in articles, insisting that the participatory Government should get the ratification of the Korea–Chile FTA from the National Assembly at the earliest time and promote more FTAs with other trading countries to embody Korea's image of openness and economic reforms. The major Korean newspapers have displayed concerns that the image of Korea as an open trading nation could be ruined if the Government is not able to cope with domestic, anti-liberalization movements, and establish FTAs with major trading partners following the international trend of economic regionalization, which has sped up since the official launch of the WTO.

Moreover, the WTO has indicated that trade amongst member countries of regional trade agreements constituted 43 per cent of the total global trading at the end of 2002 and 51 per cent in 2005. Although a late-starter in the business of preferential trade deals, South Korea has set the target of having FTAs with 50 nations by 2007. If Korea fails to establish FTAs with other nations, it will lose its competitiveness because Korean products will be treated less favourably than those of FTA member countries. Economic integrations in the Americas and in Europe are also speeding up. The European Union accepted ten Eastern European countries in May 2004 and has been promoting FTAs with various regions such as Mediterranean countries and the MERCOSUR of the South America. As for the Americas, the United States is taking the initiative by creating the Free Trade Area of the Americas (FTAA) by 2005 as the next agenda of the North America Free Trade Agreement (NAFTA).

Meanwhile, Korea's participatory Government considers the promotion of FTAs as necessary for Korea to develop into an open trading nation. President Rho insisted on actively dealing with the international trend of FTAs, while taking care of the sectors that will be damaged from the opening of markets. While some of the agricultural organizations are strongly against the approval of the Korea–Chile FTA, the general sentiment, such as that of the media, is that the Korean Government should actively promote FTAs. Furthermore, it has also been inevitable for the Government to pay attention to the fact that East Asian countries are actively promoting FTAs with other East Asian countries and with non-East Asian nations, which is different from the previous situation in that discussion on FTA issues in East Asia had been inactive. The Japan–Singapore Economic Partnership Agreement (EPA) was reached in 2002. Also, China and the Association of South East Asian Nations (ASEAN) agreed on a framework agreement of a bilateral FTA in November 2002 and reached an FTA in July 2004. Negotiations were ongoing in 2005. The Japanese Government launched a committee to promote a Closer Economic Partnership (CEP) with ASEAN.

One of backgrounds for Korean government's pursuit of FTAs can be related to the goal of Korea becoming the business hub of North East Asia. One of the new government's policy goals is to develop Korea into a business hub in the region. It is hoping to take advantage of Korea's geopolitical position in North East Asia, to realize the potential economic gains from economic integration, to promote the development and identity of North East Asia and to eventually develop the region into an economic union like the European Union (EU).

To achieve the goal of developing Korea into a business hub of North East Asia, there needs to be cooperation in various sectors, such as industries, finance, IT, energy and environment. However, the inflow of foreign direct investment (FDI) through opening domestic markets and improving economic rules and systems is the most essential. Also, political stabilization and national security would be important factors for foreign investors. As we have seen in the cases of the Netherlands and Singapore, economic reform, opening of markets and political stabilization are the first things that are needed in order to become a business hub. These pre-conditions for a business hub can be achieved through FTAs with neighbouring countries. A China–Japan–Korea FTA, which officially and systemically promotes economic cooperation among the three countries, is also closely related to the establishment of a North East Asian business hub.

KOREA'S FTA UNDER NEGOTIATION/DISCUSSION

Korea had reached an FTA with Chile after the three-year negotiations. Besides this FTA, Korea has discussed FTAs with many other countries. First of all, Japan and Singapore are the nations with which the Government is working on bilateral FTAs. As for an FTA with Japan, there were eight conferences by the joint research group of industry, government and academia after July 2002. The Korean President and the Japanese Prime Minister agreed to start a negotiation on the Japan–Korea FTA in the near future at the Japan–Korea summit of June 2003. As for an FTA with Singapore, the joint research group was launched in March 2003 for a period of six months. Although discussions between the two countries were delayed due to the SARS outbreak early in 2003, both parties could launch a negotiation earlier than expected since there is no agricultural issue, which is a sensitive matter in Korea. Korea concluded negotiation for an FTA with Singapore in early 2005.

As for the countries with which the Korean Government is actively investigating possible FTAs, there are Mexico, the ASEAN and the European Free Trade Association (EFTA). Among these, the EFTA–Korea FTA progressed most rapidly and was signed in the second half of 2005. However, Korea experienced problems with an FTA with Mexico. Since Mexico is a gateway to the North American market and has a great potential as a market for exports, Korean industrial sectors have strongly emphasized the importance of having an FTA with Mexico. The Mexican economy ranks 12th in the world economy ($481.4 billion), which is 1.1 times the Korean economy. Moreover, since Mexico currently holds FTAs with 32 countries, the disadvantages of Korean companies in Korea have been increasing. Therefore, there is a great need to promote a Korea–Mexico FTA. However, in November 2003, as Mexico declared a moratorium against further FTAs except an FTA with Japan, which was under negotiation, discussion for a bilateral FTA between the two countries could not continue until the Korean Trade Minister, Mr Hwang Doo-Hyun, met his Mexican counterpart in May 2004, to resume official dialogue. When Korean President Noh made a state visit to Mexico in September 2005, both countries agreed to start negotiation for a Strategic Economic Complementarity Agreement (SECA).

Korea was also internally considering the possibility of establishing an FTA with the ASEAN in 2003. In light of the situation where competitor countries of Korea such as Japan and China are actively seeking to reach bilateral FTAs with ASEAN, there would be great economic disadvantages for Korea if only Korea is excluded from an FTA with ASEAN. Both parties agreed to introduce a joint study group for studying a bilateral FTA at the end of 2003, and the first meeting was held in Jakarta, Indonesia, in March 2004. The report by the study group was presented to the ASEAN-Korea Leaders' Meeting (November 2004).

Following current discussion on a FTA between ASEAN and Korea, both regions started negotiation for a FTA in early 2005, and both parties were expected to conclude negotiation for market access in late 2005.

It is expected that Korea's participatory Government will consider the China–Japan–Korea FTA as a relatively important issue along with the Korea–Japan FTA. The three concerned countries – China, Japan and Korea – agreed to study a trilateral FTA at the summit among the three countries in November 2002. At present, a joint research group on the economic effects of the China–Japan–Korea FTA is in the works by economic research institutes of the three countries (China's Development Research Center of the State Council (DRC), Japan's National Institute for Research Advancement (NIRA) and Korea's Institute for International Economic Policy (KIEP)).

The three countries constitute 20 per cent of the world's GDP and 13 per cent of the world's trade. It is expected that the China–Japan–Korea FTA will bring great economic benefits to the three countries and contribute to the opening of North Korea and stabilization of the Korean peninsula. Korean industries have insisted on the necessity of this FTA, and it is true that the importance is acknowledged in Korea in light of economic and strategic benefits. However, the three countries are not clearly motivated at this time, and Korea is greatly concerned about some aspects, such as trade liberalization for the agricultural sectors.

It has been observed that Korea has not shown intentions to promote official negotiations for a trilateral FTA of China–Japan–Korea in the governmental level at present. However, affiliated research institutes of the Government have set forth research results that emphasize the positive effect of a China–Japan–Korean FTA. Meanwhile, the Japanese Government states that it will prioritize the Korea–Japan FTA and investigate the FTA with China in the long term. In addition, the short-term promotion of a FTA with China will place a burden on Korea in a situation where Korea is not fully prepared for a complete market opening in the agriculture and manufacturing industry.

The East Asian Free Trade Area (EAFTA) is one of the FTAs that Korea needs to investigate in the long term. The East Asian Study Group has

Table 8.1   Current progress of FTAs in Korea (at October 2005)

Stage	Region	Current Status	Remark
Implementation	Chile	Implementation (April, 2004)	
Officially Signed	Singapore		Ratification by the National Assembly is required
	EFTA		Ratification by the National Assembly is required
Official Negotiation	Japan		No progress since November 2004
	Canada		Negotiation started July 2005
	ASEAN	Negotiation per 2–3 month period	Negotiation for market opening of goods concluded in 2006, other sectors under negotiation
	Mexico		Strategic Economic Complementarity Agreement
Joint Research or Official Discussion	USA	Governmental level talks	
	India	Governmental level talks	
	• Joint Study for a FTA with MERCOSUR (South American Customs Union)		
	• Joint research for a China–Japan–Korea FTA		

Source: Authors' summary.

submitted a report that encourages the EAFTA, and the leaders of the 13 countries of ASEAN + 3 adopted the report at the ASEAN + 3 summit (at Cambodia) in November 2002. Although the importance of the EAFTA is fully acknowledged in terms of economic and strategic interests, it would be difficult to proceed in the short term due to the diversity among member countries in terms of economic systems and development stages.

A bilateral FTA with the USA is also acknowledged to hold economic and strategic interests. The economic scale of the USA (GDP $10 trillion) is 20 times greater than that of the Korean economy, and the USA is the number one trade partner of Korea ($53 billion). According to the research results on a Korea–USA FTA by the US International Trade Center (ITC), it is expected that Korean exports to the USA will increase by 21 per cent ($10 billion) and that US exports to Korea will increase by 54 per cent ($19 billion). The sectors where trade is expected to increase are textiles, clothing, chemistry, and electronic products for Korea, and rice, meat and dairy products for the USA. In light of the US's passive attitude towards the FTA and the possible impact on the Korean agricultural sectors, a USA–Korea FTA was regarded as difficult to be achieved in the short term until 2005. However, the USA prioritized the FTA with Korea in 2005, and both parties had a joint research for a bilateral FTA.

KOREA'S PERSPECTIVES ON A JAPAN–KOREA FTA

Political leaders of Japan and Korea agreed to analyse the possible economic impacts of a Korea–Japan FTA. Researchers from Korea's KIEP and Japan's IDE carried out this research for two years, culminating in the release of a report that suggested that a Korea–Japan FTA is economically desirable under certain conditions. That is, although Korea may lose from the trade liberalization enabled through the FTA, such an agreement could provide significant dynamic gains to Korea by realizing economies of scale, enhancing the competitive business environment, increasing investment inflows and expanding strategic alliances among companies. Both institutes state that a Japan–Korea FTA could alleviate the pressures of industrial structure adjustment based on the understanding that there are differences in the structure of tariff rates and industrial competitiveness (KIEP and IDE 2000). However, the Ministry of Commerce, Industry and Energy (MOCIE) of Korea, representing manufacturing industries, still did not support the FTA, arguing that the Government should accept the general opposition from businesses while worrying about the impacts a FTA would have on manufacturing.

In late 2001, at the Japanese–Korean summit meeting, leaders agreed to establish a Japan–Korea FTA Business Forum to facilitate exchanges over a bilateral FTA and deliver opinions in the business sector to the Governments of both countries. In 2002, the leaders of businesses from both countries released a report based on the discussions of the Business Forum. The statement indicated support for the proposed Korea–Japan FTA and sought the immediate promotion of such an agreement. Major participants in the Forum were the Federation of Korea Industries (FKI) representing large businesses, the Korean Chamber of Commerce and Industry (KCCI) representing the small and medium-sized enterprises (SMEs) and executives from conglomerates (*chaebols*) such as Samsung, LG, Hyundai and SK. The Forum submitted its report to the Governments of Korea and Japan, strongly recommending the promotion of a bilateral FTA between two countries.

A lot of Korean companies are sceptical as to whether the FTA has the potential to increase Korean exports to Japan because Japanese industries are more competitive; Japanese average tariff rates are as low as 2.7 per cent (Korean 7.8 per cent), and there are still non-tariff barriers that cannot be eliminated through an FTA. Moreover, they argue that Korean imports from Japan will increase on a large scale. Examining the impacts of trade liberalization under the FTA on Korean industries, clothing, agriculture and processed food, textiles and fibre are potential beneficiaries. There will be no significant effects on steel and iron, semi-conductors and shipbuilding. Nevertheless, it is expected that an FTA would be disadvantageous for automobiles, machineries and household electronic appliances.

Although the Government of Korea sees its industries as losers in bilateral trade liberalization through an FTA with Japan, it evaluates the FTA to be advantageous to Korean industries for the following reasons. First of all, the FTA could facilitate structural adjustment for Korean industries, which will be beneficial to Korea in the long-term, although it can bring in adjustment pains in the short run. Korea has introduced various policies for structural adjustment during previous decades but has not seen satisfactory outcomes so far. While there is no sign that the problem of overlapping and excessive investments will be resolved in the near future, competition between Korean and Japanese companies for overseas markets continues to intensify. The growing competition for the US market can be clearly seen in the export similarity index. The export similarity index between Korea and Japan from 1995 to 2003 shows that Korea is not differentiating its products from Japanese goods, resulting in prolonged bilateral competition. In addition, the competition between Korea and China is increasing. In order to maintain market shares in major importing countries, Korean companies have reduced the prices of exported goods and thus Korea's terms of trade have deteriorated so far.

Another rationale for a Korea–Japan FTA is that trade liberalization under the FTA can force Korean companies to improve their international competitiveness. With the accession of China to the WTO at the Doha Ministerial Meeting in November 2001, China is in a position to gain increased international recognition as well as rapid economic growth. China's economic growth is creating business opportunities in China for Korean companies, but it can be regarded as a threat for them in the near future, as China is catching up with Korea rapidly. Booz, Allen and Hamilton (1997) warned that Korea could be trapped in a 'nutcracker' – caught between China's low costs and Japan's technical excellence. They state that 'Korea is too small to compete directly with either Japan or China over the long term in its core industries', suggesting that market size be expanded by establishing FTAs with major trading partners.

A Korea–Japan FTA is expected to influence North East Asian economic integration in the long run. Given the recent discussions on a Northeast Asian FTA, consisting of China, Japan and Korea, as well as an East Asian FTA, both Korea and Japan would like to conclude a bilateral FTA first and then branch out to larger regional FTAs based on that experience. Following the proposal by then-Chinese Premier Zhu Rongji, the economic feasibility of a China–Japan–Korea (CJK) FTA was officially studied in 2003–5 by the Trilateral Joint Research Project of the DRC in China, the NIRA in Japan and KIEP in Korea. The three research institutes, representing their respective countries, have jointly studied how to strengthen economic cooperation in North East Asia since 2001. In 2004 the joint study group presented to the political leaders of the three countries a summary report of the research topic for 2003 entitled 'Economic effects of possible Free Trade Area among China, Japan and Korea (CJK)'. Considering current internal and external conditions, a CJK FTA will be feasible in the mid- to long term. However, the progress of a Korea–Japan FTA will encourage China to be more positive towards economic integration in North East Asia. Thus, it can be said that a Korea–Japan FTA will contribute to the progress of a CJK FTA.

Korean companies' concerns over the FTA are increasing as the negotiation with Japan has been sped up since mid-2004. It is known that the two countries were scheduled to start negotiations for tariff concessions in the second half of 2004. The FKI, which had supported a Korea–Japan FTA, now requests the Government of Korea to slow the speed in concluding the FTA. Academia and labour unions have also shown a negative stance. In mid-May 2004, during the third round negotiation for a Korea–Japan FTA, Korean Confederation of Labour Unions (KCFL) physically demonstrated against a Korea–Japan FTA in front of the Government complex in Seoul.

The recent growing trend of negative stances against a Korea–Japan FTA seems to be related with the following aspects. First, while business executives delivered pro-FTA positions before the start of negotiations recognizing economic gains coming from various forms of closer economic cooperation, now trade managers have become concerned with the FTA, focusing on weakening price competitiveness under the FTA and a disadvantageous position in market access. Second, they might deliver strategic comments in order to minimize market liberalization in the FTA, although they accept the necessity for the FTA. Third, they might expect the Government's compensation or supports for damaged industries as the Korea–Chile FTA did for agriculture. Fourth, generally, opposing

opinions against FTAs may be covered more by the press than supporting positions.

Some people such as KCFL argue that the Korea–Japan FTA should be
reconsidered. They insist that it is evident that Korea will be damaged in
the short-run and the dynamic (long-term) benefits are still ambiguous and
uncertain. In some points, they may be right, but their arguments are not
complete. First of all, in the short-term, they estimate an FTA with Japan
is disadvantageous to Korea due to Japan's strong industrial competitiveness and low tariff rates. But this argument is based on across-the-board
elimination of tariffs. However, there is little possibility that such results
occur under the current negotiation, since many sensitive Korean manufacturing sectors will be exempted from trade liberalization. These sectors
will be given a longer period for eliminating tariffs on these sensitive items,
when they are included in the liberalization package. Moreover, Korea will
not be impatient to conclude the FTA with Japan, unless there is strong evidence that economic gains resulting from the agreement will be more or less
evenly distributed between the two countries. As Korea is in a disadvantageous stance in industrial competitiveness, it seems to take a cautious step
in preparing tariff concession proposals. A number of stake-holders are
against a FTA with Japan.

Preliminary studies on the impact of an FTA with Japan demonstrate
that a number of sensitive industries such as automobiles, machinery and
household electronics will be seriously affected if Japan gains free access
to these markets in Korea. The mid- to long-term dynamic gains based on
economies of scale, adjustment of industrial structure and inflows of
foreign direct investment are uncertain in some aspects. However, these economic gains will be eventually determined by Korea's endeavours in
improving its economic and trade rules, fostering a pro-competitive environment, facilitating technological innovation, reducing the costs for businesses and developing Korea as an FTA hub by concluding various FTAs
with major trading partners.

The Government of Korea and Japan agreed to conclude the negotiation
for a bilateral FTA by the end of 2005, but this goal was not reached, with
negotiations stalled in the beginning of 2006. Above all, market access has
been the most difficult issue for negotiation. Although Japan insists on
complete market opening, it still put an emphasis on exemption on agricultural products. Moreover, it has been difficult to set up preferential rules
of origin. Because the two countries' industries are overlapped and competitive, it is not easy for companies of both countries to figure out what
are desirable rules of origin for them. It has also been difficult for the
Government of Korea to persuade labour unions especially NGOs that are
against an FTA with Japan. And as the negotiation progresses, opposite

public opinion towards an FTA with Japan will be expanded. Overall, it is expected that it might take more than two years to conclude an FTA with Japan.

REFERENCES

Booz, Allen and Hamilton (1997), *Revitalizing the Korean Economy Towards the 21st Century*, Report for Vision Korea Committee, Booz-Allen-Hamilton Inc.

Korea Institute for International Economic Policy (KIEP) and Institute for Developing Economies (IDE) (2000), *Toward a Korea–Japan FTA: Assessment and Prospects.* Presented at an international seminar Towards Closer Korea–Japan Economic Relations: Proposal for Formulating a 21st Century Partnership, Seoul.

9. AUSFTA and its implications for the Australian stock market

David Allen, Lee K. Lim and Trent Winduss

INTRODUCTION

The relationship between economic fundamentals and stock returns in developed markets such as the United States of America (USA) and Europe has been well researched; (Fama 1990; Schwert 1990; Nasseh and Strauss 2000; Chen *et al.* 1986; Cheung and Ng 1998; Choi *et al.* 1999; Chen 1991). However the role of the economy in stock returns in the Australian market is not nearly as well documented. Attention to this issue is particularly timely, given the recently arranged Free Trade Agreement between Australia and the USA. A possible implication of this agreement is that the capital markets and financial services sectors in Australia and in the USA will become more closely integrated. One of the purposes of this chapter is to take stock of how things stand at the moment in terms of the linkages between the Australian and US capital markets. Bilson *et al.* (2001) address this general issue in an international context using the multivariate model below including local factors and global factors to explain realized returns in 20 emerging markets.

$$R_{it} = \alpha_i + \sum_{m=1}^{G} \beta_{im} F_{imt}^{G} + \sum_{j=1}^{L} \gamma_{ij} F_{ijt}^{L} + \varepsilon_{it} \qquad (9.1)$$

where R_{it}, F_{imt}^{G}, F_{ijt}^{L}, represent return, a set of global factors and a set of local factors, respectively. More specifically Bilson *et al.* (2001) selected the return on a value weighted world index and based on past evidence selected narrow money (M1), exchange rate, industrial production and the consumer price index as potential local influences to form the following model:

$$R_{it} = \beta_i + \beta_{i1} R_{Gt} + \beta_{i2} MS_{it-1} + \beta_{i3} GP_{it-1} + \beta_{i4} RA_{it-2} + \beta_{i5} ER_{it} + \varepsilon_{it} \qquad (9.2)$$

This chapter attempts to improve and extend the work of Bilson *et al.* (2001) in a number of ways and to apply it in an Australian context. The variables chosen to explain stock market behaviour are variables implied by the present value model. Bilson *et al.* (2001) use a global stock market index as the global factor, in order to prove more relevant to policy makers this chapter uses the economic variables implied by historical trade patterns, and pays particular attention to the USA. It is imperative that researchers and policy makers definitively establish the pass through effect US economic developments may have on the Australian economy.

The chapter examines relationships between local and foreign macroeconomic variables and share prices in an Australian context. A key question is how macroeconomic variables affect share prices in Australia. In addition, this chapter explores the informational efficiency of the Australian market. It is well accepted that stock markets should be a leading indicator of economic activity. Using an aggregate proxy for cash flows such as GNP and industrial production the relationship inherent in the present value model can be tested, suggesting that if current cash flows are found to be significant causes of current prices the present value model is violated. Cheung and Ng (1998) (Canada, Germany, Italy, Japan and the USA) and Nasseh and Strauss (2000) (France, Italy, Netherlands, Switzerland and the UK) find evidence that current cash flow proxies are a significant source of stock return variation. It has been suggested (Groenewold 1997) that the existence of cointegration and causality is a violation of the efficient market hypothesis, thus if current industrial production is found to cause stock prices stock markets may be inefficient. To qualify this assumption further, cash flows must be bisected into an expected and unexpected component. If the efficient market hypothesis holds, only the unexpected component should be able to explain stock returns, and this component should be random.

Much past research has been conducted on international globalization and increased capital market integration. The majority of this has concluded that the USA is the world's dominant economy and as a result research has generally found that US stock markets are exogenous and lead other world markets (Arshanapelli *et al.* 1995; Masih and Masih 1999). Given these findings it is reasonable to expect that American domestic macroeconomic variables may influence Australian stock prices because of the information these variables are likely to contain about future economic activity. For three consecutive years ending 30 June 2001, Japan was the largest Australian trading partner, followed by the USA.[1] We aim to extend the literature available on the Australian share markets by not only considering the effect of domestic macroeconomic variables but also by examining the effect of US influences.

The Australia–United States Free Trade Agreement (AUSFTA) is likely to have a significant future impact on the linkages between the US and

Australian economies. It prohibits export taxes on goods and replicates World Trade Organization protection against discriminatory taxes on goods. Beyond this the Agreement does not apply to any existing taxes (DFAT 2004a), but does place limits on the ability of both Australian and United States federal and state governments to implement discriminatory taxes in the future. The agreement features arrangements with respect to trade in services (DFAT 2004b, ch. 10). It ensures that service suppliers from each Party receive national treatment or Most Favoured Nation treatment (whichever is better) from the other Party. It prohibits a range of market access restrictions on service suppliers, as well as restrictions on transfers. Similar provisions apply to investments (DFAT 2004b, ch. 11). There are provisions for the lifting of any restrictions on the supply of financial services:

> Article 13.4 prohibits each Party from placing limits, either on the basis of a regional subdivision or on the basis of its entire territory, on:
>
> - the number of financial institutions;
> - the value of financial service transactions or assets;
> - the number of financial service operations or the quantity of financial services output; or
> - the number of natural persons that may be employed in a particular financial service sector or that a financial service supplier may employ.
>
> It also prohibits each Party from placing controls on the type of legal entity or joint venture through which a financial institution can supply a service. (DFAT 2004b, ch. 13)

The likely implication of the implementation of AUSFTA is that the financial markets and financial services sectors in the two countries, as well as many other segments of the economy will display a much greater degree of linkage in the future. This chapter provides an assessment of the current degree of linkage, utilising a variety of time-series techniques.

The chapter is organized as follows: the following section provides the research procedure used to test the theoretical relationships. The third section outlines the econometric methodology used and the fourth section describes the results. A conclusion brings an end to the chapter.

RESEARCH PROCEDURE

Three models will be utilized to test the validity of the present value model and the relationship between economic variables and the Australian stock market. The first model uses current industrial production to test for the relationship between current economic activity and stock prices:

$$SP_t = IP_t - IR_t \qquad (9.3)$$

where SP denotes domestic stock prices, IP is industrial production and IR is a domestic interest rate series. The present value model will be tested using Model (9.4).

$$SP_t = IP_{t+1} - IR_t \qquad (9.4)$$

where IP_{t+1} denotes domestic industrial production leading one quarter.

According to the present value model, current share prices should be caused by future industrial production. As a proxy for future industrial production, share prices will be led by industrial production by one quarter. It may be the case that share prices share a significant positive relationship with industrial production more than one quarter ahead, however, the objective of the chapter is to establish whether stock prices are significantly related to future industrial production, not how far ahead stock markets predict economic activity.

Using American industrial production one quarter ahead and American interest rates as the external factors most likely to influence the Australian stock market Model (9.5) will test the existence of a relationship and whether domestic or the USA factors have greater influence on Australian share prices.

$$SP_t = USIP_{t+1} - USIR_t + IP_{t+1} - IR_t \qquad (9.5)$$

where $USIP_{t+1}$ is American industrial production leading one quarter ahead and $USIR_t$ is American interest rates.

METHODOLOGY AND DATA

To test the above relationships cointegration and Granger causality tests are employed. We commence with unit root tests, and having established that our series are $I(1)$ proceed with Johansen maximum likelihood (ML) tests for cointegration (Johansen and Juselius 1990). A finding of cointegration suggests causal links between variables (Engle and Granger 1987). We further explore these via long run structural modelling (LRSM) of the cointegrating vectors, estimate the vector error correction model (VECM) and undertake variance decomposition (VDC) analysis. After normalizing share prices as the dependent variable LRSM will be used to determine the existence of a long run causal relationship by placing a restriction of zero on the variable in the cointegrating vector. The rejection of such a restriction implies the variable must enter the cointegrating vector significantly and a long run causal relationship is said to exist.

The VECM is a vector autoregressive (VAR) model where the non-stationary variables have been transformed into a stationary series by first differencing. Such tests can allow the researcher to examine the relative exogeneity and endogeneity of each variable in the system over the short run as well as examining the significance of the long run adjustment to the short run dynamics of the system. A VDC can further enhance the above tests of causality by estimating the relative exogeneity and endogeneity of a system of variables in an out of sample test. Furthermore a VDC can demonstrate the relative significance of each individual variable thus assisting comparison between domestic and international economic variables in this current chapter.

Our sample of quarterly data runs from 1974 Q1 to 2000 Q4. The total return share market indexes comprising 80 per cent of the market capitalization used for Australia were sourced from the Datastream International finance database. Interest rates, consumer price index (CPI) and industrial production indexes were sourced from the International Financial Statistics published by the International Monetary Fund. The interest rate selected was a Government Bond rate in both cases. The data was deflated using the quarterly CPI, and all data apart from interest rates was examined in natural logarithmic form.

RESULTS

Unit Root Tests

We applied tests of data stationarity using Augmented Dickey-Fuller (ADF) tests supplemented by Phillips-Perron tests. When the results obtained from the ADF tests were ambiguous the Phillips-Perron test was then applied. For the sake of brevity the results of the ADF tests are not presented but are available upon request. The null hypothesis that each time series contains a unit root could not be rejected for all variables.

Tests for Cointegration

The presence of cointegration in our data set provides strong preliminary evidence in favour of the present value model. The model implies that a

Table 9.1 Johansen ML cointegration test

	Current Economic Activity		Future Economic Activity		External Factors	
	ME	Trace	ME	Trace	ME	Trace
Australia	$r=2$	$r=1$	$r=2$	$r=2$	$r=1$	$r=1$

stationary long run relationship must exist between share prices, interest rates and industrial production. The existence of cointegration implies that at least uni-direction causality must exist. Following Pesaran and Pesaran (1997) unrestricted intercepts and restricted trends were included as exogenous variables in the cointegrating VAR. It is a strong prior that one cointegrating relationship exists in one of the three models outlined in the second section, based on the fact that domestic share prices must be caused by the variables that make up either the domestic or foreign present value models. In the case that more than one cointegrating vector is found then a priori information is used to determine the correct present value model. The results of the Johansen ML test for cointegration are presented in Table 9.1. It can be seen from the results that a finding of cointegration is accepted.

This table shows the results from the Johansen ML cointegration tests for the number of stationary linear relationships present in the group of variables including industrial production, interest rates and share prices. A finding of cointegration in this chapter provides preliminary evidence in support of the present value model of share prices, which defines a long run relationship between cash flows (aggregate industrial production), interest rates (Government bond rate) and share prices (total return indexes). The cointegrating vector tested for current economic activity includes only domestic economic variables and takes the form $\{SP_t, IP_t, IR_t\}$, while the tests for future economic activity includes industrial production leading domestic share prices by one quarter and the cointegrating vector takes the form $\{SP_t, IP_{t+1}, IR_t\}$. The cointegration test for external factors includes domestic industrial production leading domestic share prices by one quarter, the external factors used in this test are economic variables from the USA including industrial production one quarter ahead, the external factor cointegrating vector is given as $\{SP_t, IP_{t+1}, IR_t, USIP_{t+1}, USIR\}$. r indicates the number of cointegrating relationships found in the Johansen ML cointegration tests, significant at the 5 per cent level. To ascertain the existence of cointegration both the maximal eigenvalue (ME) statistic and the trace statistic were considered and are reported in Table 9.2.

Causality Tests

Long run structural modelling
Table 9.2 shows the results of the LRSM test, which are used in this chapter
to examine for the presence of long run causality. It can be seen from Panel
A that current industrial production is a significant cause of share prices in
Australia, whilst interest rates also significantly cause share prices in
Australia. The significance of current industrial production violates the
present value model and indicates that there is an unexpected portion of
industrial production that influences share prices. Panel B indicates that
future industrial production significantly causes share prices in Australia.

Panel C of Table 9.2 illustrates share price causality stemming from
domestic and external economic factors. The inclusion of USA economic
factors does not alter the composition of the Australian model, indicating
that the domestic economy has greater importance for share prices than the
USA economy.

Table 9.2 summarizes the results obtained from the LRSM analysis,
which is used to determine the existence of long run causal relationships
from economic variables to the domestic share market. Each cointegrating
equation was normalized on share prices so that the estimated equations be
identified as $SP_t = IP_t - IR_t$ for the current economic activity model;
$SP_t = IP_{t+1} - IR_t$ for the future economic activity model that is treated as
the proxy for the present value model and $SP_t = IP_{t+1} - IR_t + USIP_{t+1} -
USIR_t$ for the external factor model, which uses the USA as a foreign
influence. Uni-directional causality could then be examined by placing a
restriction of zero on each variable in question. If that restriction could not

*Table 9.2   Country share returns variables in the cointegrating vector:
summary of LRSM*

	IP	IR	Trend		
Panel A: Current economic activity					
Australia	5.26	0.046	0.00		
	IP_{t+1}	IR	Trend		
Panel B: Future economic activity					
Australia	1.00	0.00	0.00		
	IP_{t+1}	IR	$USIP_{t+1}$	USIR	Trend
Panel C: External factors					
Australia	1.00	0.00	0.00	0.00	0.00

be rejected then the restriction remained in the long run cointegrating vector, therefore the variables that appear as zero in Table 9.2 are insignificant in causing share prices in the long run. *IP* refers to current industrial production while Ip_{t+1} refers to industrial production leading share prices by a quarter; *IR* refers to the domestic interest rates used; while $USIP_{t+1}$ and *USIR* refers to the future USA industrial production and USA interest rates, respectively.

Vector Error Correction Model

Once the cointegrating vectors have been modelled via LRSM, thus eliminating insignificant variables, a vector error correction model (VECM) can be estimated. A VECM provides evidence of short-term causality as well as indicating the significance and speed of the long run error adjustment via the error correction term. The results of the VECM are presented in Table 9.3. It was expected that the error correction terms in the current activity model would not be significant as this model does not represent the present value model, it is expected that in the future economic activity model the error correction terms will be significant to represent the correction to the long run relationship implied by the present value model.

Evidence of significant short-term causality in the model for future economic activity is also rare. Past share prices are surprisingly a significant short-term cause of future share prices in Australia. As expected the majority of error correction terms are significant in the future economic activity models. As displayed in Panel C, US future industrial production and interest rate in the VECM have a short-term causal relationship with Australia, while there is little change to the significance or size of the error correction terms.

Variance Decomposition

A VDC analysis of current economic activity, future economic activity and external factor models was undertaken (the full results are available from the authors on request) whilst a summary is provided in Table 9.4. VDC analysis can be useful in deciphering the relative importance of each variable in explaining the error variance of the dependent variable: share prices. As expected the influence of future industrial production is significantly more prominent than current industrial production, which suggests that at a domestic level the present value model is upheld. Australian investors look forward to domestic future economic activity to explain share prices.

In Table 9.3 Panel A summarizes the results for the error correction model including current economic activity, Panel B meanwhile includes the results for the error correction model including future economic activity. Panel C summarizes the error correction models that include US influences. The respective structure of the VECM for the current economic activity model, the future economic activity model (the proxy for the present value model) and external factor model are estimated as:

$$\Delta SP_t = a_1 Z_{t-1} + \beta_{SPi}\Delta SP_{t-1} + \beta_{PRi}\Delta IP_{t-1} + \beta_{IRi}IR_{t-1} + \varepsilon_t$$

$$\Delta SP_t = a_1 Z_{t-1} + \beta_{SPi}\Delta SP_{t-1} + \beta_{PRi}\Delta IP_{t+1_{t-1}} + \beta_{IRi}IR_{t-1} + \varepsilon_t$$

$$\Delta SP_t = a_1 Z_{t-1} + \beta_{SPi}\Delta SP_{t-1} + \beta_{PRi}\Delta IP_{t-1} + \beta_{IRi}\Delta IR_{t-1}$$
$$+ \beta_{USIP_{t+1}i}\Delta USIP_{t+1_{T-1}} + \beta_{USIRi}\Delta USIR_{t-1} + \varepsilon_t$$

The dependent variable in each model is change in domestic share prices, ΔSP_{t-1}, while ΔIR_{t-1}, ΔIP_{t-1}, $\Delta USIP_{t+1_{T-1}}$ and $\Delta USIR_{t-1}$ are the differenced temporary, lagged explanatory variables for domestic share prices, domestic industrial production, domestic interest rates, US industrial production and the US Government bond rate, denoted by dSP1, dIP1, dIR1, dUSIP1 and dUSIR1 in Table 9.3, the significance of these variables describe a short-term causal relationship with share price return. The error correction term is taken from the cointegrating VAR and highlights $a_1 Z_{t-1}$ influence of the speed and significance of the long run adjustment on domestic share returns; it is denoted by ECT(1) in Table 9.3. The symbol * denotes significant at the 5 per cent level.

The table shows the results of the generalized forecast error variance decomposition for the cointegrating vectors $\{SP_t, IP_t, IR_t\}$ and $\{SP_t, IP_{t+1}, IR_t\}$ with unrestricted intercepts and restricted trends in the VAR for each country for the variable used to proxy cash flow in the present value model, industrial production. The restrictions placed on the cointegrating vector via LRSM hold, such that share prices have been normalized and the coefficient for insignificant variables remains at zero. The variable to be shocked is SP_t. By comparing the relative influence of current and future industrial production we are able to comment on the level of market informational efficiency – as previously mentioned an efficient market should predict future economic activity, hence future economic activity should be more influential than current industrial production. The percentages given are taken from the VDC for current economic activity and future economic activity after a one-year time period. In Australia; current industrial production explains 0.8 per cent of the share price error variance, while future industrial production explains 93.4 per cent; it may be said that the market processes information efficiently.

In Table 9.4 Australia appears to be highly efficient at processing information, in that current industrial production explains less than 1 per cent of

Table 9.3 Summary of error correction models

Explanatory variable	Australia
Panel A: Current economic activity	
Intercept	0.996
dSP1	−0.043
dIP1	−0.021
dIR1	−0.031
ECT(1)	0.056
Panel B: Future economic activity	
Intercept	−0.029*
$dSP1_{t+1}$	0.065*
dIP1	−0.046
dIR1	0.001
ECT(1)	−1.060*
Panel C: External factors	
Intercept	−0.025*
dSP1	0.051*
$dIP1_{t+1}$	−0.085
dIR1	0.002
$dUSIP1_{t+1}$	0.361*
USIR1	−0.003
ECT(1)	−1.091*

Note: * = 5 per cent level of significance.

Table 9.4 Summary of VDC results for current and future industrial production

Country	Current industrial production	Future industrial production
Australia	0.80%	93.41%

the share prices forecast error variance while future industrial production explains approximately 93 per cent of share price forecast error variance.

CONCLUSION

This chapter has attempted to model Australian share markets in terms of a domestic or external present value model for share prices. A current economic activity model, a future economic activity model and an external factor model were estimated using various time-series techniques and applied to the Australian market. The prior that the Australian share market should adhere to either a domestic or external present value model (as tested via the presence of cointegration) was upheld. As expected economic variables were generally a significant cause of share prices as shown via LRSM, generally domestic industrial production was more prominent than domestic interest rates, while US interest rates were more prominent than US industrial production. Furthermore a number of short run causal relationships were also found giving different implications for policy makers interested in long run and short run contagion. The VDC test uncovered the surprising finding that generally Australian share markets do not look to future economic developments in the USA as a guide to future domestic economic performance, instead domestic factors are generally more important. This finding is consistent with the findings of Bilson *et al.* (2001). The findings in this chapter also suggest that the previous research concentrating on perfect segmentation or perfect integration is unrealistic and both domestic and external factors need to be considered when setting policy. The implementation of free trade policies under the auspices of AUSFTA is likely to lead to more pronounced linkage in future between Australian and US financial markets and to an increase in the impact of US macroeconomic variables on Australian markets.

NOTE

1. The largest trading partner is defined in terms of volume of exports and imports of the external trade for the Australian economy.

REFERENCES

Arshanapelli, B., J. Doukas and L. Lang (1995), 'Pre and post-October 1987 stock market linkages between US and Asian markets', *Pacific-Basin Finance Journal*, **3** (1), 57–73.

Bilson, C.M., T.J. Brailsford and V.J. Hooper (2001), 'Selecting macroeconomic variables as explanatory factors of emerging stock market returns', *Pacific-Basin Finance Journal*, **9** (4), 401–26.

Chen, N.F. (1991), 'Financial investment opportunities and the macroeconomy', *Journal of Finance*, **46** (2), 529–54.

Chen, N., R. Roll and S. Ross (1986), 'Economic forces and the stock market', *Journal of Business*, **59** (3), 383–403.

Cheung, Y. and L. Ng (1998), 'International evidence on the stock market and aggregate economic activity', *Journal of Empirical Finance*, **5** (3), 281–96.

Choi, J., S. Hauser and J. Kopecky (1999), 'Does the stock market predict real activity? Time series evidence from the G-7 countries', *Journal of Banking and Finance*, **23** (12), 1771–92.

Department of Foreign Affairs and Trade (DFAT) (2004a), 'Australia–United States Free Trade Agreement – Chapter Twenty Two – General Provisions and Exceptions', www.dfat.gov.au/trade/negotiations/us_fta/final-text/chapter_22.html, 3 February.

DFAT (2004b), *Australia–United States Free Trade Agreement – Guide to the Agreement*, Canberra: Commonwealth of Australia.

Engle, R.F. and C.W.J. Granger (1987), 'Cointegration and error correction: representation estimation and testing', *Econometrica*, **55** (2), 251–76.

Fama, F. (1990), 'Stock returns, expected returns, and real activity', *Journal of Finance*, **45** (4), 1089–108.

Granger, C.W.J. (1986), 'Developments in the study of cointegrated economic variables', *Oxford Bulletin of Economics and Statistics*, **48** (3), 213–28.

Groenewold, N. (1997), 'Share market efficiency: tests using daily data for Australia and New Zealand', *Applied Financial Economics*, **7** (6), 645–57.

Johansen, S. and K. Juselius (1990), 'Maximum likelihood estimation and inference on cointegration – with applications to the demand for money', *Oxford Bulletin of Economics and Statistics*, **52** (2), 169–210.

Masih, A. and R. Masih (1999), 'Are Asian stock market fluctuations due mainly to intra-regional contagion effects?', *Pacific-Basin Finance Journal*, **7** (3–4), 251–82.

Nasseh, A. and J. Strauss (2000), 'Stock prices and domestic and international macroeconomic activity: a cointegration approach', *The Quarterly Review of Economics and Finance*, **40** (2), 229–45.

Pesaran, M.H. and B. Pesaran (1997), *Working with Microfit 4.0: Interactive Econometric Analysis*, Oxford: Oxford University Press.

Schwert, G. (1990), 'Stock returns and real activity: a century of evidence', *Journal of Finance*, **45** (4), 1237–57.

PART IV

Southeast Asia

10. US–Singapore free trade agreement: implications for Singapore, Australia and other ASEAN countries

Jose Tongzon

INTRODUCTION

Singapore believes that multilateralism through an open and stable global environment, facilitated by the World Trade Organization (WTO), will allow for the smooth flow of goods and services. However, Singapore also believes that to augment the multilateral trade regime, like-minded countries could work together in bilateral and regional trade agreements to accelerate trade liberalization. Hence, Singapore takes a strategy of 'additive regionalism' by signing bilateral free trade agreements with her main trading partners while actively supporting multilateralism (Harrison *et al.* 2002). By February 2004, Singapore had signed six FTAs, is currently negotiating eight FTAs and has intentions to start negotiating two more.

Singapore's economy with scarce natural resources and a small domestic market depends on imports of raw materials and on the markets of trading partners to absorb exports. Therefore, trade is highly important to sustain Singapore's economic growth. Table 10.1 shows the extent of its trade to GDP ratio. Trade in goods as of the year 2001 makes up 277 per cent of Singapore's GDP. Singapore is ranked as the world's 15th largest exporter and importer of goods, accounting for 2 per cent and 1.7 per cent of the world's merchandise export and import trade in 2002, respectively. With respect to commercial services, Singapore is ranked as the world's 16th and 20th largest exporter and importer, respectively. Foreign direct investment (FDI) flows into Singapore stood at US$8.61 billion, illustrating that Singapore is dependent on FDI for her economic growth as well (Wong 2004).

Figures 10.1 and 10.2 exhibit trends in Singapore's total exports and imports with her major trading partners over the period of 1990–2002.

Table 10.1　Singapore's macroeconomic data

	Series Name	1980	1985	1990	1995	1999	2000	2001
Singapore	GDP growth (annual %)	9.70	−1.62	8.97	8.01	6.93	10.25	−2.04
	GDP per capita (constant 1995 US$)	11 003	13 109	17 620	23 565	26 246	28 462	27 118
	Exports of goods and services (% of GDP)	–	–	184.05	178.25	168.45	178.79	173.56
	Imports of goods and services (% of GDP)	–	–	177.13	162.29	149.47	160.85	151.84
	Trade in goods (% of GDP)	204.87	277.53	309.53	292.19	273.17	293.66	277.59
	Trade (% of GDP)	–	–	361.18	340.54	317.92	339.63	325.40

Source:　World Development Indicators (2002).

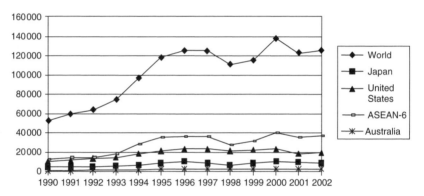

Source:　Calculated from *IMF, Direction of Trade Statistics Yearbook*, various issues.

Figure 10.1　Singapore's exports to its major trading partners

ASEAN-6's (Indonesia, Malaysia, Philippines, Singapore, Thailand and Vietnam) is currently Singapore's largest trading partner with 30 per cent of Singapore's goods traded with the ASEAN countries. This figure has increased by approximately 8 per cent from 1990–2002. The USA, Japan, Australia trade constituted about 15 per cent, 10 per cent and 2 per cent, respectively, of Singapore's trade with the world in 2002.[1] In particular, trade with the USA decreased by about 3 per cent from 1998 to 2002. While the USA and Japan continue to be important external trading partners, in comparison with the increasing volume of trade with ASEAN, the rising intra-ASEAN trade indicates that ASEAN countries are becoming an

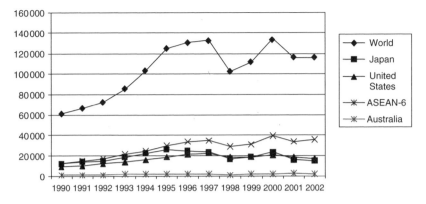

Source: Calculated from *IMF, Direction of Trade Statistics Yearbook*, various issues.

Figure 10.2 Singapore's imports from its major trading partners

increasingly more important trading partner for Singapore. In contrast, Singapore constitutes 2 per cent and 3 per cent respectively of USA and Japan's total global trade.

On average, USA, Japan and Australia constitute about 15 per cent, 7 per cent and 2.5 per cent of Singapore's exports, as shown in Figure 10.1. Over the period from 1990 to 2002, while the exports to Japan have remained in the 7 per cent to 9 per cent and 2 per cent to 3 per cent range, respectively, exports to the USA declined from 21 per cent to 15 per cent.

For Singapore's import sources, USA, Japan and Australia contributes to 14 per cent, 12 per cent and 2 per cent of Singapore's imports, as indicated in Figure 10.2. Over the period from 1990 to 2002, imports from Australia remained on average at a constant level of 2 per cent, while imports from Japan decreased from 21 per cent in 1995 to 12 per cent in 2002. Imports from the USA fluctuated over the range of 16 per cent in the 1990s and remained at 14 per cent in 2002.

Singapore ranks as the USA's 10th largest export market and the 12th largest import source in 1998. Singapore was the sixth largest export market for Japanese goods and Japan's 13th largest source of imports in 1999 (Rajan *et al.* 2000). Overall, Singapore's domestic exports to its FTA partners represent 51.1 per cent of its total domestic exports, amounting to S$61.01 billion (Wong 2004).

In 2002, the two major sectors contributing to Singapore's exports were the machinery and electrical sectors, which accounted for 57.4 per cent of total domestic exports. The third largest sector was petroleum and petrol products with 12.6 per cent. The chemical and chemical products sector was the fourth biggest contributor to domestic exports with a share of

9.8 per cent. However, the machinery and electrical sectors faced a –5.3 per cent and –17.4 per cent average annual growth from 2000 to 2002. This reflects the outsourcing of manufacturing to low-cost locations such as China and India. Petroleum and petroleum products similarly faced a decline of 6.8 per cent due to the competition from new refineries in foreign markets and the weak demand for oil products in the region. On the contrary, Singapore's chemical, plastics and optical precision instruments products grew by 20.1 per cent, 11.2 per cent and 10.1 per cent, respectively, indicating the key areas that Singapore may specialize in (Wong 2004).

Given Singapore's dependence on trade (goods and services) and on FDI for the sustenance of her economy, it is therefore not surprising that Singapore has taken the FTA route so as to remain competitive in her exports and attractive as a destination for FDI. This also ensures that her companies are not disadvantaged, allowing for expansion in the global market.

UNITED STATES–SINGAPORE TRADE PARTNERSHIP

The US–Singapore FTA (USSFTA) was signed on 6 May 2003 and has been in force since January 2004. As the first bilateral FTA with an Asian country, the US–Singapore FTA serves as a catalyst towards deeper economic integration for Asia and to spur ASEAN-wide FTAs.

With 1300 USA companies and 15 000 US citizens residing in Singapore and with many United States MNCs using Singapore as a base to export around the world, the USA is one of the most important trading and investment partners for Singapore. As at the end of 2001, United States was Singapore's largest foreign direct investor with US$27.3 billion in Singapore, consisting of 2.2 per cent of US investment overseas. Currently, Singapore is the second largest Asian investor in the USA after Japan (Koh 2003).

The base of Singapore's trade with the USA is in manufactures with machinery and electrical equipment consisting of a huge 75 per cent of Singapore's exports and imports to the USA. Miscellaneous manufactures take up 11 per cent and the third largest traded goods are chemicals and chemical products totalling 7 per cent. In 2002, according to statistics from Industry Enterprise (IE) Singapore, Singapore's top three imports from the USA are machinery and equipment making up 66 per cent and miscellaneous manufactures and chemicals totalling approximately 10 per cent. The top export, including re-exports, to the USA is the machinery and equipment sector (80 per cent), followed by miscellaneous manufactures at

11 per cent and chemicals and petroleum products taking up 4 per cent. Therefore, tariff reductions in the manufacturing sector for machinery and electronics will benefit Singapore largely.

In the USSFTA, Singapore has committed to zero tariffs for all imports upon entry into force of the FTA, thereby eliminating tariffs on the following alcoholic products: beer, stout, samsoo and medicated samsoo. Before the FTA, all goods imported from the USA are duty free besides the four products as stated above.

The United States commitment is to eliminate 92 per cent of current tariffs on exports from Singapore to the USA, within the first four years of entry into force of the USSFTA and almost all the rest will be eliminated within eight years. The sectors that are likely to benefit most from the reduction of tariffs are electronics, chemicals and petrochemicals, agricultural products, instrumentation equipment, processed foods and mineral products.

Besides the elimination of tariff barriers, the FTA covers rules of origin, non-tariff barriers, customs administration and technical barriers to trade, trade remedies, cross-border trade in services, temporary entry, telecommunications and e-commerce, investment, competition policies, government procurement, intellectual property protection, transparency, general provisions, labour and environment standards and dispute settlement.

ECONOMIC IMPLICATIONS OF US–SINGAPORE FTA FOR SINGAPORE AND ITS TRADING PARTNERS

To date, no quantitative analysis has yet been undertaken on the economic implications of US–Singapore FTA. Only qualitative assessments have so far been done, for example, Tongzon (2003a and 2003b) and Malaysian Institute of Economic Research (2001). These qualitative studies have concluded that Singapore would benefit greatly in terms of more tariff savings, greater market access to the US market and in terms of strengthening her position as the bridge between the USA and other neighbouring Asian countries. Second, they have concluded that there would be trade and investment diversions suffered by other ASEAN countries that have similar export structures in the US market.

To quantify the gains and costs of the US–Singapore FTA from the perspective of Singapore and its other trading partners, this chapter employs a Computable General Equilibrium (CGE) model of the Global Trade Analysis Project (GTAP). The structure, aggregation strategy and experimental design are discussed in the subsequent sub-sections.

Model Structure

The standard GTAP model is a multi-region, multi-sector, computable general equilibrium model with perfect competition and constant returns to scale. The Armington structure accounts for bilateral trade. The description below explains the relationships in a GTAP model, which does not take into account government intervention (taxes and subsidies).

The model starts with the Regional Household deriving its income from the sale of primary factors to producers. It then allocates expenditure to three sectors: private households, global savings and government. Producers use primary factors and combine them with domestically produced and imported intermediates to produce the final goods which are sold to private households and the government while exporting a portion to the rest of the world. Final goods are also imported from the rest of the world by the government and private household. The Global Bank acts as an intermediary between global savings and regional investments. It assembles a portfolio of regional investment goods and sells this portfolio to regional households to meet their savings demand (Hertel 1997).

The firm behaviour is next examined and the production structure in the GTAP model is described below. Here, the production process assumes constant returns to scale and output assumes a Leontief aggregation function specified between value-added and intermediate demands. This implies that composite intermediates and primary factors are non-substitutable. Value-added demand is specified in a CES aggregation of three primary factors: labour, land and capital. Labour and capital are perfectly mobile within the region while land is specific to agriculture. Demand for intermediates is an aggregation of domestic and imported intermediates, with imported intermediates sourced from different regions. Imported intermediates are treated according to the Armington specification (Hertel 1997).

The Armington structure handles bilateral trade by assuming that products are differentiated by their country-of-origin such that products produced in different regions are heterogeneous rather than homogeneous across countries.

Aggregation of Data

This model uses the latest version GTAP.TAB 6.2 which was released in 2003. The data used are from the GTAP database Version 5.4 which identifies 66 countries, each producing 57 commodities. In this chapter, the world is aggregated into nine regions and 16 sectors. ASEAN countries are separate components and Singapore's major trading partners, Japan and Australia, are included so as to distinguish their individual welfare and trade effects of policy simulation of the US–Singapore FTA. The nine regions are: Singapore (SGP), United States (US), Malaysia (MYS), Indonesia (IDN), Thailand (THA), Philippines (PHL), Vietnam (VIET), Australia (AUS), Japan (JPN) and Rest-of-World (ROW). A 16-sector aggregation for commodities was chosen based on sectoral characteristics and to account for the relative importance of the sectors to the Singapore economy.

In addition, to obtain a baseline for this study, the tariff data have to be processed in three stages. The first stage is to take into account the import tariffs for Japan, Australia and ASEAN five countries due to Japan–Singapore Economic Partnership Agreement (JESPA), Singapore–Australia Free Trade Agreement (SAFTA) and ASEAN Free Trade Agreement (AFTA). This is to ensure that when the USSFTA is simulated, the analysis will be reflective of the current situation where AFTA, JESPA and SAFTA are already in force. For simulation purposes, the underlying scenario for Japan and Australia is a 100 per cent reduction in import and export tariff for goods while the service liberalization effort is assumed to reduce services tariff equivalents by 50 per cent. In this chapter, services tariff equivalents are not reduced fully. This is due to the fact that there are other 'man-made' non-tariff barriers such as geographical proximity, culture and so on and as a result, we are unable to assume that once services tariffs are reduced to zero, services will be traded freely like traded goods. To account for AFTA, simplified average tariffs as scheduled for year 2004 in the AFTA agreement are used.

The second stage consists of updating the US–Singapore import tariff rates to reflect the tariff rates before the US–Singapore FTA came into effect, where Singapore's import tariffs are at zero per cent, except for certain alcohol products. To reflect a realistic situation of non-tariff barriers, services taxes to tariffs for business, financial, communication, construction, transport and other services are updated according to the Australian Productivity Commission.

Simulation Design

The USSFTA came into effect on 1 January 2004. The simulated scenario uses the standard closure and captures the effects of the trade liberalization of *ad valorem* import tariffs and tariff equivalents of services. Tariffs are reduced by 100 per cent in all sectors and a 50 per cent reduction in services tariffs equivalents for simulation purposes. This is based on the USSFTA, whereby in the tenth year, all goods tariffs will be reduced to zero per cent and services would have been liberated in certain sectors. A 100 per cent reduction in services is not simulated as some restrictions on foreign firms will still be present even in the event of a liberalization of the services sector.

SIMULATION RESULTS

This section presents and discusses the macroeconomic, bilateral and international trade flows and microeconomic (sectoral impacts) results of the simulation, which simulates the complete import liberalization between Singapore and the United States. Comparisons between the macroeconomic and microeconomic results are also discussed in the last section of the chapter.

Macroeconomic Effects of the Policy

The macroeconomic effects of the USSFTA are presented in Table 10.2. Looking at the welfare changes, we notice that Singapore and the United States enjoy positive welfare gains. However, while the welfare gains for Singapore are $678.1m, the distribution of gains translates to less than 1 per cent in terms of per capita utility. For the United States, the welfare gains are negligible with a US$1.8m gain and in terms of per capita utility there is a zero per cent gain. This signals that the welfare gains for both countries in the USSFTA are relatively small. Similarly, the effect on output as measured by real GDP is small, with Singapore experiencing only a 1.3 per cent change and United States suffers from a negligible 0.003 per cent loss in real GDP.

Examining the welfare losses for Singapore's major trading partners, the losses are negligible; an overall $118.9m for ASEAN countries, $15.5m for Japan, $12.1m for Australia and $75.8m for China. These negligible losses reflect the distribution of dependence of Singapore's trade with her major trading partners and with the Rest-of-the World (ROW). Comparing among Singapore's major trading partners, ASEAN registers the biggest loss as compared to Japan, Australia and China, reflecting the higher dependence of Singapore's trade on ASEAN countries.

Welfare changes can be decomposed into allocative and terms of trade distribution. In this model, the welfare gains are attributed more to the terms of trade movements than to the allocative efficiency, therefore, the positive terms of trade (*tot*) of 0.47 per cent for Singapore are reflective of the positive welfare gains. The changes in terms of trade are linked by the equation:

$$tot = psw - pdw$$

The improvement in export prices (*psw*) in Singapore signals that there is a switch to Singapore's exports at the expense of Singapore's other trading partners. The losses in the terms of trade for other countries are however negligible.

Table 10.2 Macroeconomic effects of simulation

	Welfare (US$m)	Allocative efficiency (US$m)	Per Capita utility (%)	Change in Real GDP (%)	Real Exports (%)	Real Imports (%)	psw (%)	pdw (%)	Terms of Trade (tot) (%)	Rate of return (%)	Current Account (US$m)
SGP	678.10	53.41	0.931	1.275	-0.069	0.682	0.473	-0.001	0.474	2.003	-385.12
USA	1.83	67.95	0	-0.003	0.112	0.103	-0.002	0.005	-0.006	0.011	-137.62
IDN	-17.10	-2.56	-0.008	-0.011	-0.005	-0.037	-0.004	0.021	-0.025	-0.014	3.72
MAL	-56.15	-0.82	-0.047	-0.023	-0.017	-0.086	0.007	0.068	-0.061	-0.098	5.53
PHL	-23.63	-6.52	-0.034	-0.044	-0.004	-0.070	-0.012	0.023	-0.035	-0.068	17.76
THA	-18.09	0.48	-0.011	-0.017	-0.001	-0.045	-0.002	0.025	-0.027	-0.031	10.85
VIET	-3.99	1.87	-0.022	-0.048	0.045	-0.057	-0.011	0.040	-0.050	-0.092	5.30
ASEAN	-118.96	-7.55	–	-0.028	-0.007	-0.061	-0.002	0.034	-0.040	–	8.63
JPN	-15.49	4.74	0	-0.001	0.007	-0.012	0.000	0.004	-0.004	-0.001	63.94
AUST	-12.10	-0.04	-0.003	-0.011	0.010	-0.023	-0.008	0.009	-0.017	-0.009	11.13
CHN	-75.78	-10.79	-0.008	-0.013	-0.009	-0.038	-0.006	0.015	-0.021	-0.014	24.83
ROW	-501.75	-150.19	-0.004	-0.010	0.005	-0.013	-0.007	0.001	-0.008	-0.007	379.68

Notes:
1. ASEAN consists of Indonesia, Malaysia, Philippines, Thailand, Vietnam.
2. Welfare is defined by the Hicksian Equivalent Variation.
3. All percentage figures refer to a percentage change from the base data.
4. psw represents the change in the price index received for exports.
5. pdw represents the change in the price index paid for imports.

In the standard closure used in this simulation, where investments are responsive to the changes in the rates of return across regions, there is a rise in the rate of return to investment in Singapore and the United States and correspondingly, a current account deficit. The increase in the rate of return to investment signals that investments are diverted from Singapore's trading partners.

Within ASEAN, Malaysia suffers the greatest diversion in investments. Likewise, Malaysia's welfare losses, per capita utility, negative per cent change in real exports and imports and declining terms of trade is a result of Malaysia's closer relations and trade links with Singapore. Overall, the macroeconomic gains from trade liberalization to Singapore and the United States from the USSFTA and the subsequent effects on Singapore's major trading partners such as ASEAN are negligible.

Bilateral and International Trade Flows

Table 10.3 highlights the percentage change in the volume of bilateral exports. Singapore is projected to enjoy an 8.6 per cent increase in goods and services exports to the USA, with about half resulting from the reduction in the USA's import tariffs in goods. Singapore's exports are however diverted from the other regions to the USA because of the USSFTA reductions in the USA's import tariffs for Singapore. This diversion occurs as the reduction in tariffs translates into cost savings for US firms importing their goods from Singapore, resulting in an increase in the demand for certain goods from Singapore. The reductions in the exports of Singapore to other countries have changed by a small percentage of about 2 per cent and less. The changes in bilateral exports are explained by the initial tariff rates, such that trade would expand the most in sectors which have the greatest reduction in tariffs. Hence, in sectors such as textiles and processed food, the increases in volume of exports are the greatest.

Bilateral trade with Australia and Japan has minimal effects due to the USSFTA with a reduction of 1.9 per cent and 2 per cent in Singapore's exports to Australia and Japan, respectively. While these figures are insignificant because Singapore is already facing zero tariffs in Australian and Japanese markets with the SAFTA and JESPA in force, the USSFTA results in a small reduction in the increase of Singapore exports to the two countries. This occurs since Singaporean exporters are now able to export their products to the USA at a cheaper price and there is more competition between Australian, Japanese and the US markets.

Looking at the increase of US exported goods to Singapore (see Table 10.4), this figure of 0.42 per cent is negligible. This results from the fact that Singapore's import tariffs for the USA's imports were mostly at

Table 10.3   Percentage change in volume of exports from Singapore to Singapore's major trading partners

	USA	IDN	MAL	PHL	THA	VIET	ASEAN	JPN	AUST	CHN	ROW
AGR	49.76	-2.53	-2.45	-2.53	-2.52	-2.36	-2.52	-2.21	-2.45	-2.46	-2.48
PFD	60.03	-2.32	-2.26	-2.37	-2.31	-2.34	-2.35	-2.35	-2.34	-2.21	-2.37
MIN	-1.49	-1.40	-1.20	-1.36	-1.36	-1.44	-1.40	-1.50	-1.15	-1.24	-1.36
CHM	18.16	-1.19	-1.07	-1.30	-1.31	-1.25	-1.18	-1.38	-1.37	-1.25	-1.42
TXC	133.17	-3.24	-2.76	-3.26	-3.23	-3.22	-2.97	-3.31	-3.26	-3.17	-3.29
OMF	3.79	-3.40	-3.08	-3.30	-3.31	-3.29	-3.29	-3.42	-3.39	-3.40	-3.49
BMM	16.26	-2.79	-2.67	-2.84	-2.78	-2.72	-2.80	-2.87	-2.87	-2.87	-2.90
ME	15.27	-2.14	-1.94	-2.11	-2.09	-2.00	-2.06	-2.18	-2.20	-2.15	-2.22
TRE	4.46	-5.68	-5.70	-5.82	-5.85	-5.88	-6.10	-5.92	-5.89	-5.82	-5.92
EE	1.39	-1.76	-1.36	-1.65	-1.54	-1.26	-1.44	-1.65	-1.53	-1.60	-1.69
Total Goods	**5.40**	**-1.63**	**-1.59**	**-1.96**	**-1.87**	**-1.76**	**-1.69**	**-1.84**	**-1.76**	**-1.78**	**-2.04**
BizSvc	30.55	-3.41	-3.42	-3.45	-3.44	-3.56	-3.55	-3.47	-3.46	-3.44	-3.43
FinSvc	7.90	-3.76	-3.75	-3.82	-3.78	-3.84	-3.99	-3.76	-3.77	-3.78	-3.77
ComSvc	-4.79	-4.78	-4.79	-4.82	-4.82	-4.82	-4.43	-4.78	-4.80	-4.80	-4.80
TransSvc	79.97	-2.52	-2.55	-2.57	-2.54	-2.51	-2.61	-2.52	-2.54	-2.54	-2.53
ConsSvc	16.92	-3.05	-3.03	-3.18	-3.08	-3.11	-2.84	-3.07	-3.08	-3.08	-3.08
OtherSvc	28.64	-3.15	-3.17	-3.23	-3.16	-3.24	-3.31	-3.13	-3.15	-3.15	-3.15
Total	**8.65**	**-1.86**	**-1.65**	**-2.18**	**-1.97**	**-1.76**	**-1.79**	**-2.02**	**-1.91**	**-1.85**	**-2.46**

Notes:
1. ASEAN consists of Indonesia, Malaysia, Philippines, Thailand, Vietnam.
2. Volume changes here refer to a percentage deviation from the base data. The volume change used to calculate the percentage change is valued at initial export prices in US$.
3. Under the USSFTA, services barriers are reduced. We therefore reduce services tariffs by 50 per cent, as explained earlier in the Aggregation of data section.

Table 10.4 Percentage change in volume of imports from Singapore's major trading partners to Singapore

	USA	IDN	MAL	PHL	THA	VIET	ASEAN	JPN	AUST	CHN	ROW
AGR	0.71	0.72	0.61	0.83	0.68	0.69	0.71	0.69	0.70	0.73	0.72
PFD	0.88	0.91	0.89	1.04	0.89	0.92	0.93	0.87	0.90	0.91	0.90
MIN	-0.32	-0.32	-0.34	-0.31	-0.30	-0.23	-0.30	-0.36	-0.32	-0.34	-0.31
CHM	0.49	0.46	0.46	0.51	0.51	0.53	0.49	0.48	0.51	0.50	0.51
TXC	4.59	4.52	4.46	4.60	4.58	4.56	4.54	4.52	4.56	4.56	4.56
OMF	0.82	0.86	0.77	0.91	0.88	0.86	0.86	0.83	0.87	0.87	0.86
BMM	0.11	0.12	0.07	0.23	0.13	0.21	0.15	0.11	0.15	0.14	0.14
ME	0.47	0.45	0.44	0.45	0.47	0.48	0.46	0.47	0.51	0.49	0.51
TRE	1.89	1.91	1.95	1.95	1.91	1.91	1.93	1.87	1.95	1.94	1.94
EE	-0.19	-0.19	-0.29	-0.26	-0.28	-0.31	-0.27	-0.21	-0.22	-0.24	-0.18
Total in goods	**0.42**	**0.62**	**0.13**	**0.00**	**0.10**	**0.49**	**0.15**	**0.35**	**0.54**	**0.74**	**0.42**
BizSvc	50.98	-3.55	-3.51	-3.44	-3.52	-3.43	-3.49	-3.58	-3.55	-3.55	-3.55
FinSvc	46.38	-4.03	-3.99	-3.91	-3.99	-3.87	-3.96	-4.06	-4.02	-4.02	-4.03
ComSvc	19.91	0.20	0.26	0.28	0.24	0.27	0.25	0.17	0.20	0.20	0.20
TransSvc	17.97	-1.56	-1.53	-1.49	-1.53	-1.57	-1.54	-1.58	-1.55	-1.55	-1.55
ConsSvc	18.17	2.83	2.79	2.92	2.86	2.90	2.86	2.82	2.85	2.85	2.85
OtherSvc	39.06	-7.71	-7.69	-7.59	-7.68	-7.55	-7.64	-7.74	-7.71	-7.71	-7.71
Total	**4.06**	**0.49**	**0.10**	**-0.36**	**0.03**	**0.47**	**0.08**	**0.25**	**0.13**	**0.35**	**-0.16**

Notes:
1. ASEAN consists of Indonesia, Malaysia, Philippines, Thailand, Vietnam.
2. Volume changes here refer to a percentage deviation from the base data. The volume change used to calculate the percentage change is valued at initial export prices in US$.

zero per cent before the FTA was concluded, consequently, the gains for the USA's exports from the reduction in Singapore's import tariffs are little. Mostly, USA will gain from the reduction in services barriers.

Singapore's major trading partners also experience an increase in exports to Singapore due to the USSFTA. Nevertheless, the changes in goods imports from ASEAN, Japan and Australia are small as Singaporean importers already face a near zero tariff for most products. Therefore most of the products from Australia and Japan are on an equal footing with the US products. Looking at the specific sectors where Singapore–Australia trade is important such as the agricultural sector, the results show that agricultural imports are not diverted to the USA. In 2002, Singapore's percentage volume of agricultural trade with Australia was 8.5 per cent while the percentage volume of agricultural trade with the USA was only at 1 per cent. In addition, agricultural products from both Australia and the USA are at zero per cent before the USSFTA commenced.

Since there is a small proportion of US agricultural imports and with Singapore's low base import tariffs, as a result, there is no significant diversion of agricultural imports. For the services sector, given that Singapore has relatively high tariffs equivalents for sectors such as the financial sector, there is a potential diversion of imports of services from other countries towards the USA with the reduction in services barriers.

For the USA, imports are diverted from ASEAN, Japan, Australia, China and Rest of the World. Therefore, Singapore gains but other regions including ASEAN lose in terms of the volume of exports to the USA. Nonetheless, there are no adverse effects from the USSFTA on the exports of other regions to the USA due to the small changes in the volume of trade. The negligible changes in the volume of trade shows that ASEAN goods are not much less competitive even with the reduction in tariffs for Singapore products. This reflects the situation that the major export products differ between Singapore and the other ASEAN countries.

The results also show that there is a significant percentage increase in the volume of agricultural exports to the USA. Although Singapore is not a major exporter of agriculture to the USA, the significant increase is a result of the high import tariffs base in the USA facing Singapore exports, reflecting the USA's protection of its agriculture sector.

Sectoral Effects

Sectoral output in sectors of processed food, textiles, transport, construction and other services in Singapore face an increase in demand due to the USSFTA. Given the high US MFN tariff levels for textiles, Singapore becomes an attractive exporting market which can be shown by the substantial increase of 22 per cent in textiles output. However, to enjoy the zero per cent tariffs for textiles, Singaporean exporters need to use Singapore-made or US made yarn or fabrics (Tongzon 2003a, 2003b). Other restrictions included in the rules of origin may also prevent a substantial increase in Singapore's textiles output. With regard to Singapore's major export markets, chemicals, machinery and electrical goods face a drop in demand due to the USSFTA. The scope for an increase in the price competitiveness for chemicals, machinery and electrical goods compared with processed food and textiles are limited due to the relatively low tariff barriers erected by the United States. It is observed that there are no significant contractions in sectoral output for ASEAN countries as a result of the USSFTA.

CONCLUSION

This chapter has provided a quantitative assessment of the Singapore–United States FTA using a nine-region, 16-sector, static CGE model focusing mainly on Singapore, ASEAN and Australia.

Based on the simulation results, the static welfare effects from the removal of goods and services tariff barriers under the USSFTA are insignificant with a net gain of 'US$678m for Singapore which also translates to 0.9 per cent per capita utility. The corresponding GDP percentage change due to the USSFTA is at a minimal 1.3 per cent. Overall, although Singapore gains, the slight expansion in the volume of goods exports from Singapore to the USA at 5.4 per cent also indicate that the gains are not substantial. Therefore, one of the policy implications is that Singapore can further realize other gains from trade liberalization through dynamic effects. These dynamic effects include the gains from increased investment, economies of scale, external economies and learning-by-doing effects. From the USA and other countries' investors' view, Singapore is a more lucrative market for investments since there are fewer restrictions and more concessions for trade with the USA. In addition, with the multiple FTAs that Singapore has signed with other major countries such as Japan and Australia, and will be signing with other countries, these FTAs can work together to bring about a more liberal trading system for Singapore and her neighbouring countries.

With respect to ASEAN, the simulation above which incorporates tariff reductions in AFTA shows that ASEAN countries lose an insignificant amount in terms of welfare, percentage changes in GDP and the percentage changes of exports and imports. Therefore, this chapter quantifies that the negative effects of the USSFTA on ASEAN countries that critics of the USSFTA have concluded, are negligible.

How will the USSFTA affect current FTAs that Singapore has signed with Australia and Japan? The conclusions are that in terms of welfare, percentage changes in GDP and percentage changes in exports and imports, the negative impacts are smaller than that for ASEAN and are insignificant. The responses of Australia and Japan to the USA import tariff reduction towards Singapore do not result in large changes in individual sector demand. Therefore, bilateral trade between Singapore and the above two countries will not be severely affected. Instead, with the USA–Australia FTA, there will be more scope for joint cooperation between Australia, Singapore and the United States to further liberalize the trading system and to reap potential benefits.

Since this chapter only quantifies the static effects of the USSFTA, there are a number of limitations encountered: the use of simplified AFTA tariff rates, the use of Alter Tax in the GTAP model, the aggregated GTAP sectors, the failure to include non-tariff barriers in the simulation and lastly, a dynamic model could not be simulated. However, the study does indicate the general direction in terms of the economic impact of the recently concluded USSFTA.

NOTE

1. Singapore is Australia's largest trade and investment partner in ASEAN and its eighth largest trading partner overall. In 2003 Australian merchandise exports to Singapore were valued at A$3.5 billion and imports from Singapore were valued at A$4.5 billion. As at June 2003, Australian investment in Singapore was valued at A$10 billion while total Singaporean investment in Australia was A$33.5 billion in the area of telecommunications, energy, healthcare, waste management, piggery and aviation (Business Times 2004).

REFERENCES

Business Times (2004), 'Singapore investors warm to Aussie investments', 8–9 May, p. 1.

Harrison, G.W., T.F. Ruthford and D.G. Tarr (2002), 'Trade policy options for Chile: the importance of market access', *The World Bank Economic Review*, **16** (1), 49–79.

Hertel, T. (1997), *Global Trade Analysis: Modelling and Applications*, New York: Cambridge University Press.

Koh, T. (2003), 'Introductory remarks', in T. Koh, K. Paulson, J. Tongzon and V. Khanna, *US–Singapore FTA: Implications and Prospects*, Trends in Southeast Asia Series: 5 (2003), Singapore: Institute of Southeast Asian Studies, pp. 1–4.

Malaysian Institute of Economic Research (2001), *Singapore Bilateral FTA and AFTA*, Malaysian Institute of Economic Research.

Rajan, R.S., R. Sen and R. Siregar (2000), *Singapore and Free Trade Agreements: Economic Relations with Japan and the United States*, Singapore: Institute of Southeast Asian Studies.

Tongzon, J.L. (2003a), 'US–Singapore FTA: economic implications for Singapore and the ASEAN region', in T. Koh, K. Paulson, J. Tongzon and V. Khanna, *US–Singapore FTA: Implications and Prospects*, Trends in Southeast Asia Series: 5(2003), Singapore: Institute of Southeast Asian Studies, pp. 13–19.

Tongzon, J.L. (2003b), 'US–Singapore free trade agreement: implications for ASEAN', *ASEAN Economic Bulletin*, **20** (2), 174–8.

Wong Chian Voen (ed.) (2004), *Making Business Sense of the Singapore FTAs*, Singapore: Times Editions.

World Bank (2002), *World Development Indicators*, Washington, DC: World Bank.

11. Comparative advantage in Thailand and Indonesia and potential free trade agreements: implications for trade diversion

William E. James

INTRODUCTION

The recent trend for Thailand to enter into bilateral free trade agreements (FTAs) with major trade partners outside of the Association for South East Asian Nations (ASEAN) such as Australia is in marked contrast to Indonesia. The Thai Government is second only to Singapore among the ten South East Asian nations in the vigorous pursuit of free trade agreements on a bilateral basis with numerous trading partners.[1] The proclivity to negotiate bilateral preferential trade agreements by Thailand is of possibly greater concern to ASEAN partners like Indonesia than is the case with Singapore. Thailand's average MFN tariff for WTO members is 14.6 per cent and its average manufacturing tariff (also for WTO members) is 16.5 per cent (WTO 2003b). Thailand has bound 74 per cent of its 5505 tariff lines with the simple average bound rate of 28.4 per cent in 2003.[2] Thailand also maintains tariff quotas on 23 agricultural products (WTO 2003a, pp. 38–9). In contrast, 99.9 per cent of Singapore's tariff lines are duty-free, with only four tariff lines subject to specific duties (WTO 2000). Singapore has bound 70.5 per cent of its tariff lines with an average bound tariff rate of 9.7 per cent.[3] The high levels of protection in Thailand compared with Singapore imply larger potential for trade diversion in the Thai case. Preferential agreements between Thailand and major markets for Indonesian exports like the US and Japan are also of concern because of the potential for such agreements to lead to diversion of Indonesian exports in favour of those of Thailand.[4]

Trade diversion effects of discriminatory preferential trade agreements are not the only source of concern over their proliferation. Investment diversion and the subsequent restriction of intra-industry trade because of rules of origin that exclude intermediate inputs from non-members is another source of worry (Garnaut and Song 2003). The threat of 'truncated globalization' is particularly worrisome for East Asia as the recent trade boom fuelled by intra-industry trade in components, particularly in electronics and electrical and non-electrical machinery, preceded the formation of the new wave of FTAs involving East Asian entities. If rules of origin are used to restrict members of free trade agreements from using components from non-member sources, this would interfere with firm decisions to locate production facilities in non-members and would further be debilitating to trade by raising costs of production inside the FTA.

FREE TRADE AGREEMENTS AND THE WTO

The World Trade Organization provides for exceptions to the fundamental principle of non-discrimination in the form of free trade agreements under GATT Article XXIV, GATS article V and under the so-called 'enabling clause' instituted during the Tokyo Round (Srinivasan 1998). The fundamental theoretical debate over whether free trade agreements are 'stepping stones' or 'stumbling blocks' to global free trade aside, the characteristics of such agreements do matter.[5] Figure 11.1 is an attempt to develop a simple classification scheme for agreements. The intuition underlying Figure 11.1 is that 'WTO-compliant' free trade agreements minimally cover 'substantially all trade', meaning trade in goods with some exceptions (usually for agriculture) and do not raise overall average tariffs on non-members. However, 'WTO (+)' free trade agreements are now coming into vogue and go well beyond the minimal requirements in coverage, as suggested in the bottom two quadrants of the matrix.

Free trade agreements may be judged to be 'closed' or 'open' depending on whether they maintain or lower tariff barriers to non-members and whether or not they impose strict rules of origin that lead to reductions in imports of intermediate goods from non-members. Such closed agreements were characteristic of many Latin American trade agreements in the 1970s and recent agreements in Africa and South Asia. North American Free Trade Agreement (NAFTA) rules of origin in textiles and automobiles are highly restrictive with respect to intermediate inputs of non-members, but are quite liberal for other machinery sectors, particularly for electronics, telecommunications equipment and computers.[6] Some preferential trade agreements have augmented tariff preferences with favourable quota treatment. This is the case in the NAFTA, whereby textile and clothing items produced in Mexico under the 'yarn forward' or 'triple transformation' rule of origin are free of quotas and pay very low tariffs (see, Hufbauer and Schott 1993; James and Umemoto 2000; James 2004).

	Closed	Open	
			Weaker
WTO	Maintain high external tariffs; basic commitments to lower duties	Lower external tariffs; basic commitments to lower duties	
WTO (+)	Maintain high external tariffs; make commitments to reforms that go beyond the WTO	Lower external tariffs; make commitments to reform that go beyond the WTO	
	(Services, Investment laws, property rights, customs, dispute settlement)	(Services, Investment laws, property rights, customs, dispute settlement)	

Weaker ⟶ Stronger

Source: James and Wendel (2004).

Figure 11.1 Classification matrix for free-trade agreements

Movement from left to right and from top to bottom in the matrix implies agreements have substantial effects in terms of deepening economic integration between member states. Closed and weak agreements are those that maintain high external tariffs and merely comply with the minimal standards and that lack development of institutions such as dispute settlement mechanisms. Such agreements do little to encourage reform and are mainly political in nature. Open and strong agreements provide support to 'lock-in' reforms that liberalize trade and investment and develop strong institutions for resolution of disputes with clear legal guidance and time-bound schedules. NAFTA has been instrumental in Mexico's reform efforts in the areas of trade and customs, financial services and foreign direct investment rules.

Thailand is launching negotiations for a FTA with the US in Honolulu at the East–West Center in late June 2004. There are several reasons for the US–Thai decision to pursue a free trade agreement. A long-term bilateral treaty between the two countries that grants national treatment to US companies that invest and operate in Thailand is due to expire shortly and the US side is keen to preserve this preferential treatment. Thailand is a front-line state in the war on terror and has strongly backed the US in Iraq and Afghanistan by committing Thai troops to the effort. A free trade agreement is one way to reward Thailand for its support in the global fight against the terrorists. Nonetheless, the Thai government's decision to explore the bilateral path to trade liberalization is ironic in that it coincides with the term of Thai Director-General Supachai Panitchpakdi as the head of the World Trade Organization (WTO). Thailand states that its bilateral agreements will allow benefits to accrue to third parties yet there are no specifics on the mechanism by which this may occur (WTO 2003b, p. 26).

The adoption of rules of origin (or what might more aptly be termed rules of preference) to enforce preferential trade agreements is to exclude benefits from accruing to non-members (third parties) except where exemptions are granted to non-members for certain products.[7] The import-weighted average tariff for textile and clothing products in the US market paid by various major suppliers reveals that a preferential arrangement may confer a very substantial margin of preference for products deemed to originate in the territory of a preferential supplier (Table 11.1). While such arrangements are obviously in the interest of states receiving preferences, they may have adverse consequences for non-members in terms of market access.

Complex rules of origin and overlapping sets of rules of origin (and numerous different preferential tariff rates) may impose substantial costs upon businesses that are seeking to obtain origin within a preferential trade area. A recent study of the rules of origin in the Australia–New Zealand Closer Economic Relations (CER) agreement by the Australian Productivity Commission (PC 2003) reveals that compliance with rules of origin could cost between 1 and 6 per cent of the value of imported goods. Complex and overlapping sets of rules of origin may give rise to customs problems and could lead to corrupt practices in developing countries when the benefits of conference of origin are large.

Free trade agreements have ambiguous effects on global economic welfare and much turns on the details of negotiated outcomes. Empirical

Table 11.1   US imported weighted tariffs on apparel in 2001 as percentage of FOB value

Customs Territory	Import-Weighted Tariff %	PTA Status
Indonesia	17.5	No
Bangladesh	15.5	No
Pakistan	15.8	No
Malaysia	11.1	No
Thailand	13.7	Negotiations under way
Costa Rica	2.3	CAFTA/CBERA
Mexico	1.3	NAFTA
China	12.0	No
Dominican Republic	3.3	CAFTA/CBERA

Source: USITC (2004).

evaluations of free trade agreements are best undertaken through *ex post* studies that carefully assess their economic effects on members and non-members.

Open free trade agreements allow member states to use third country intermediate inputs, provided these undergo 'substantial transformation' under liberal cumulation clauses. Without provisions allowing Central American countries to use third party inputs, including those from Mexico, the United States–Central American Free Trade Agreement (US–CAFTA) would be of greatly diminished value to the Central American countries. The African Growth and Opportunity Act (AGOA) is set to extend special cumulation rules that enable sub-Saharan African countries to export apparel made from third-country fabric duty-free subject to certain volume limits to the US for another three years beginning in 2005. Without such a clause and with the end of quotas on 1 January 2005, it is unlikely these countries could maintain a share of the US apparel market.

In the case of preferential trade agreements involving Thailand, rules of origin are likely to be important, as MFN tariffs remain quite high on a number of key industrial and agricultural products in Japan and the US. Possible trade diversion impacts of new free trade agreements between Thailand and the US and Thailand and Japan are explored in the following sections.

COMPARATIVE ADVANTAGE IN THAILAND AND INDONESIA

Comparative advantage has evolved rapidly in newly industrializing economies of Asia and Thailand and Indonesia are no exceptions. Evolution over the past 50 years has seen comparative advantage shift from primary exports of logs, minerals, fish and agricultural commodities, to processed products such as plywood, metals, canned fruit and fish, and prepared food products, to light manufactures of footwear, textiles and clothing and toys, and finally, to electrical machinery, office and computing equipment and transportation equipment. In some industries, comparative advantage is sustainable for relatively long periods (for example, textile and clothing sectors, minerals and plantation crops such as natural rubber). However, careful analysis of major manufacturing exports reveals that comparative advantage is rapidly being transformed as educational levels rise and as foreign investment and intra-industry trade link these economies to the global markets. Indeed, multinational enterprises have played a key role in structural transformation of the manufacturing industries in these two economies (Ramstetter 1991; James and Ramstetter 1997, 2004).

Comparative advantage in Thai and Indonesian manufacturing industries, represented by revealed comparative advantage (RCA) indices over
the period of 1985–2001, has undergone some change (Table 11.2). Both
countries kept a revealed comparative advantage in the apparel sector over
the entire period. Yet, it appears that Indonesia has become relatively more
competitive in apparel than Thailand in the period since the financial crisis
of 1997–8. Both countries have also maintained a revealed comparative
advantage in textiles over the entire period for Thailand and since 1988 for
Indonesia. The major change is in office and computing machinery with
both countries attaining a revealed comparative advantage by year 2000,
with Thailand achieving this more than a decade earlier than Indonesia.
Thailand also has a revealed comparative advantage in other electrical
machinery since 1988.

Market shares and growth are key indicators of export competitiveness,
which is also affected by supply-side factors in addition to external demand
conditions. Clearly, on the demand side, terms of market access may
strongly influence performance in market share and growth because market
access conditions will directly or indirectly affect the prices of the products
imported from various sources compared with prices of domestically produced goods. If Indonesian exports are taxed more heavily than those of
competitors, then Indonesian producers will have to cut costs or they will
lose market share, given normal profits and assuming no or little change in
real exchange rates.[8]

Indonesia's export competitiveness in its two largest markets, the US
and Japan, was evaluated over the period of 2001–3 using quarterly
import data from official sources in both the US and Japan. The advantage of using import data is that these data are more accurate and timely
than the data from the exporting country. Performance of the top 50
SITC 3-digit products in the two largest markets was examined over the
most recent three years, with the products being the top Indonesian non-
oil exports to the US and Japan, as recorded in these countries' import
data. In the case of Japan, the top 50 products accounted for over 89 per
cent of total Indonesian non-oil exports in 2003. In the case of the US,
these products accounted for over 92 per cent of US non-oil imports from
Indonesia in 2003.

In the US case, of the 50 top products in 2003, import market share fell
in 23 cases, was unchanged in 11 and rose in 16. In Japan, import market
share fell in 22 cases and rose in 22 cases while in six cases it remained
unchanged.[9] Upon examination of the results, it was found that Thailand
competes directly with Indonesia in many of these products in both the US
and Japan. An evaluation of the products with which Thailand is a major
competitor with Indonesia is provided for 2003 (Tables 11.3 and 11.4).

Table 11.2 Trade with the world and revealed comparative advantage (period averages, annual totals)

Country, commodity group	1985–87	1988–90	1991–93	1994–96	1997	1998	1999	2000	2001
Revealed comparative advantage indices									
Indonesia									
Manufactures	0.348	0.485	0.664	0.685	0.565	0.569	0.700	0.757	0.750
Textiles	0.891	1.292	2.055	1.822	1.243	1.361	1.805	1.749	1.714
Apparel	2.040	2.732	3.289	2.416	1.813	1.836	2.897	3.000	3.216
Nonelectric machinery	0.010	0.015	0.035	0.075	0.080	0.139	0.136	0.180	0.149
Office & computing mach.	0.017	0.012	0.096	0.371	0.550	0.533	0.854	1.846	1.380
Other electric machinery	0.050	0.058	0.274	0.475	0.429	0.386	0.422	0.646	0.729
Transportation machinery	0.007	0.018	0.069	0.093	0.068	0.113	0.091	0.082	0.082
Thailand									
Manufactures	0.689	0.784	0.906	0.949	0.929	0.931	0.941	0.986	0.973
Textiles	2.017	1.492	1.085	1.079	2.887	2.818	2.648	2.588	2.540
Apparel	3.273	3.674	3.536	2.653	2.072	2.215	2.141	2.127	2.172
Nonelectric machinery	0.176	0.208	0.352	0.448	0.501	0.484	0.524	0.574	0.597
Office & computing mach.	0.301	1.287	2.123	3.254	4.044	4.834	4.882	4.773	4.656
Other electric machinery	0.998	1.148	1.446	1.413	1.416	1.430	1.400	1.457	1.448
Transportation machinery	0.028	0.065	0.135	0.244	0.255	0.194	0.285	0.334	0.367

Source: James and Ramstetter (2004).

Table 11.3 Japanese imports of top Indonesian non-oil products in 2003 (current prices US$ million)

SITC and Description	Imports from Indonesia	Imports from Thailand
036 Crustaceans	486.4	317.9
288 Nonferrous Base Metal & Scrap	365.3	18.2
641 Paper and Paperboard	296.1	22.1
752 Automatic Data Process Mach.	223.7	245.3
231 Natural Rubber	223.6	525.3
821 Furniture & Bedding	207.0	329.0
763 Sound and TV Recorders	200.4	80.3
651 Textile Yarn	185.5	61.6
776 Thermionic Cold Cathode	168.2	694.8
764 Telecommunications Equip.	152.2	481.1
034 Fresh Fish	150.5	231.6
037 Fish, Crustaceans and Molluscs	148.7	391.1
773 Equip. for Distributing Elec.	148.3	156.3
635 Wood Manufactures	138.4	48.9
771 Electric Power Mach. & Parts	108.8	109.6
851 Footwear	103.1	54.3
778 Elec. Machinery & Appar.	99.6	188.0
574 Polyacetals & Epoxide Resins	96.0	26.9
893 Articles of Plastics	91.6	171.6
772 Elec. Appar. for Switching	88.2	274.2
761 Television Receivers	84.1	79.5
784 Parts of Motor Vehicles	83.1	208.7
716 Rotating Electric Plant & Parts	77.7	79.4
625 Rubber Tires & Accessories	73.3	43.0
642 Paper & Paperboard Cut to Size	65.4	16.8
713 Internal Combustion Engines	64.7	56.6
512 Alcohols, Phenols & Deriv.	63.1	24.5
000 Unclassified Products	59.8	529.9
687 Tin	57.5	21.4
667 Pearls, Precious Stones	56.5	66.1
582 Plates Foil & Strip of Plastics	54.4	17.1
841 Men's Boy's Coats, Not Knit	44.9	42.0
653 Manmade Woven Fabrics	44.1	12.9
775 Household Type Elec. Equip.	42.4	384.1
699 Manufactures of Base Metal	36.1	95.1
598 Miscellaneous Chemicals	34.9	82.4
658 Made-Up Articles of Textiles	33.9	12.7
845 Articles of Apparel	32.8	77.7
759 Parts for Office Mach.	31.9	152.9
652 Cotton Fabrics, Woven	30.5	8.1
TOTAL	4752.7	6439.0

Source: James and Minor (2004).

*Table 11.4   US imports of top Indonesian non-oil products in 2003
(current prices of US$ million)*

SITC and Description	Imports from Indonesia	Imports from Thailand
842 Women's/Girl's Coats, not knit	836.3	413.0
845 Articles of Apparel of Textiles	616.4	753.2
231 Natural Rubber	595.9	258.0
851 Footwear	569.6	284.7
763 Sound & Television Recorders	552.1	336.3
821 Furniture & Bedding	524.4	412.0
752 Automatic Data Process Mach.	338.7	1659.4
762 Radiobroadcast Receivers	171.0	148.0
036 Crustaceans	169.1	597.7
894 Toys & Sporting Goods	163.2	295.2
037 Fish, Crustaceans & Molluscs	154.9	772.8
776 Thermionic Cold Cathodes	141.1	616.4
635 Wood Manufactures	127.0	138.5
034 Fresh Fish	106.7	53.7
843 Men's/Boy's Coats Knitted	93.6	218.1
761 Television Receivers	86.3	664.4
759 Parts for Office Mach.	83.8	262.2
848 Apparel & Access. Headgear	80.7	413.8
773 Equip. for Distributing Elec.	80.5	174.4
897 Jewelry, Gold & Silver Ware	69.5	806.5
831 Trunks, Suitcases	68.1	114.5
574 Polyacetals & Epoxide Resins	56.0	115.3
697 Household Equip. Base Metal	47.8	205.6
658 Made-Up Articles of Textiles	47.4	142.8
666 Pottery	46.7	81.8
652 Cotton Fabrics, Woven	46.3	41.7
893 Articles of Plastics	44.7	133.1
662 Clay & Refractory Cons. Mats.	33.5	21.8
TOTAL	5951.3	10 134.9

Source: James and Minor (2004).

In Japan (Table 11.3) imports from Indonesia and Thailand are concentrated in natural resource-based industries, including minerals, fisheries and forestry products. Of the 50 top items imported from Indonesia, 40 directly compete with similar products from Thailand (80 per cent). Japan's imports are still relatively heavily concentrated in natural resource-based items. For example, in 2003, 19 of the top 50 imports from Indonesia are in these resource-based sectors, 14 of which are subject to competition with similar Thai products.

Thailand does not export the following products of interest to Indonesia or Japan: copper, aluminium, plywood and wood, and coffee. Indonesia and Thailand compete in six textile and apparel product groups in Japan. In 2003, these product groups accounted for $371.9 million in export receipts for Indonesia and $215.0 million in Thailand. From these data, we estimate trade diversion from Indonesia to Thailand under a Japan–Thai FTA to have the potential to affect trade with a value in the range of $4–5 billion. Further analysis of trade barriers and the margin of preference offered to Thai producers would be necessary to more rigorously estimate the likely range of trade diversion. In addition, sector and product specific rules of origin applied to auto parts and electronic components could lead companies to divert investment in production facilities and eventually to divert trade in components from Indonesia to Thailand and stifle the future development of components trade with Indonesia.

In the US (Table 11.4) of the top 50 imports from Indonesia, 28 compete directly with similar Thai products (56 per cent). US imports are heavily concentrated in textile and apparel manufactures with ten items in the top 50 from Indonesia, in eight of which Thailand is a major competitor. These textile and apparel items accounted for $2751.9 million in export receipts for Indonesia in 2003 and $2797.1 million for Thailand. This presents a huge trade diversion potential as the average import weighted tariff on these textile and apparel items from Indonesia is nearly 18 per cent for clothing and 10 per cent for textiles (Table 11.1; USITC 2004). If Thai products gained duty-free access after quotas are eliminated next year, there would be a very large margin of preference in Thailand's favour. Overall, the maximum potential for trade diversion from Indonesia should there be a Thai–US FTA is $6.3 billion (Table 11.4). Again it is important to examine tariff and non-tariff barriers to assess more rigorously the actual likelihood for trade diversion in the US market.

Clearly, it is not possible to a priori forecast trade diversion from a free trade agreement with any precision. This is why *ex post* rather than *ex ante* studies are necessary to accurately assess the benefits and costs of such trade agreements. While this issue cannot be settled for several years, it is important for countries like Indonesia to recognize that much is at stake, even if the precise amount of 'much' is not known.

IMPLICATIONS FOR INDONESIA

Thomas Friedman (2002, p. 4) points out: 'whether you are a company or a country, your threats and opportunities increasingly derive from who you are connected to'. In the game of trade negotiations, being connected to the big markets through free trade agreements is becoming more and more important. With the demise of the global system of textile quotas in the coming year, preferential market access could be a crucial determinant of export performance and industry profitability. This seems to help explain the vigorous pro-active efforts of Singapore and Thailand in securing free trade agreements with major trade partners and the largest markets. If one evaluates the risks faced by not acting, the scramble to negotiate seems logical.[10]

From an Indonesian perspective, then, it follows that if Thailand succeeds in negotiating free trade agreements with Japan and the US, nearly $10 billion in non-oil exports would be at risk from enhanced Thai competitiveness in these markets. The immediate implication is that Indonesia can ill-afford to stand pat while major competitors enhance their market access terms in the major world markets. If Indonesia is unable to come to the negotiating table, it will have to drastically improve its supply chain performance and cut costs to the bone to compete. It will also need to enhance services, which is one of the main advantages of joining into FTA arrangements with advanced economies in the first place.

A first-best solution would be for the Doha Round to succeed in cutting peak tariffs on products of export interest to Indonesia, but this may be several years in the offing. If that is the case, creative solutions might be sought under existing regional or bilateral arrangements.

NOTES

1. Thailand's most recent trade policy review report to the World Trade Organization (WTO 2003a) mentions bilateral FTA negotiations with Australia, Bahrain, Japan, India, Peru, Mexico, New Zealand, South Korea, the US and China. Press reports indicate that six of the above negotiations have been successfully concluded (Australia, Bahrain, India, Peru, New Zealand and China), and that Thailand is preparing to enter into negotiations with Canada, and Hong Kong. The WTO reports Thailand has a bilateral trade agreement with Laos, implying that a total of 13 bilateral agreements are in process. In contrast, Indonesia has just entered into bilateral negotiations with Australia and Japan and is planning talks with a few others but has yet to conclude a single bilateral free trade agreement, although it is a member of the ASEAN Free Trade Agreement (AFTA).
2. See WTO (2003b), 72.1 per cent of the tariff lines are fully bound, with another 1.8 per cent partially bound.
3. About 55 bound tariffs are specific rather than *ad valorem* (0.9 per cent of all lines), and 1.9 per cent of all lines are partially bound (WTO 2000).
4. James and Wendel (2004) report a Spearman Rank Correlation Coefficient between imports from Thailand and Indonesia into the US market (excluding values below $0.5 mil.) of 0.643.
5. For a review of the literature see Panagariya (1999, 2001).
6. Hufbauer and Schott (1993) and James and Umemoto (2000) provide evidence of the trade diversion in textiles and apparel from East Asia in the North American markets resulting from the restrictive textiles rules of origin in the NAFTA.

7. For example, the Singapore–US FTA allows duty-free importation of certain Indonesian electronic products produced on Batam Island (a free trade zone). The exemption under the rules of origin is granted to a few specific products that are produced by electronic assembly plants possibly owned by Singaporeans.
8. Market share in this exercise refers to the share of total imports of a 3-digit SITC category coming from Indonesia versus other customs territories. This approach abstracts from domestic production and is less comprehensive than market share measured as imports over domestic apparent consumption. However, import market share is available for 2003, whereas market share of apparent consumption can only be calculated through 1998 or 1999.
9. This summarizes the results of a comprehensive study of market shares of Indonesian non-oil exports in these two large markets (James and Minor 2004). The import market shares of Indonesia and its 15 top competitors are evaluated over the course of 2002–3 in this study. A previous study did the same comparing 2001 and 2000 data (James 2002). All these data are available from the author upon request.
10. James and Minor (2004) provide an assessment of the risk facing various Southeast Asian apparel exporters once quotas are lifted on 1 January 2005. It turns out that Thailand faces greater risk than Indonesia and this may help explain the differences in negotiating positions.

REFERENCES

Friedman, T. (2002), *Longitudes and Attitudes: Exploring the World Before and After September 11*, London: Penguin Books.

Garnaut, R. and L. Song. (2003), 'Progress and obstacles in Asia Pacific economic integration', paper presented at the Pacific Trade and Development Conference (PAFTAD) 29, 15–17 December, Jakarta.

Hufbauer, G.C. and J. Schott. (1993), *NAFTA: An Assessment*, Washington, DC: Institute for International Economics.

James, W.E. (2002), *The Competitiveness of Indonesian Non-Oil Products in Major Markets: Market Shares in the United States and Japan*, Jakarta: Partnership for Economic Growth.

James, W.E. (2004), 'Rules of origin, tariff discrimination and trade diversion: a case study of Asian textiles and apparel exports', paper presented at Rules of Origin in Regional Trade Agreements: Conceptual and Empirical Approaches, Washington, DC: Inter-American Development Bank, 20–21 February.

James, W.E. and P.J. Minor (2004), *Performance of Indonesian Non-Oil Exports to Major Markets: United States, Japan, EU*, Growth through Investment, Agriculture and Trade Project, Jakarta, 30 April.

James, W.E. and E.D. Ramstetter (1997), 'Globalization's implications for Indonesia: trade policy, multinationals and competition', in Satya Dev Gupta (ed.), *Dynamics of Globalization and Development*, Boston: Kluwer Academic Publishers, pp. 153–86.

James, W.E. and E.D. Ramstetter (2004), 'Export performance, foreign firms and economic policy in textiles and apparel, electric machinery and transportation equipment industries in Indonesia and Thailand', paper presented at East–West Center, Honolulu, 22 May.

James, W.E. and M. Umemoto (2000), 'NAFTA trade with East Asia: rules of origin and market access in textiles, apparel, footwear and electrical machinery', *ASEAN Economic Bulletin*, **17** (3), 293–311.

James, W.E. and S. Wendel (2004), *Implications of Indonesian Free Trade Agreements*, Growth through Investment, Agriculture and Trade Project, Jakarta, 13 August.

Panagariya, A. (1999), *Regionalism in Trade Policy: Essays on Preferential Trading*, Singapore: World Scientific.

Panagariya, A. (2000), 'Preferential trade liberalization: the traditional theory and new developments', *Journal of Economic Literature*, **38** (2), 287–311.

Productivity Commission (2003), *Rules of Origin under the Australia–New Zealand Closer Economic Relations Trade Agreement*, Canberra: Commonwealth of Australia, Interim Research Report.

Ramstetter, E.D. (ed.) (1991), *Direct Foreign Investment in Asia's Developing Economies and Structural Change in the Asia-Pacific Region*, Boulder, CO: Westview Press.

Srinivasan, T.N. (1998), 'Regionalism and the WTO: is nondiscrimination passé?', in A.O. Krueger (ed.), *The WTO as an International Organization*, Chicago, IL: University of Chicago Press, pp. 329–49.

United States International Trade Commission (2004), *Textiles and Apparel: Assessment of the Competitiveness of Certain Foreign Suppliers to the US Market*, 2 Volumes, Publication 3671, January, Washington, DC.

World Trade Organization (2000), *Trade Policy Review Singapore*, *WTO Document WT/TPR/S/67*. Available from: http://docsonline.wto.org/DDFDocuments/t/WT/TPR/S67-0.DOC, 3 February.

World Trade Organization (2003a), *Trade Policy Review Thailand*, *WTO Document WT/TPR/S/123*. Available from: http://docsonline.wto.org/DDFDocuments/t/WT/TPR/S123-0.doc, 3 February.

World Trade Organization (2003b), *Trade Policy Review Thailand*, *WTO Document WT/TPR/G/123*. Available from: http://docsonline.wto.org/DDFDocuments/t/WT/TPR/G123.doc, 3 February.

12. The Singapore–Australia free trade agreement (SAFTA): motivations and implications for the Asia-Pacific economies

Rahul Sen

INTRODUCTION

Singapore's economic performance over the past three decades has been enviable, with its economy registering one of the highest rates of growth in the world.[1] It was counted among the few stories of economic success in Asia during the later part of the previous century, with its economy evolving into a modern city-state economy from a modest trading post in just about four decades. Being a manufacturing and trading hub for Southeast Asia, Singapore remains one of the most open economies in the region with a trade to GDP ratio of over 250 per cent in recent years (World Bank 2003). It is thus not surprising that its international trade policy remains the cornerstone in defining the shape of Singapore's economic success, and that Singapore policymakers have been consciously attempting to find ways and means towards achieving freer trade in East Asia.

In recent years, following the aftermath of the East Asian crisis in 1997–1998, and its resultant adverse impact on trade and liberalization efforts within ASEAN as well as APEC, Singapore's economic performance has been adversely affected, and its ability to sustain global competitiveness is now challenged by several factors. These include an increased reliance on the electronics industry for its growth, its erstwhile excessive dependence on the region for its growth prospects and the increasing ability of its regional rivals to compete for global investments, skills and exports, thus eroding its competitive edge in manufacturing as well as service sectors (Rajan 2003). These challenges have prompted Singapore to expand its market access beyond the region, besides attempting to enhance the attractiveness of the region for foreign investors through active participation in regional economic integration efforts. The continuing slow progress at the multilateral level has prompted Singapore to look for alternative means towards achieving liberalizing trade and investment within the global economy, and thus retain its competitiveness as a 'super-trading' nation. As pointed out in a recent study on Singapore's competitiveness by Rajan (2003):

> the need for Singapore is to be particularly aware of and responsive to the powerful forces that are transforming markets and dramatically changing ways of doing business, so as to remain 'ahead of the game'.

It is against this backdrop that apart from regionalism, Singapore has been actively pursuing bilateralism through negotiation of regional trading agreements (RTAs) as a key strategy of its commercial trade policy. The principal objectives behind the pursual of such a strategy has been two-fold. First, these RTAs (commonly referred to as FTAs) are aimed to enhance and deepen its economic and strategic links with its major trading partners in the global economy, namely the USA and Japan. Singapore has now a working FTA with both of these economies. Second, the RTA strategy aims to forge new economic and strategic partnerships by seeking market access in the economies of its other trading partners which have hitherto not been contributing substantially to Singapore's merchandise trade. This would help it to diversify its external economic linkages beyond Southeast Asia (Rajan *et al.* 2001). Towards achieving this objective, Singapore has a working bilateral FTA with New Zealand, the EFTA countries, Australia, the USA, Hashemite Kingdom of Jordan, India and Korea and has also recently concluded a plurilateral FTA involving New Zealand, Chile and Brunei named as the Trans-Pacific Strategic Economic Partnership (SEP). It is continuing to negotiate FTA pacts with Canada, Mexico, Kuwait, Sri Lanka, United Arab Emirates, Panama, Egypt and Pakistan among others (Rajan and Sen 2003a; Sen 2004). Although Singapore's FTA moves were greeted with much scepticism by other ASEAN members in its initial stages, it has now been widely accepted as the viable alternative to multilateral trade liberalization within Southeast Asia, with negotiations now ongoing for an ASEAN-wide FTA with China, Japan, Korea, India and the Closer Economic Relations Grouping consisting of Australia and New Zealand besides other bilateral initiatives.[2] Very recently, plans have been announced to launch an ASEAN-wide FTA with Australia and New Zealand, although any details on timeframe and framework for negotiations are yet unknown (Lyall 2004).

Specifically, the SAFTA, which is Australia's first bilateral FTA involving South East Asian countries, came into effect from July 2003. Negotiations for SAFTA were launched on 15 November 2000 by the Prime Ministers of both sides at the fringe of the APEC Leaders' Summit. In November 2002,

after ten formal rounds of negotiations, Singapore and Australia successfully finalized a free trade agreement that was signed in Singapore on 17
February 2003, and came into force on 28 July 2003. As in the case of
Singapore's other bilateral FTAs, the SAFTA has been a comprehensive
Agreement covering key and diverse areas such as trade in goods, trade in
services, investment, telecommunication and financial services, movement
of business persons, government procurement, intellectual property rights,
competition policy, e-commerce and education cooperation.

The SAFTA, which is much more comprehensive than a traditional FTA,
assumes economic and strategic importance, being Australia's first bilateral
FTA with any Southeast Asian country, and Singapore being the largest
trade and investment partner of Australia in ASEAN. This FTA hopes to
build upon the strong and productive bilateral relationship between
Singapore and Australia that has been based on long-standing links in the
area of political, defence, educational, trade and tourism spheres. The
SAFTA is likely to build upon the foundations laid by the two countries
towards closer economic and strategic relationship through the establishment of a biennial Singapore–Australia Joint Ministerial Committee
(SAJMC) since 1996.

This chapter analyses the rationale for and implications of the recently
implemented SAFTA in the backdrop of their bilateral economic linkages,
and highlights the benefits of SAFTA for the Australian economy. It
further attempts to analyse the implications of this agreement for other
Asia-Pacific economies in the region.

The remainder of the chapter is organized as follows. The next two sections analyse the extent of bilateral economic linkages between Singapore
and Australia in terms of merchandise trade and trade in services and
investment flows. This is followed by highlighting some salient features of
the SAFTA agreement and its likely impact on businesses in Singapore and
Australia. The final section analyses the implications of the SAFTA agreement for other Asia-Pacific economies in the region, and concludes the
chapter.

SINGAPORE'S BILATERAL MERCHANDISE TRADE LINKAGES WITH AUSTRALIA

Trends in Merchandise Trade

Figure 12.1 displays the trends in Singapore's total merchandise trade with
Australia over the past two decades (1980–2004). The share of Australia in
Singapore's overall trade during this period averaged 2.8 per cent, with a

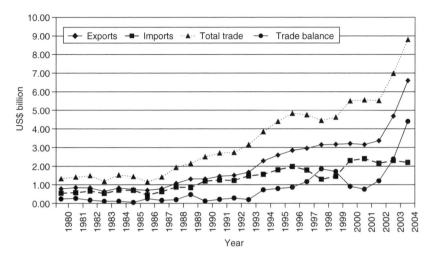

Source: International Monetary Fund, *Direction of Trade Statistics Yearbook*, various issues.

Figure 12.1 Singapore's merchandise trade with Australia

significant increasing trend observed after 1986, which was adversely affected during the crisis in East Asian economies in 1997–98, largely due to a decline in Singapore's imports from Australia. However, this increase in volume of trade has not been matched by a concomitant trend increase in Australia's share in Singapore's merchandise trade. The share was about 2.7 per cent of the total in 2004, almost similar to the levels in the 1987–98 period. It is further observed that Singapore has registered a continuous bilateral trade surplus with Australia over this period, which has been steadily peaking since 2001.

It is important to note that Singapore–Australia merchandise trade constitutes a significant entrepôt component of re-exports. Thus, in 2004, nearly 38 per cent of Singapore's total exports constituted of re-exports, which constituted of goods that underwent some value-adding in Singapore, while they were transshipped from other ASEAN countries through Singapore.[3] Figure 12.2 indicates that over the past decade, the share of re-exports peaked at about 58 per cent of Singapore's total exports to Australia in 1998, which thereafter has seen a sharp decline. This indicates that in recent years, the importance of Singapore's domestic exports (exports that originate from Singapore) has increased in Singapore–Australia merchandise trade. Indeed, if calculated as a share of Singapore's total domestic exports, the share of domestic exports destined

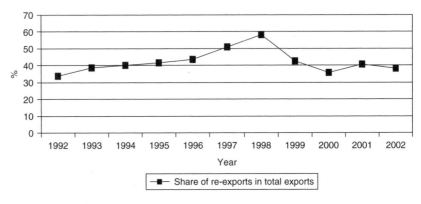

Source: Computed from IE Singapore (2003).

*Figure 12.2   The entrepôt component in Singapore's merchandise exports
to Australia, 1992–2002*

for Australia has increased from 2.1 per cent to 4.1 per cent over the period
1998–2004.

In contrast, trade with Singapore has constituted an average of about
3.8 per cent of Australia's global trade in the same period. Singapore was
Australia's eighth largest trading partner, with Australian merchandise
exports to Singapore valued at A\$3.3 billion in 2004. Australia's imports
from Singapore were valued at A\$7.3 billion during the same period, thus
making Singapore the fifth largest source for Australian imports as compared to the eighth largest in 2003 (DFAT 2004a). Figure 12.3 displays
the trends in Australia's total merchandise trade with Singapore, over the
period 1988–2004. It is observed that the volume of merchandise
trade has been growing over the middle of the 1990s, but has been declining in recent years. As of 2005, Australian exports to Singapore increased
to A\$3.9 billion, while its imports increased to A\$8.6 billion, suggesting
a significant expansion in exports from Singapore in the post-SAFTA
period.

Comparing Figures 12.1 and 12.3, it is observed that interestingly, both
Singapore and Australia seem to be reporting bilateral trade surpluses with
each other, which is statistically impossible. This is likely due to the fact that
Australia reports its imports from Singapore according to country of
origin, and therefore does not include Singapore's reported re-exports in its
import data. Studies by Sen (2000) on Singapore's entrepôt trade role
observed that trading partners of Singapore that have a high entrepôt component do report such discrepancies with respect to the consistency and
variations in their bilateral trade statistics.[4]

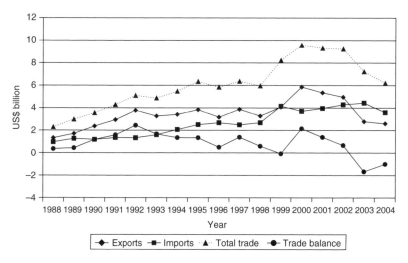

Source: Computed from International Monetary Fund, *Direction of Trade Statistics Yearbook*, various issues.

Figure 12.3   *Australia's merchandise trade with Singapore, 1988–2003*

Trade Intensity Indices

Trade intensity indices are often considered as a useful tool for analysing bilateral trade linkages, since it is a relative measure of bilateral trade shares of two countries with respect to their trade with the rest of the world. In the context of this chapter, the indices are designed to capture the extent to which the home country (Singapore) regards its trading partners (Australia) as being important in relation to the former's trade with the rest of the world (ROW), and vice versa. An index value above unity indicates a relative 'over-representation' of the trading partner in the home country's trade.[5]

Singapore's trade (exports plus imports) intensity indices with Australia over the period 1988–2002 are highlighted in Figure 12.4a and 12.4b. It is evident from Figure 12.4a that Singapore's trade intensity with Australia has declined over the period. In particular, the index values for trade intensities of Singapore's merchandise trade with Australia was above unity until 1998, indicating an over-representation of Australia as a trading partner for Singapore *vis-à-vis* ROW. The decline thereafter, suggests an under-representation of the same. On the other hand, Singapore's export intensity with Australia, although declining continuously over the earlier part of the 1987–2002 period, has remained higher than unity over the entire period, indicating an over-representation for Australia as one of the export

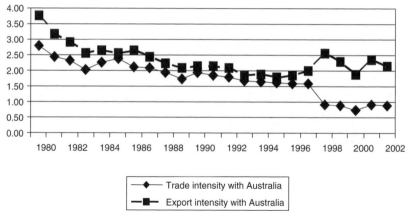

Source: Computed from International Monetary Fund, *Direction of Trade Statistics Yearbook*, various issues.

Figure 12.4a   Singapore's merchandise trade intensities with Australia

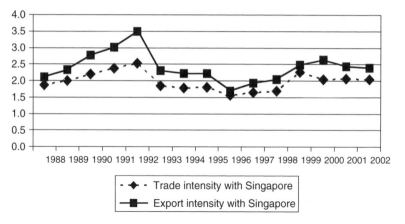

Source: Computed from International Monetary Fund, *Direction of Trade Statistics Yearbook*, various issues.

Figure 12.4b   Australia's merchandise trade intensities with Singapore

destinations for Singapore's exports. This suggests that compared with the ROW, Australia has probably not been among its preferred source for imports, indicating a declining import intensity. Singapore's average trade intensity with Australia over the past decades has been about 1.7 (Figure 12.4a), mainly because of the relatively high export intensity that averaged about 2.3 during this period. From Australia's perspective, Singapore has continued to remain an important trading partner *vis-à-vis* ROW, as indicated by higher average trade intensity with Singapore at 2.0 over the 1988–2002 (Figure 12.4b). Australia's export intensity with Singapore has also been above unity and has continued to increase since 1996, averaging about 2.4 for the entire period, implying that Singapore has been and continues to be increasingly over-represented as an export destination for Australia. Since both trade and export intensities are above unity, it is suggestive that Australia's import intensity with Singapore has also been above unity, indicating that Singapore is also over-represented as an import source for Australian imports.

TRADE IN SERVICES AND DIRECT INVESTMENT

Importance of Services Trade to Australia and Singapore

The services sector has been rapidly expanding and increasing its prominence in production and employment structures of developed as well as developing countries in the world. The impact of this trend is profound in the case of Australia and Singapore, where the services sector has emerged as the largest contributor to GDP in these economies (about 70 per cent in 2001) (The World Bank 2003). With increased globalization, various activities in the services sector are now being opened up for commercial trading purposes among international service providers. It is this increasing importance of services in the world trading system that led to the conceptualization of a multilateral framework for liberalizing trade and investments in the services sectors under the General Agreement Trade in Services (GATS), wherein multilateral services trade began to be negotiated under the aegis of the WTO as part of the Uruguay Round. With increasing deadlock in the WTO, liberalization of trade in services began to be increasingly negotiated at the regional level, with recent RTAs, including the SAFTA, focusing on the same.

It is important to take note of the fact that analysing services trade is inherently more complex than merchandise trade, especially as available data on services trade are not comprehensive, detailed, timely or internationally comparable, largely due to the distinct nature of services trade that separate it from merchandise trade.[6] However, with rapid internationalization of services, data are now being made available for trade in commercial services.

There is no known source of data on bilateral service trade in Singapore. However, the Department of Foreign Affairs and Trade (DFAT) in Australia does provide the same on a country basis. However, before

analysing the linkages with respect to bilateral services trade, it is imperative to analyse the aggregate trends in overall services trade and its composition in Singapore and Australia.

It is observed that Australia's service exports were nearly similar in
volume as its imports during most of this period. Specifically, its services
exports increased from US$10 billion in 1990 to almost US$37 billion by
2005. A similar trend was noted for its service imports, which increased from
about US$14 billion to US$38 billion over 1990–2005. Australia's services
trade remained in deficit by less than US$1 billion over most of this period,
with travel and tourism services accounting on an average for about 47 per
cent of Australia's services exports over 1995–2001 (World Bank 2003).

Singapore's overall service exports increased significantly from US$13
billion to over US$41 billion over 1990–2004. Singapore's service imports
more than quadrupled from about US$9 billion to almost US$40 billion
over the 1990–2004 period. Singapore maintained an aggregate overall
surplus in service trade, with ICT and related services constituting the bulk
of Singapore's service exports during the entire period (averaging about 56
per cent over the 1995–2001 period), followed by travel and transport services (World Bank 2003).

In recent years, Singapore has aimed to strengthen and consolidate its
position as a regional and global services hub, in the area of trade logistics,
financial services, media, entertainment and education services. Strategies
are being chalked out by the Economic Development Board of Singapore
(EDB) to develop the services hub of Singapore as stated out in its objectives in the Industry 21 (I21) plan launched in January 1999. The strategies
are broadly directed at boosting manpower and skills in knowledge-based
industries and encouraging overseas businesses to set up their headquarters
in Singapore under the Overseas Headquarters/Regional Headquarters
(OHQ/RHQ) scheme, besides facilitating the promotion of innovation and
R&D in the production process for local companies using IT-related applications (Rajan and Sen 2003b).

Bilateral Services Trade Between Australia and Singapore

Given the available trade data on bilateral services trade for Australia,
Figure 12.5 charts the trends in Australia's services trade with Singapore,
comparing it with that of ASEAN as a grouping. The data here are
observed in terms of fiscal years from the Australian Bureau of Statistics.
It is observed that Australia–Singapore services trade has been increasing
in volume over the 1996–7 to 2001–2002 period.[7] During the same period,
Australia's services trade with ASEAN increased from about A$7.0 billion
to A$9.8 billion, indicating an increase in Singapore's share in Australia's

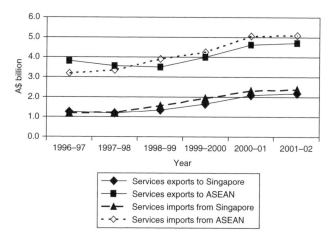

Source: DFAT (2004b).

*Figure 12.5   Australia's services trade with Singapore and ASEAN,
1996–2002*

service trade with ASEAN, from 37 per cent to 47 per cent. Australia has
been running a bilateral services trade deficit with Singapore since 1997–8,
which has significantly increased in magnitude thereafter. In 2005,
Singapore constituted about 7 per cent of Australia's total services exports
as well as imports, becoming the fourth largest trading partner for
Australia's services trade after the USA, UK and Japan.

According to the latest available data from DFAT (2006), Australia's services exports to Singapore in 2005 consisted of travel services (including
tourism) (constituting 37 per cent of the total share), transportation services (including logistics, storage and freight) (43 per cent), and other services[8] (20 per cent). The composition of Australia's services imports from
Singapore during the same year was highly skewed towards transportation
services, (including logistics, storage and freight) constituting 75 per cent of
the total share, followed by travel services (including tourism) (9 per cent),
and other services (16 per cent).

Tourism and travel services has therefore been the major constituent of
Australian services exports to Singapore. In 2002, Singapore ranked as
Australia's second largest tourist market in Asia after Japan, and the fifth
largest source of short term visitors (0.3 million) overall in recent years.
Among other services, education services have been a key constituent of
Australian services exports to Singapore. Thus in 2002, Singapore became
the largest source of overseas students to both on- and off-shore Australian
educational institutions (with 29 956 students being enrolled).

Although detailed bilateral data on Singapore's services trade with Australia remains unavailable, the above evidence from the Australian side indicates that a similar trend is likely to be observed from the Singapore side. This is more than likely as Singapore is not only ranked higher in global services trade compared to Australia, but has been actively targeting service providers from its major trading partners to locate in Singapore and establish it as a regional services hub. This suggests that the SAFTA agreement, which focuses at length on services trade liberalization, is likely to generate major economic opportunities for both countries in expansion of their bilateral services trade links.

Direct Investment Flows between Singapore and Australia

Direct investment flows, in the form of Foreign Direct Investment (FDI), have been a key instrument of economic development in the case of Singapore, being a city-state economy. Notably, FDI inflows have been and continue to play a pivotal role in its economy and constitute a significantly high proportion of gross capital formation in the economy. In contrast, being a large economy consisting of a domestic market of about 20 million people, nearly five times that of Singapore, Australia has used FDI inflows much more generously in it's economy, as a key constituent of domestic capital formation.

Bilateral flows of FDI have been a major instrument in the development of economic linkages between Singapore and Australia in recent years. A largely open and transparent economy, a business friendly environment for foreign investors, similarities in the legal system, close geographical proximity and the presence of a pool of internationally competitive and skilled workforce in both countries, have been the driving force behind these investment flows.

Singapore's cumulative investments amounted to about A$25 billion, making it Australia's fifth-largest foreign investor while, coincidentally, Australia was also Singapore's fifth-largest foreign investor, with cumulative investments worth about A$13.89 billion (Tan 2003). However, the trends in Singapore's net FDI inflows over the period 1995 to 2001, on a BoP basis, indicate that Australia's investments in Singapore have been rather negligible in magnitude, with Australia recording a net disinvestment in Singapore to the tune of about US$0.3 billion in 2001 (ASEAN Secretariat 2002). The data indicate that since 1997, Australia has been recording net disinvestments in Singapore, which implies that FDI outflows from Singapore into Australia have remained higher in magnitude than the inflows over the 1997–2001 period, peaking at about US$1 billion in 1999. This trend is also indicated by the fact that the share of Australia in

Singapore's outward equity investments (2.6 per cent in the year 2000) was higher than that of Japan, one of the major foreign investors in Singapore.[9]

The above indicates that while Australian investors may not fully have utilized the investment potential of Singapore as a regional investment hub in Asia, Singapore investors have aggressively ventured into Australia for investment opportunities.[10] Singapore's investments in Australia have traditionally been concentrated in real estate, but diversification is taking place in recent years, with investments flowing into the services sector, for example, telecommunications, power generation and air transport services.[11]

The investment linkages between Singapore and Australia are predicted to grow significantly with the liberalization of investment norms under the SAFTA agreement. The agreement, which has focused to a large extent on liberalization of investment rules as well as on protection of intellectual property rights, is likely to provide a strong impetus for knowledge-based investments to flow between the two countries.

THE SINGAPORE–AUSTRALIA FREE TRADE AGREEMENT

Having analysed the extent of existing bilateral economic linkages that exists between Singapore and Australia, this section provides the brief highlights of the SAFTA agreement that came into force between the two countries in July 2003, and their possible implications for expansion of the existing economic linkages. The SAFTA negotiations have covered a wide range of areas from trade in goods and Rules of Origin, to trade facilitation, trade in services (focusing on professional, financial and telecommunication services), movement of natural persons, intellectual property rights, investment cooperation, government procurement and setting up of appropriate dispute settlement mechanisms.[12]

Some of the salient features of the agreement are:

1. Tariffs have been reduced or eliminated by both parties in a range of manufacturing industries including chemicals and petroleum products, electrical and electronic products, plastic products, pharmaceuticals, instrumentation equipment, transport equipment and fabricated metal products. The tariffs on most product lines in Singapore have already been removed, and tariffs on all other goods from Australia, including on Australian Beer and Stout will be removed.
2. Appropriate rules of origin have been designed and all products need only fulfil a general rule of a specified threshold of a local value content

of either 30 per cent or 50 per cent, depending on importance of the product for and its current and future production trends in Singapore. The SAFTA also commits both countries to improve the speed and efficiency of customs clearance of goods on a mutual basis by streamlining and simplifying existing procedures and via the use of informational technologies. In this context, the Mutual Recognition Agreement (MRA) on conformity assessment between the two countries that was signed in 2001 has been strengthened to cover sanitary and phytosanitary measures.

3.   Singapore and Australia have guaranteed market access for service providers in a wide range of services sectors in the SAFTA, which goes beyond what has been committed at the WTO. The services sectors covered by this agreement include professional services, transportation services, distribution services, tourism services, environmental services and recreational, cultural and sporting services. All the committed sectors are subject to market access, national treatment and domestic regulation disciplines.

4.   Both countries have agreed to ease restrictions on movement of natural persons to facilitate services trade liberalization.

5.   The SAFTA has also aimed at expansion of the scope for promoting trade between Australia and Singapore through government procurement. The SAFTA contains comprehensive provisions on investment promotion and protection, and aims to foster an open international environment for cross-border investment.

6.   The SAFTA also seeks to provide enhanced IPP standards, beyond the requirements under the Trade-Related aspects of Intellectual Property Rights (TRIPS) Agreement in areas that are of mutual benefit. The objective is to increase dialogue and cooperation between Australia and Singapore on IPP protection and review current and future areas of cooperation in this area. Both countries have committed to ensure effective enforcement of IPP standards by agreeing to take efforts to improve communication between enforcement agencies as well as cooperating on information exchange on education and awareness programmes.

7.   The SAFTA aims to enhance the bilateral trade and investment relationship between Singapore and Australia by promoting mutual cooperation in education.

8.   SAFTA has also focused on competition policy issues by committing to curtail anti-competitive business practices in both countries and promote a fair and competitive business environment. It has appropriate dispute settlement provisions in place for resolving any probable disputes arising between investors from both countries.

Overall, the SAFTA confers a range of benefits for Australian businesses and for its economy that are elaborated in DFAT (2004a).

It is evident from the contents of the SAFTA that from an Australian perspective, since trade in goods between Australia and Singapore was already substantially liberalized before the FTA (due to a close to zero-tariff regime in Singapore), the impact of the SAFTA on the Australian economy with respect to merchandise trade is unlikely to be large, and is likely to be restricted to marginal benefits arising from lower input costs of production of some goods. This corroborates Access Economics (2001) study on the costs and benefits of SAFTA on the Australian economy that highlighted that the significant gains to Australia from SAFTA would be reaped in the area of services trade with Singapore.

The overall structure of the agreement indicates that the SAFTA is a comprehensive FTA, and attempts at being 'WTO-Plus' in many aspects.[13] This agreement, in force for about a year now, aims to strengthen Singapore's trade and investment linkages with Australia.

IMPLICATIONS OF SAFTA FOR ASIA-PACIFIC ECONOMIES

The SAFTA is one of the many bilateral FTAs that have been negotiated in recent years among the Asia-Pacific economies that involve countries in the Asia-Pacific Economic Cooperation (APEC) grouping. While both Singapore and Australia continue to negotiate bilateral FTAs with other trading partners consisting of both developed and developing countries,[14] other APEC economies, including ASEAN economies as well as Japan, USA, China, India, New Zealand, Canada, Mexico, Korea and Chile also continue to jump on to the FTA bandwagon, with a myriad of bilateral and regional FTAs/RTAs being negotiated among them. The current impasse at the WTO and the failure of multilateral trade talks at Cancun in 2003 have increased the likelihood of these countries continuing to resort to bilateralism at a rapid pace, as a major tool of trade liberalization among them. Indeed, many bilateral FTAs involving the APEC economies intend to complement the efforts towards an APEC wide FTA, which is envisioned to be created by 2020 according to the Bogor declaration signed at the APEC Summit in 1994 in Bogor, Indonesia.

The analysis of the SAFTA indicates that on a bilateral basis, similar FTA initiatives (possibly involving APEC economies) are likely to be beneficial for its members in terms of greater market access in goods and services due to reductions in trade barriers, increased investment opportunities in overseas markets and reduction of business costs arising from dismantling of tariffs and non-tariff barriers. However, it must be empha-sized that by definition, FTAs such as SAFTA allow member countries to pursue discriminatory policies *vis-à-vis* non-members, and could, in certain instances become a stumbling block for multilateral liberalization.

This could be particularly so wherein the compliance costs of the Rules of Origin (ROOs) across several FTAs can increase the cost of doing busi-ness and place significant burden on origin-certifying institutions, which can indeed lead to opportunities for rent-seeking activities[15] (Rajan and Sen 2004). This problem is likely to be even more acute in the presence of trade involving product fragmentation, which has become an important feature of global merchandise trade, particularly in East Asia (Athukorala 2003). Further, cross-membership of a country in multiple FTAs (for example, Australia's membership in an FTA with Singapore as well as with ASEAN at some stage (also involving Singapore)) could leave investors confused as to which set of rules, obligations and incentives correspond to which partner. Proliferation of FTAs could also enhance the scarcity of negotiat-ing resources for multilateral negotiations and may thus undermine the efforts undertaken by the WTO for global free trade (Rajan *et al.* 2001).

One of the increasing concerns in the emerging regionalism in the Asia-Pacific economies is a rise of a highly complex and untidy hub-and-spokes trading systems, of which SAFTA also happens to be a part. Although the SAFTA appears to be a comprehensive and WTO-plus FTA which could probably be more of a building block for free trade than a stumbling block, the other FTAs proliferating in this system may not be necessarily so, as they may exclude certain sectors from negotiations, or may have a more complex system of ROOs. Indeed, it is unlikely that the SAFTA model could be extended to other ASEAN countries when Australia considers an FTA with ASEAN, given the wide differences in the levels of economic development among the member countries. The absence of a common framework for negotiating comprehensive bilateral FTAs in ASEAN would certainly make the negotiating process much more difficult.

The above implies that although the SAFTA appears to be trade creat-ing in nature for Australia and Singapore, its benefits may be undermined by the other ongoing APEC-wide FTA initiatives, many of which may not necessarily be WTO-plus or even comprehensive in nature. Although the idea of an APEC-wide FTA by 2020 could be realistic, it would still be a second best alternative to multilateral liberalization at the WTO, and would also require member countries to adhere to some sort of a common frame-work, for example the Pacific Economic Cooperation Council (PECC) proposal for a common understanding on PTAs[16] to achieve a degree of consistency and avoid welfare losses from inconsistencies among the myriad agreements that could come into existence. As observed by Scollay

(2004), the most likely alternative in the absence of multilateralism will be a hub and spoke system of FTAs, wherein it would be more beneficial if individual economies could seek such agreements with as many trading partners as possible and in order to avoid being discriminatory, instil mechanisms for multilateralization of the existing bilateral FTAs. However, this may not necessarily lead to free trade for most Asia-Pacific economies.

Thus, multilateralism continues to remain the first-best option for free trade and is indispensable to a well-ordered, open and rational international trading system. It would therefore need to be pursued on a parallel track, in order to reap full benefits of global free trade. The success achieved at the Geneva meeting in July 2004 was expected to revive the ongoing Doha Round negotiations to achieve this outcome. However, in the blind pursuit of FTAs, details on the modalities of these negotiations remain to be worked out, and one can only hope for a more positive outcome for global free trade in the near future.

NOTES

1. Singapore's Gross Domestic Product (GDP) has been appreciating at an annual average rate of about 8 per cent during the past three decades, and its average real per capita income is close to US$30 000, which is higher than many developed countries (Rajan 2003).
2. These include Thailand's recent spree towards FTAs with Bahrain, India, China, Japan, Australia, Korea, New Zealand, the USA, and Malaysia's ongoing negotiations with Japan, India, Australia, Korea, and more recently, the USA.
3. It is thus indicative of the fact that some of the observed increase in Singapore–Australia trade has actually been due to Australia's increasing trade with other ASEAN countries, with goods being transshipped through Singapore. This has important implications while applying Rules of Origin for trade in goods under the SAFTA.
4. This is due to the fact that Singapore uses the GTS system under which, all goods imported into or exported from Singapore are included in its external trade statistics, barring a few exceptions (Sen 2000).
5. See Rajan (1996a), Sen (2002) for details on the formulation of these indices.
6. Notably, trade in services cannot be modelled in a perfectly competitive market and a model of vertical product differentiation suits better for this purpose. Also, due to the simultaneous interaction of producer and consumers, asymmetric information among producers and consumers lead to problems of adverse selection or moral hazard. Since services are non-storable by nature, the quantification of its trade in value terms is quite difficult (Stibora and De Vaal 1995).
7. Australia's exports of services to and imports of services from Singapore have both increased by an average of about 11 per cent per annum over the past decade (DFAT 2004b).
8. These include other commercial services – professional business services, ICT related services, health and education services.
9. According to Foreign Investment Review Board (FIRB) Australia, the stock of foreign direct investment in Australia by Singapore steadily increased from A$2.1 billion in 1998 to A$19.1 billion by 31 December 2004. In contrast, Australian foreign direct investment in Singapore has fluctuated over the period from A$1.3 billion in 1998,

A$2.9 billion in 2001 to A$1.3 billion in 2002. The stock of total Australian investment in Singapore at 30 June 2002 was A$11.7 billion, compared with A$14.3 billion in 2001 (ABS 2003).

10. Recent estimates indicate that as at 31 December 2004, Australian investments in Singapore were valued at A$14.0 billion, while Singapore's investments in Australia were valued at A$19.1 billion.

11. Examples of these are the Singapore Telecommunications (Singtel), A$14 billion investment in acquiring Cable & Wireless Optus that now operates under the name SingTel Optus, and investments of A$25 million by SembCorp Industries of Singapore for a 30 per cent equity stake in the Kwinana co-generation gas-fired power plant in Western Australia. In September 2003, Australia and Singapore settled a range of new aviation arrangements, which includes an unrestricted capacity for airlines of both countries to fly between Singapore, via most intermediate points, and through any points in Australia. Effectively, this means that the number of services that can now be operated by Australian carriers and Singaporean carriers between Europe and Australia via Singapore is limited only by each country's bilateral arrangements with European countries. The new arrangements provide greater opportunities for Australian airlines to explore establishing ground handling enterprises in Singapore, and also provide rights for airlines operating all-cargo services to base aircraft in the other country for operations to third countries, besides streamlining code sharing provisions that facilitate alliance arrangements with other airlines (Vo-Van 2003).

12. See Sen (2004), MTI (2003), DFAT (2004a) as well as various media reports on the details of this agreement, and their benefits for Singapore.

13. Although the term 'WTO-Plus' remains undefined, it largely indicates that the agreement has attempted to negotiate in areas wherein consensus has not yet been reached at the multilateral level in the WTO.

14. Within the APEC economies, while Singapore continues to negotiate bilateral FTAs with Korea, Canada, Mexico and even trilateral arrangements, including P-3 (involving New Zealand and Chile), Australia has recently signed a bilateral FTA with the USA and Thailand, and is studying the feasibility of the same with Japan and China.

15. Bhagwati (1995) terms this situation as a 'spaghetti-bowl' problem.

16. See Scollay (2004) for more details on this issue.

REFERENCES

Access Economics (2001), *The Costs and Benefits of a Free Trade Agreement with Singapore*, Access Economics.

ASEAN Secretariat (2002), 'ASEAN FDI Database', www.aseansec.org, 2 February.

Australian Bureau of Statistics (ABS) (2003), 'ABS catalogue 5352.0 international investment position: supplementary country statistics', www.abs.gov.au/AUSSTATS/abs@.nsf/Lookup/5352.0Main+Features12004?OpenDocument, 2 February.

Athukorala, P.C. (2003), 'Product fragmentation and trade patterns in East Asia', Trade and Development Discussion paper 2003/21, Division of Economics, Research School of Pacific and Asian Studies, The Australian National University, Canberra.

Bhagwati, J. (1995), 'US trade policy: the infatuation with free trade areas', in J. Bhagwati and A.O. Krueger (eds), *The Dangerous Drift to Preferential Trade Agreements*, Washington, DC: The AEI Press, pp. 1–18.

Department of Foreign Affairs and Trade (DFAT) (2004a), 'Singapore–Australia

Free Trade Agreement (SAFTA): a business guide', www.dfat.gov.au/trade/negotiations/safta/safta_guide.html, 2 February.

Department of Foreign Affairs and Trade (DFAT) (2004b), *Trade in Services Australia 2002–03*, Market Information and Analysis section, Canberra: Commonwealth of Australia.

Department of Foreign Affairs and Trade (DFAT) (2006), 'Singapore: fact sheet', www.dfat.gov.au/geo/fs/sing.pdf.

International Enterprise (IE) Singapore (2003), *Singapore Trade Connection CD-Rom*, International Enterprise Singapore.

Lyall, K. (2004), 'The China free trade syndrome', *The Australian*, 7 May, News Corporation.

Ministry of Trade and Industry Singapore (2003), 'Media-Info Kit on the SAFTA', http://app.fta.gov.sg/data/fta/file/FTA_SAFTA_Mediakit.pdf, 2 February.

Rajan, R.S. (ed.) (2003), *Sustaining Competitiveness in the New Global Economy: The Experience of Singapore*, Cheltenham, UK and Northampton, MA, US: Edward Elgar.

Rajan, R. and R. Sen (2003a), 'Singapore's drive to form cross-regional trade pacts: rationale and implications', in R. Rajan (ed.), *Economic Globalization and Asia: Essays on Finance, Trade and Taxation*, Singapore: World Scientific.

Rajan, R. and R. Sen (2003b), 'The Japan–Singapore trade pact: a "new age" economic partnership agreement for the new millennium', in *Trading Arrangements in the Pacific Rim*, New York: Oceana Publications.

Rajan, R. and R. Sen (2004), *New Regionalism in Asia: ASEAN's trade with China and India*, mimeo, June.

Rajan, R., R. Sen and R. Siregar (2001), *Singapore's Attraction to Free Trade Areas: Bilateral Trade Relations with Japan and the US*, Singapore: Institute of Southeast Asian Studies.

Sampson, G. and R.H. Snape (1985), 'Identifying the issues in trade in services', *World Economy*, **8** (2), 171–82.

Scollay, R. (2004), 'Thoughts on Sequencing of Preferential Trading Initiatives in the Asia-Pacific Region', paper presented at the APEC Study Centre Consortium (ASCC)/Pacific Economic Cooperation Council (PECC) meeting, Vina del Mar, Chile, 28 May.

Sen, R. (2000), 'Analyzing entrepôt trade in a small open economy: the case of Singapore', *ASEAN Economic Bulletin*, **17** (1), 23–35.

Sen, R. (2002), 'Singapore–India economic relations in the context of their globalization strategies', unpublished PhD thesis, National University of Singapore, Singapore.

Sen, R. (2004), 'Free trade agreements in Southeast Asia', *Southeast Asia Background Series no. 1*, Singapore: Institute of Southeast Asian Studies (ISEAS).

Stibora, J.J. and A. De Vaal (1995), 'Services and services trade: a theoretical inquiry', *Tinbergen Institute Research series 97*, Amsterdam: Thesis publishers.

Tan, T. (2003), 'Exposed down under', *Smart Investor*, Singapore edition, February.

The World Bank (2003), *World Development Indicators 2003*, Washington, DC: The World Bank.

Vo-Van, C. (2003), 'Singapore settles new aviation arrangements with Australia', *Asialine Online*, Department of Foreign Affairs and Trade, Canberra: Commonwealth of Australia. Available from: www.asialine.dfat.gov.au/asialine/Asialine.nsf/WebCurrentIssue/5BAF160B801104ABCA256DFD001DEE54.

PART V

Sector studies

13. The commodity coverage of PTAs: does agriculture matter?

Donald MacLaren

INTRODUCTION

Preferential trade agreements (PTAs) have recently taken centre stage in trade relations between countries. The Asia-Pacific region has been no exception.[1] Several reasons have been suggested to explain the development of bilateral and plurilateral preferential trade agreements. These include: first, negotiations are likely to be more straightforward with fewer countries and the gains from trade will arrive sooner than with multilateral negotiations; second, the fewer the number of countries involved, the greater the number of issues which can be included (the notion of 'deep integration'); third, the economic costs of adjustment may be smaller with an agreement amongst similar economies; fourth, a PTA may make inward FDI more attractive; and fifth, countries fear being left out of agreements, thereby forgoing any net benefits to be derived from membership and, therefore, losing from being a non-member country in a world replete with PTAs.

In the past decade, with the substantial increase in PTAs being negotiated and the hub and spokes arrangements that are now emerging amongst intersecting PTAs, discriminatory treatment has grown and the WTO has failed the excluded members, many of which are developing and least-developed countries. These excluded Members suffer from diminished social welfare.[2] This hub and spokes architecture has created the 'spaghetti bowl effect' (see Bhagwati et al. 1998, p. 1138; Crawford and Fiorentino 2005; and Lloyd and MacLaren 2004, Figure 1) and, increasingly, multi-layered discrimination. This form of discrimination in turn leads to complex rules of origin with attendant substantial costs of compliance for exporting firms in the PTA and to additional costs for the customs authorities administering them.[3] As a consequence, even if the net gains to an individual country would be more immediate when they are achieved through a PTA than they would be if achieved through multilateral negotiations in the WTO, when such net gains are discounted to present value terms, it is highly probable that the multilateral gains will exceed the gains from a PTA.

This outcome is probable because the reciprocal benefits received multilaterally from Members of the WTO (numbering 149 in total) will be larger than the reciprocal benefits received from a bilateral or plurilateral partner.

Discrimination exists not only between members and non-members but between sectors amongst members. It is common in PTAs to find that not all traded goods sectors are treated with the same degree of preferential treatment and, indeed, some sectors may be entirely excluded from preferential treatment. Agriculture, or at least some of its sub-sectors, is a sector typically discriminated against in the formation of PTAs. This form of discrimination is not consistent with Article XXIV of GATT 1994 which requires that all duties and other barriers to trade are eliminated: for customs unions on 'substantially all trade in products originating in such territories' (Article XXIV:8(a)(i)); and for free trade areas on 'substantially all trade between constituent territories in products originating in such territories' (Article XXIV:8(b)) (see WTO 2006). Despite such requirements, PTAs which are inconsistent with these Articles were not challenged in the GATT, pre-1995, nor have they been challenged subsequently in the WTO (Panagariya 2000, p. 289).

One of the difficulties for excluded countries with mounting a challenge to a non-conforming PTA has been the lack of a sufficiently precise definition of the phrase 'substantially all trade'. An attempt to clarify the meaning of this phrase is to be found in the Understanding on the Interpretation of Article XXIV of the General Agreement on Tariffs and Trade 1994 (hereafter, the 'Understanding') (see WTO 1995, pp. 31–4). Presumably the intention of those who drafted the original Article was to ensure that all goods traded amongst members of a PTA would have tariffs and other barriers entirely removed, while recognizing that, in some situations, for example, those covered by the exemptions which are underpinned by Article XX of the GATT, trade barriers would remain on trade within the PTA. However, in current practice, tariffs are not removed on all goods traded amongst members and the justifications are not based on Article XX. A second difficulty has been the time scale over which preferential rates are phased in. In the Understanding, this period has been defined as ten years (WTO 1995, p. 32, para. 3).

There are three purposes to this chapter. The first is to explain why agriculture is so often treated in PTAs in the same way as it is in the multilateral negotiations. The second is to review some elements of one of the recent PTAs in the Asia-Pacific region, namely the Australia–United States Free Trade Agreement (AUSFTA). The third is to answer the question: does the partial exclusion of agriculture matter for the potential welfare benefits to be derived from membership of a PTA? An answer to this question is provided in the concluding section.

WHY IS AGRICULTURE EXCLUDED?

One of the sectors which tends to be excluded, partially or totally from the elimination of trade barriers within PTAs, or which has been given substantial periods of time over which to make the adjustment to freer intra-PTA trade, is agriculture. In the multilateral trade context it is well known that agriculture remained largely outside the GATT in the years prior to the introduction of the WTO Agreement on Agriculture. It is also clear that the negotiations on agriculture which began in the WTO during 2000 and which, subsequently, became part of the Doha Round, have made little progress when measured against the requirement that is set out in Article 20 of the Agreement (see WTO 1995, p. 55). The stated goal, which was reiterated in the Doha Declaration, is 'to establish a fair and market-oriented trading system through a programme of fundamental reform' (WTO 2001, para 13). The outcome at the Cancún WTO Ministerial Conference in 2003 and the slow progress made since the 'July package' was agreed in 2004 (see WTO 2004a), point to a continuation of protracted negotiations, especially on the pillar of market access but also on the other two pillars of domestic support and export competition.

But why should such difficulties arise in a bilateral negotiation to form a PTA? There are several reasons but fundamentally there are two. First, there remains a conflict between the greater economic efficiency to be achieved as the outcome of trade liberalization on the one hand and the pursuit by many governments of non-economic (that is, non-efficiency objectives) in their agricultural sectors on the other. Such intervention takes many forms but the policy instruments can be classified broadly into those providing import protection, domestic support and export assistance. The objectives being pursued include, *inter alia*, raising the level and reducing the variability of the incomes of farm households, and providing security of food supplies.

The second explanation is that some governments appear to believe that the principles of economics ought not to be applied to the agricultural sector.[4] It is claimed that the sector has special characteristics. For example, it is claimed that farming is more than just a business; it is a way of life; that there is an essential link between food production and culture; between food production and landscape; and between food production and the viability of rural communities. Each of these characteristics is believed to make economics largely irrelevant and its application inappropriate in the design of public policy for the agricultural sector. However, these characteristics can be recognized as examples of public goods and externalities and, as such, each is amenable to the application of economics.

Some, but not all, of the governments which eschew the application of economics to agriculture belong to the set of governments which pursue the multifunctional agenda (see, OECD 2001 for more details). This agenda includes the links listed above as well as other items such as animal welfare, the rural environment and geographic indications. Multifunctionality may be viewed in one of two ways. The first is that each of the elements on the agenda, for example, food production and landscape, can be viewed as an objective. Then, given this objective, the targeting principle of applied welfare economics could be applied, taking the externality into account. In the second way, multifunctionality is less amenable to economic analysis because it is viewed as an objective peculiar to agriculture: 'agriculture as an activity is entrusted with fulfilling certain functions in society' (OECD 2001, p. 9). Clearly, this view of multifunctionality is a much broader one than the first and is based on a set of social norms which go well beyond the pursuit of economic efficiency. From this perspective, the multifunctionality of agriculture is an objective which, it is argued by its proponents, can only be pursued through the continued use of price-distorting and hence trade-distorting, instruments, thus to attain a vibrant agricultural sector which will achieve higher-level objectives for society. The reality is that this policy objective, to a greater or lesser extent, has been pursued throughout the post-war period by governments of many of the developed countries and yet it has not been achieved. There are many reasons for this failure but perhaps the most important three are: first, the rents transferred to the agricultural sector have become capitalized in land values; second, the size or scale of many farms in many instances remains just too small to generate an adequate household income; and, third, the means used to transfer income have been regressive with the greatest transfers accruing to the largest farms.

For governments which adhere in varying degrees to the multifunctional agenda, the liberalization of agriculture, even within a PTA, is unlikely to be an option and the sector will be excluded either partially or wholly from the negotiations which are designed to eliminate barriers to trade. However, it is also the case that some governments which do not subscribe to the multifunctional agenda, for example, that of the United States, nevertheless continue to intervene in their agricultural sectors through trade distorting instruments and they are reluctant to allow a PTA to compromise their ability to achieve their non-economic objectives for agriculture. The alternative to exclusion from the terms of an agreement is to provide a time period of adjustment to free trade that runs one to two decades and which also includes various forms of special safeguards against surges in imports. Such a time period for adjustment violates the ten-year rule in the 'Understanding'.

AGRICULTURE IN AUSFTA

To illustrate these points, consider the outcome for three agricultural sub-sectors in the Australia–United States FTA.[5] The first is sugar. Because of the weight of the US sugar lobby and the political economy of sugar policy in the USA (including its regional bias), sugar was never placed on the negotiating table by the USA. Clearly, this outcome was not advantageous to the Australian sugar industry which had looked forward to improved access to an otherwise very restricted market. Currently, Australia's share of the sugar tariff rate quota (TRQ) in the USA for sugar is 8 per cent (de Gorter and Sheldon 2001, p. 75).[6]

Second, the USA is currently the most important single market for exports of Australian beef with around 40 per cent of exports going to that market (CIE 2004, p. 100). It is also a market which is protected from imports by a TRQ. Under the Agreement, Australia's annual quota will expand from its current level of 378 214 tonnes by annual increments over a 18-year period until it reaches 448 214 tonnes. The current within-quota specific tariff of US¢4.4/kg (CIE 2004, p. 101) was to be removed immediately when the Agreement took effect (1 January 2005) and the current over-quota *ad valorem* tariff of 26.4 per cent will remain unchanged for the first eight years (CIE 2004, p. 102). Thereafter, it will be reduced until it reaches zero in the 18th year of the Agreement. However, there are safeguard provisions in the Agreement (Annex 3-A) which enables the USA to restrict imports of beef if there is a surge in the volume of imports (the quantity trigger) or a fall in import prices (the price trigger) (DFAT 2004b).

The third sub-sector is that of dairy products. Currently, Australia's access to the US market for dairy products is very heavily restricted. The TRQs are 7000 tonnes for cheese, 600 tonnes for skim milk powder and 3108 tonnes of other products (CIE 2004, p. 103). Together, by value, these exports to the USA represent less than 5 per cent of Australia's exports of dairy products. As in the case of beef, improved access is to be phased in over a substantial number of years. In this case the phase-in period is 17 years with annual increments in access thereafter of three per cent (DFAT 2004a, p. 12). The current within-quota tariff rate on cheese of 12 per cent was to be abolished immediately but the above-quota tariff remains high at over US¢50/lb (de Gorter and Sheldon 2001, p. 86).

Australia's imports of agricultural products tend not to be impeded by tariffs. There are a few exceptions, for example, cheese for which there is a TRQ (see de Gorter and Sheldon 2001, p. 143). Hence, the only impediment to US exports of agricultural products to Australia are quarantine regulations. Under the Agreement (Article 7.4), a Committee on Sanitary and

Phytosanitary (SPS) matters is established with the aim of enhancing each country's implementation of the WTO SPS Agreement.

It is clear from this brief sketch of the realities of bilateral trade in agricultural products between Australia and the USA that the Agreement contains very little, if any, free trade in the important sub-sectors covered.[7] This outcome contrasts with the selling of the need to engage the USA in free trade negotiations which stressed the benefits to Australian agriculture: 'The Government will give a high priority to reducing the most significant market access barriers facing Australian exports, *particularly in the agricultural sector*' (emphasis added) (cited in Parliament of Australia 2004, para 1.12). The overall benefits to Australia of the partial liberalization of agriculture are less than those anticipated originally. Winchester and Richardson (2005) used a computable general equilibrium model to quantify the effects on Australia of the exclusion of certain agricultural sectors from the Agreement. They found that total liberalization in the FTA would cause Australia to gain US$516 million measured against a pre-FTA base line (ibid. Table 7.4); and with agriculture excluded from the FTA, Australia would gain US$256.4 million (Table 7.10), that is, the gains are halved by the exclusion of agriculture.[8]

THE ECONOMIC CONSEQUENCES OF EXCLUDING SECTORS

In the theoretical economic analysis of PTAs, it is usually assumed that all tariff barriers on trade in goods amongst members of the PTA are set to zero upon formation of the agreement. The analysis is then conducted to identify the sign of the welfare effects of the formation of a PTA on its members. As far as the theoretical analysis of FTAs is concerned, there is an existence proof, due to Panagariya and Krishna (2002), in which they show that an FTA can create a Pareto improvement for each citizen of each member country of the FTA. This outcome is accomplished through the use of lump-sum transfers within the FTA which are financed through tariff revenues received on members' trade with non-members. Moreover, by fixing the volume of trade between each member of the FTA and non-members at its pre-FTA level, they show that non-member countries will be no worse off. Therefore, such an FTA is a Pareto improvement for the global economy. The crucial assumption made to derive this result is that each country in the FTA adjusts its tariff on each commodity traded with non-members in such as way that its volume of imports of each good does not change with the formation of the FTA. In practice, of course, FTAs do not satisfy this assumption. Hence, the conclusions about the welfare gains of a member need not carry over, nor need it be the case that non-members are not harmed.

Instead of fixing traded quantities and allowing tariffs to be endogenous, the analysis can be done in a way which is consistent with Article XXIV of the GATT, namely, ensuring that the level of tariffs after the formation of the FTA are no greater than they were before. Then the quantities traded are endogenous. Panagariya (1999) has shown that the joint welfare of the members from the formation of an FTA depends upon the sign of the change in the joint output of the FTA valued at (unchanged) world prices. His result will now be explained and applied to a hypothetical FTA involving Australia and the United States, assuming first of all the total elimination of internal tariffs and then assuming that the USA does not remove its tariffs on imports of one of the goods imported from Australia.

Assume that there are two countries, namely, Australia (A), the United States (S) and the Rest of the World region (W); and there are four goods 0, 1, 2, 3. This is the minimum number of goods which allows for all possible patterns of trade. These goods are assumed to be normal in consumption and are final goods. The pre-FTA situation is labelled with superscript 0 and the FTA situation with superscript 1. Following Panagariya, the initial pattern of trade is such that good 0 is exported by countries A and S, good 1 is imported by countries A and S, good 2 is imported by country A and exported by country S, and good 3 is exported by country A and imported by country S. It is assumed that countries A and S are small countries and that when they form an FTA, the FTA remains small in this three-region global economy. This last assumption permits constant terms of trade for all countries.

In the pre-FTA situation, country A (S) has a tariff t_i (T_i) on good i with t_i (T_i) > 0 if good i is imported and zero otherwise. The consumer and producer price of good i in country A is p_i and in country S is P_i. Let the price vector faced by both consumers and producers in country A be $\mathbf{p}^0 = (1, 1 + t_1, 1 + t_2, 1)$ and that in country S be $\mathbf{P}^0 = (1, 1 + T_1, 1, 1 + T_3)$. The prices in region W are unity for each good by choice of units, and are fixed by assumption. The expenditure function for country A is $e(\mathbf{p}^0, u^0)$, where u^0 is the pre-FTA utility level, with $e_i(.)$ the compensated demand function for good i; and the corresponding functions for country S are $E(\mathbf{P}^0, U^0)$ and $E_i(.)$. The revenue function for country A is given by $r(\mathbf{p}^0)$ and for country S is $R(\mathbf{P}^0)$. The output of each good in country A is given by $r_i(.)$ and in country S by $R_i(.)$.

The equilibrium for each country is defined as expenditure equal to revenue from production plus tariff revenue from imports. Hence, for country A, pre-FTA, the equilibrium is given by

$$e^0(\mathbf{p}^0, u^0) = r^0(\mathbf{p}^0) + t_1(e_1^0 - r_1^0) + t_2(e_2^0 - r_2^0) \tag{13.1}$$

and for country S is

$$E^0(\mathbf{P}^0, U^0) = R^0(\mathbf{P}^0) + T_1(E_1^0 - R_1^0) + T_3(E_3^0 - R_3^0) \tag{13.2}$$

Assume now that countries A and S form an FTA. Each continues to import good 1 from country W at the price $(1 + t_i)$ and $(1 + T_i)$, respectively, this assumption ensuring that the price of good 1 within the FTA remains linked to the 'world' price in region W. Hence, the price of good 1 in country A remains at $p_1^1 = p_1^0 = 1 + t_1$. In country S, good 1 also continues to be imported at price $P_1^1 = P_1^0 = 1 + T_1$. In order to determine the new pattern of trade internal to the FTA, an assumption is needed about the tariff rates on good 1 in the two countries. Assume that $t_1 > T_1$. Then the consumer price for good 1 will be higher in country A than in country S ($p_1^1 = 1 + t_1 > P_1^1 = 1 + T_1$) and the entire production of good 1 in country S will be exported to country A. Consumption in country S will be met entirely by imports from region W. It is assumed that rules of origin are such that exports by region W to country S cannot then be shipped to country A; country A has to import good 1 directly from region W. It is this feature of the set-up of Panagariya's model that allows consumers' prices for the same good to differ between the two countries which form the FTA.

Pre-FTA, country A imported good 2 and in the FTA it continues to do so at price $p_2^1 = p_2^0 = 1 + t_2$. This price exceeds the price in country S for good 2 which continues to be $P_2^1 = P_2^0 = 1$. Hence, as with good 1, all of good 2 that is produced in country S will be exported to country A in order to receive a price of $1 + t_2$ instead of a price of 1 if exported to region W. Consumption in country S is satisfied by imports from region W. For good 3, the price in country S remains at $P_3^1 = P_3^0 = 1 + T_3$ which exceeds the price in country A which remains at $p_3^1 = p_3^0 = 1$. Hence, in the FTA, all of country A's production of good 3 is exported to country S and country A's consumption is satisfied by imports from region W.

With the formation of the FTA, the price vector faced by consumers ($\mathbf{p}_C^1$) and that faced by producers ($\mathbf{p}_P^1$) now differ. For consumers, the price vectors pre-FTA and in the FTA are identical, that is, $\mathbf{p}_C^1 = \mathbf{p}^0 = (1, 1 + t_1, 1 + t_2, 1)$ and $\mathbf{P}_C^1 = \mathbf{P}^0 = (1, 1 + T_1, 1, 1 + T_3)$. For producers, the price vector in the FTA is $\mathbf{p}_P^1 = \mathbf{P}_P^1 = (1, 1 + t_1, 1 + t_2, 1 + T_3)$ which indicates that producers receive the price for each good in the higher-priced country within the FTA. The equilibrium for countries A and S are now, respectively,

$$e^1(\mathbf{p}^0, u^1) = r^1(\mathbf{p}_P^1) + t_1(e_1^1 - r_1^1 - R_1^1) + t_2(e_2^1 - r_2^1 - R_2^1) \tag{13.3}$$

where $e_i^1 - r_i^1 - R_i^1$ represents net imports by country A from region W, and

$$E^1(\mathbf{P}^0, U^1) = R^1(\mathbf{P}_P^1) + T_1 E_1^0 + T_3(E_3^0 - R_3^1 - r_3^1) \qquad (13.4)$$

To determine whether or not the welfare of country A has increased as a consequence of forming an FTA with country S, it is necessary to compare $e^1(.)$ with $e^0(.)$ as a discrete, rather than a marginal, change. Subtracting Equation (13.1) from Equation (13.3) gives

$$e^1(\mathbf{p}^0, u^1) - e^0(\mathbf{p}^0, u^0) = (r^1 - r^0) - t_1[(r_1^1 - r_1^0) +$$
$$R_1^1 - (e_1^0 - e_1^1)] - t_2[(r_2^1 - r_2^0) + R_2^1 - (e_2^0 - e_2^1)] \qquad (13.5)$$

Because the expenditure and revenue functions are homogeneous of degree one in prices, each can be expressed as the sum of prices times quantities. For example, $e^0(\mathbf{p}^0, u^0) \equiv 1e_0^0 + (1 + t_1)e_1^0 + (1 + t_2)e_2^0 + 1e_3^0$. Writing out the terms on the left-hand side of Equation (13.5) fully in this way and subtracting the terms on the right-hand side that involve consumption, $t_i e_i^j, i = 1, 2; j = 0, 1$, allows the left-hand side to be written as $\Sigma_{i=0}^3(e_i^1 - e_i^0)$. The terms remaining on the right-hand side simplify to $\Sigma_{i=0}^3(r_i^1 - r_i^0) - t_1 R_1^1 - t_2 R_2^1 + T_3 r_3^1$. Hence, Equation (13.5) can be re-written as:

$$\sum_{i=0}^3 (e_i^1 - e_i^0) = \sum_{i=0}^3 (r_i^1 - r_i^0) - t_1 R_1^1 - t_2 R_2^1 + T_3 r_3^1 \qquad (13.6)$$

The left-hand side measures the change in expenditure evaluated at world prices of unity, which are unchanged with the formation of the FTA. Hence, if the sum is positive, then it can be concluded that welfare in country A has risen, that is, $u^1 > u^0$, expenditure being a monotonically increasing function of utility. On the right-hand side of Equation (13.6), the first term measures the change in revenue evaluated at world prices, the next two terms measure the loss of tariff revenue for country A from importing from country S at tariff rates of zero on goods 1 and 2, and the final term is the additional revenue obtained from exporting to country S at the higher price $(1 + T_3)$ instead of at the pre-FTA price of 1. However, in general the sign of the right-hand side is ambiguous, thus implying that the sign of the welfare change for country A is also ambiguous in the absence, as here, of intra-FTA lump-sum transfers.

Panagariya then goes on to show the following. Suppose now that when country S forms the FTA with country A, it does not set to zero its tariff on good 3 when that good is imported from country A. Instead, it retains the MFN tariff of T_3 on imports from both country A and region W. Then the price vector faced by producers in country A will remain at its pre-FTA value. This implies that, in Equation (13.6), $r^1 = r^0$ and $T_3 = 0$ (noting that the producer price in country A for good 3 is now 1 and no longer $1 + T_3$). Equation (13.6) then becomes:

$$\sum_{i=0}^{3} (e_i^1 - e_i^0) = -t_1 R_1^1 - t_2 R_2^1 \qquad (13.7)$$

The right-hand side of Equation (13.7) is unambiguously negative which means that $u^1 < u^0$. In other words, country A loses from forming an FTA with country S if country S does not reduce to zero its MFN tariff rate preferentially in favour of country A on good 3. Note that t_1 and t_2 refer to country A's tariffs on imports of goods 1 and 2 from region W, not from S, which are zero. From Equation (13.7), it can also be seen that the loss to country A increases, the greater are its imports from country S and the higher its MFN tariffs. Hence, in this example, if country A removes its tariffs preferentially on imports of goods 1 and 2 from country S but country S continues to apply its MFN tariffs on imports of good 3 from country A, then country A loses unambiguously from the formation of the FTA.

CONCLUSIONS

The substantial increase in the number of PTAs in existence, together with the hub and spokes architecture to which they have given rise, has introduced multi-layered discrimination in world trade. So far, the WTO appears to be either helpless or compliant. In either case, Members of the WTO involved with implementing PTAs are in violation of Article XXIV of GATT 1994 and are acting in a way which is inconsistent with one of the aims of the Organization, namely, the elimination of discrimination in international commerce. Moreover, in many of the PTAs in existence barriers to trade amongst members on substantially all trade have not been removed. Agriculture is one sector in which this behaviour is very noticeable. Even in cases where some of the barriers will be removed eventually, the time scale involved is often inconsistent with the 'Understanding'.

The reasons for the total or partial exclusion of agriculture were reviewed. It appears that the reasons which make multilateral negotiations in agriculture extremely difficult carry over to bilateral and plurilateral agreements. The treatment of various sub-sectors of the agricultural sector in the AUSFTA were summarized. While one sub-sector was not even open to negotiation, others will be liberalized by the USA to a small extent and gradually over almost two decades with special safeguards used to suppress any surges in imports. This Agreement is, therefore, inconsistent with Article XXIV and the 'Understanding'.

The welfare effects of such exclusions were explored in a three-region, four-commodity model due to Panagariya (1999). It was found that if two of the countries form a small FTA and totally remove all tariffs on trade between them, then the sign of the welfare change for one of the countries is ambiguous in the absence of intra-FTA transfers. If one of the members of the FTA fails to remove the tariff preferentially on imports of one good from the other member, then the welfare effect on the latter is unambiguously negative. The welfare effect on non-members was not explored because, by assumption, there was no change in their terms of trade, this being the usual source of the loss of welfare to excluded countries. Such an outcome has been demonstrated both in the theoretical literature and through the use of CGE models.

It has been argued in this chapter that so-called FTAs do not involve free trade, because agricultural commodities are often excluded in part from the agreement. It has been shown, theoretically, that FTAs which exclude a sector such as agriculture produce a welfare loss for the member whose exports in that sector are not accorded preferential treatment. Hence, agriculture does matter for the welfare effects of membership of an FTA. Given this conclusion, together with the compliance costs for exporters within the FTA and the costs for customs of administering the increasingly complex rules of origin for both hubs and spokes, perhaps it is time for trade economists to encourage governments and their policy advisers to re-evaluate the wisdom of their head-long rush into the spaghetti bowl.

NOTES

1. In early 2003 there were only four Members of the World Trade Organization (WTO) which were not also members of a preferential trade agreement: Hong Kong, China; Macao, China; Mongolia and Chinese Taipei (WTO 2003, p. 46).
2. In the Doha Declaration (para. 29), it is recognized that it has proved difficult for the Committee on Regional Trade Agreements in the WTO to ensure that PTAs are consistent with the rules (see WTO 2001). Moreover, in the Sutherland report (see WTO 2004b), PTAs were singled out as a source of serious organizational weakness because their proliferation was creating a situation in which MFN treatment was rapidly becoming the exception rather than the norm.
3. Anson *et al.* (2003) estimated that the costs to Mexico of administering its rules of origin in NAFTA amounted to 40 per cent of the benefits to that country from its membership of NAFTA.
4. In the Asia-Pacific region, both Japan and Korea qualify as countries adhering to this view. But they are not alone: in Europe, some countries of the European Union, together with Norway and Switzerland, hold strongly to this view.

5. At the time of writing, the treatment of agriculture in the Australia–China negotiations and the Australia–Japan discussion remains to be determined.
6. A TRQ is a combination of two tariffs and an import quota. For import volumes in a given time period which are less than the quota volume, a low or sometimes zero tariff is applied, the within-quota tariff. For imports within that time period which exceed the quota, a higher tariff is applied, sometimes at a prohibitive rate, the out-of-quota tariff.
7. There is one additional sub-sector, horticulture, for which there is limited liberalization for Australian exports and it will occur only over a number of years. Even then, there are various safeguard measures in place to prevent import surges (see DFAT 2004b).
8. Computable General Equilibrium (CGE) models have been used to predict the trade and welfare effects of PTAs both actual and hypothetical. In such policy simulations, not all trade barriers are removed on intra-PTA trade nor can all aspects of an agreement be simulated because of lack of detail in the model: see, for example the study by the CIE (CIE 2004) on the Australia–United States Free Trade Agreement. However, as revealed in the modelling exercises that were conducted for the AUSFTA, CGE models are of limited use in assessing the economic benefits to members. For a succinct technical account, see Dee (2004), and for an account of why the results of CGE modelling were not used as a foundation of the Senate Select Committee's recommendation on the AUSFTA, see Parliament of Australia (2004), particularly paras 1.97–1.99.

REFERENCES

Anson, J., O. Cadot, J. de Melo, A. Estevadeoral, A. Suwa-Eisenmann and B. Tumurchudur (2003), 'Rules of origin in North–South Preferential Trading Arrangements with an application to NAFTA', Centre for Economic Policy Research Discussion Paper no. 4166.
Bhagwati, J., D. Greenaway and A. Panagariya (1998), 'Trading preferentially: theory and policy', *The Economic Journal*, **108** (449), 1128–48.
CIE (2004), *Economic Analysis of AUSFTA: Impact of the Bilateral Free Trade Agreement with the United States*, Canberra: Centre for International Economics.
Crawford, J.-A. and R.V. Fiorentino (2005), *The Changing Landscape of Regional Trade Agreements*, Geneva: World Trade Organization.
Dee, P. (2004), 'The Australia–US Free Trade Agreement: an assessment', paper prepared for the Senate Select Committee on the Free Trade Agreement between Australia and the United States of America.
de Gorter, H. and I. Sheldon (eds) (2001), 'Agriculture in the WTO: Issues in Reforming Tariff-Rate Import Quotas in the Agreement on Agriculture in the WTO', International Agricultural Trade Research Consortium, Commissioned Paper No. 13, Department of Applied Economics, University of Minnesota.
DFAT (2004a), 'Australia–United States Free Trade Agreement', Annex 2-B schedule of the United States, general notes: tariff schedule of the United States, Canberra: Commonwealth of Australia. Available from: www.dfat.gov.au/trade/negotiations/us_fta/final-text/.
DFAT (2004b), 'Australia–United States Free Trade Agreement – chapter three', www.dfat.gov.au/trade/negotiations/us_fta/final-text/chapter_3.html, 1 February.
Lloyd, P.J. and D. MacLaren (2004), 'Gains and losses from regional trading agreements: a survey', *The Economic Record*, **80** (251), 445–67.
OECD (2001), *Multifunctionality: Towards an Analytical Framework*, Paris: OECD.
Panagariya, A. (1999), 'Preferential trading and welfare: the small-union case revisited', mimeo, Department of Economics, University of Maryland.

Panagariya, A. (2000), 'Preferential trade liberalization: the traditional theory and new developments', *Journal of Economic Literature*, **38** (2), 287–331.

Panagariya, A. and P. Krishna (2002), 'On necessarily welfare-enhancing free trade areas', *Journal of International Economics*, **57** (2), 353–367.

Parliament of Australia (2004), *Select Committee on the Free Trade Agreement between Australia and the United States of America: Summary of Inquiry*, Canberra: Commonwealth of Australia.

Winchester, N. and M. Richardson (2005), 'ANZUS free trade agreements: results from a global model', in S. Jayasuriya (ed.), *Trade Policy Reforms and Development: Essays in Honour of Peter Lloyd Vol. II*, Cheltenham, UK and Northampton, USA: Edward Elgar.

WTO (1995), *The Results of the Uruguay Round of Multilateral Trade Negotiations: The Legal Texts*, Geneva: WTO.

WTO (2001), 'Implementation-related issues and concerns: decision of 14 November 2001 (the Doha Declaration)', *Document Number WT/MIN(01)/17*, Geneva: WTO.

WTO (2003), *World Trade Report 2003*, Geneva: WTO.

WTO (2004a), 'Doha work programme, draft General Council decision of 31 July 2004', *Document Number WT/GC/W/535*, Geneva: WTO.

WTO (2004b), *The Future of the WTO: Addressing Institutional Challenges in the New Millennium*, report by the Consultative Board to the Director-General Supachai Panitchpakdi, Geneva: WTO.

WTO (2006), 'Regional trade agreements – GATT Article XXIV', www.wto.org/english/tratop_e/region_e/region_art24_e.htm, 23 January.

14. Multilateral consequences of bilateral trade agreements: AUSFTA and the Australian wool industry

John Stanton, M.A.B. Siddique, Emma Kopke and Nazrul Islam

INTRODUCTION

This chapter examines the third country effect of a free trade agreement between Australia and the USA (AUSFTA) using the Australian wool industry as an example. Without considering the third country effect, an attempt to evaluate the outcome of an RTA may be superficial. The Australian wool industry was selected because of the degree of product transformation of Australian wool that occurs in third countries prior to being imported into the USA, and the significance of the Australian wool industry in the international wool textile market. The chapter is divided into three sections. The next section examines the bilateral and multilateral relevance and importance of AUSFTA, and the issues pertaining to the Australian wool industry from a third country perspective are discussed in the third section. The chapter ends with some concluding remarks.

THE BILATERAL AND MULTILATERAL RELEVANCE AND IMPORTANCE OF A FREE TRADE AGREEMENT BETWEEN AUSTRALIA AND THE USA

Traditionally Australia and the United States have experienced a close relationship with one another in many areas, including defence, a commitment to democracy and international security, and the reduction of trading barriers. These links have been reinforced recently by events surrounding the war on terror, with Australia's support for the USA and involvement in the war in Iraq highlighting the commitment and friendship between the two nations. On top of all these relations, the closer economic ties between the two countries have immensely benefited both the economies in the past and will continue to do so in the future. The United States is Australia's largest single trade and investment partner and second-largest export market. It is Australia's largest market for elaborately transformed manufactures. Australia is the eighth-largest foreign holder of US assets – some $117 billion worth of direct investment in 2000. The USA is Australia's largest source of foreign investment ($235 billion in 2000–1 (DFAT 2003, p. 89)).

It is arguably advocated by many of the supporters of a free trade agreement between Australia and the USA (AUSFTA) that such an agreement would strengthen bilateral relations between the two countries and reaffirm the friendship between the two nations. It provides a formal arrangement where both countries can reach agreements on the key trade and related regulatory issues critical to expanding business and trade opportunities. Agreement on these would make it easier and less costly for businesses to operate between the two markets. An FTA in these terms could be used to establish new benchmarks in other trade forums, including the WTO and APEC (DFAT 2003, p. 89). It is also expected that AUSFTA would provide Australian exporters with improved access and greater certainty in the US market. Australia would become a more attractive destination for US investment and Australian firms would gain from greater exposure to competition from US models of business management and technology.

But there are a number of critical issues and points of friction in the bilateral economic relationships between the USA and Australia which warrant closer and in-depth examination on the following grounds.

First, both the countries are in the process of widening their free trade agreements with a number of other countries in Asia and Latin America. Prior to establishing the AUSFTA, Australia had signed three more free trade agreements: with New Zealand (Closer Economic Relations (CER)) established in 1983, with Singapore (Singapore–Australia Free Trade Agreement (SAFTA)) and Thailand (Thailand–Australia Free Trade Agreement (TAFTA)) signed in 2003 and 2004 respectively. Consultations are being undertaken with China and Japan with the aim of securing trade and economic agreements with these countries. The FTA with the United States is an important economic relationship to enter into with importance of similar, if not greater significance than a FTA with Japan or Thailand.

The United States has, on the other hand, signed six FTAs. These are with the countries included in North American Free Trade Agreement (NAFTA) (Canada and Mexico), as well as agreements with Singapore, Chile, Israel and Jordan. The USA has also a number of FTA discussions being undertaken with other countries including an FTA for the whole of the Americas (Free Trade Area of the Americas (FTAA)), except Cuba. This is an agreement that would undoubtedly give the Americas an advantage over Australian producers in the US market and also in obtaining US investment. In particular, agricultural products that are common to both the Latin American countries and Australia would be affected. Foreign investment is vital to Australia's growth and as such having US investment go to the Americas instead of Australia would have a large negative impact on Australia's economic growth.

Second, both the USA and Australia are among the most open economies in the world with average tariff rates in 1999 being 2.8 per cent and 3.8 per cent respectively (CIE 2001, p. x), and with the USA having a third of all its tariff lines duty free. This low tariff trend does not exist in all US industries, with an approximate 80 per cent tariff on sugar and 24 per cent tariff on dairy products (CIE 2001, p. x), and other high trade barriers in cotton, lamb and metals. Without concessions on these areas it has been argued that the benefit to Australia of an FTA would be largely reduced (The Australian APEC Study Centre 2001, p. xi). However, Mexico has, through its free trade agreement with the USA, been granted long-term, unrestricted access to almost all of the USA agricultural markets. The USA's importance to Australian trade in an FTA is not, however, only in the agricultural sector. Recently the United States was the destination for 25 per cent of Australia's manufactured exports and 33 per cent of its service exports (The Australian APEC Study Centre 2001, p. xiii). This would be impacted upon by an FTA, especially in the areas of some commercial automobiles, shipbuilding and some financial services. Besides, US protectionist policies relating to its steel industries will have a negative effect on Australia's interests.

Third, while Australia and the United States are both industrialized high-income economies, the United States is much larger than Australia with over 14 times the population and around 20 times the GDP. AUSFTA is expected to facilitate both trade and investment, meaning not only that it would improve Australia's access and competitiveness to the world's largest consumer market through the elimination of tariffs, but also it would enhance the attractiveness of Australia for investment from the USA, the largest source of capital in the world.

Fourth, staying economically close to the United States is also an important aspect of Australia entering an FTA with the USA. Not only would it keep Australia linked to the USA whose growth prospects for the coming decades are expected to be strong, but it would also link Australia to the leader of the information economy which would assist the growth of Australia's own information economy and would set a level of standards and codes of practice in Australia that is recognized and accepted through-out the world. However there are fears that may lead to too much competi-tion from US companies.

Fifth, it has also been suggested that AUSFTA would set a standard for other markets opening themselves up to increased trade and similar agree-ments, both on a regional level and a global level. This, it may be surmised, would help increase the liberalization momentum in APEC and the WTO. However an FTA between Australia and the USA may be seen as a change in Australia's current strategy of strengthening its economic ties with the East Asian and Pacific regions, and would also perhaps compromise Australia's strategy of utilizing the WTO to increase trade liberalization on a multilateral basis.

It can also be asked whether the USA would include the removal of important agricultural tariffs in the FTA, without which the FTA would lose a lot of its value to Australia. For example, Washington's past decisions to protect its lamb industry has harmed Australia's interests. The new Farm Bill which has increased significantly the subsidies American farmers can expect to receive harms Australia's interests. These actions weaken US lead-ership on trade liberalization, which is crucial for the success of the current WTO round, and weaken pressure on the European Union and Japan to reform their protected agricultural sectors (DFAT 2003, p. 89). Agricultural subsidy in the USA has to be negotiated at multilateral level and can only be dealt with by the WTO.

The outcome of a FTA is usually examined in three areas:

(a)   access into each other's market by their national firms producing manufacturing goods and services;
(b)   access into each other's market by the farms producing primary com-modities; and
(c)   gain and loss of the income groups in each of the countries.

However, these outcomes are the consequences of the direct trade of a particular type of commodity (either primary agricultural or manufac-tured) between the two signatory countries. The outcome of a bilateral trade agreement such as the AUSFTA may remain vague when trade between the two signatory countries and a third country exists but is not considered. For example, when a commodity is exported from signatory country A via third country C (where it is manufactured) into signatory country B. An assessment of the outcome of the bilateral free trade agree-ment is likely to remain ambiguous unless trade between all countries is considered. We would like to call this ambiguity the 'third country effect' or the 'multilateral consequence' of a bilateral trade agreement.

AUSFTA AND THE AUSTRALIAN WOOL INDUSTRY

Introduction to the Wool Industry

Wool is an example of an agricultural commodity which is transformed in global textile and apparel industries and sold into retail sectors of major consuming economies. Wool in its raw (greasy) and washed (scoured) form is handled in the Agricultural sector of the AUSFTA. When wool is combed into a wool top, or is carded, it is handled in the Textiles and Apparel sector of the AUSFTA (Figure 14.1).

Wool is therefore an interesting vehicle for examining the effects of trade agreements on producing countries, trading countries and access to retail markets. Also, because there is significant global trade occurring at each stage along the wool processing pipeline, the multilateral effects of the bilateral agreement need to be considered when measuring the net trade benefit to the Australian wool industry. In other words, the likelihood of net trade diversion rather than net trade creation needs to be explored.

As a primary commodity, the fate of wool trade is more related to the World Trade Organization's (WTOs) initiatives (to liberalize the trade of agricultural goods at multilateral level) than to the AUSFTA. Besides, the USA purchases very little raw wool from Australia. Australia's top ten wool importers purchase raw wool mostly for manufacturing wool products.

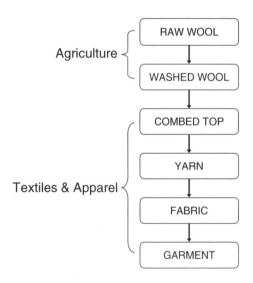

Figure 14.1   Wool is handled in the agriculture, textiles and apparel sectors of the AUSFTA

They then export these to winter-dominated countries in the world. Available trade data suggests that the USA is one of the most significant markets for wool textiles and clothing made from Australian wool. Therefore when wool textiles and clothing are traded, the implications of an FTA between Australia and the USA would depend on the nature and extent of trade barriers that exist in the US market concerning the importation of manufactured wool products. Another related area of interest in this study is whether or not NAFTA members, who trade wool textiles and clothing into the USA, are gaining market share (due to their access to this market without any barriers) at the expense of major Australian wool importers who are also major manufacturers.

Wool Fibre and the AUSFTA

Australian wool production has declined steadily since production peaked in 1989/90 (ABARE 2003). Figure 14.2 shows that the decline in the share of total wool produced has occurred mostly for medium and broad wool, and in the past 15 years the share of fine wool in Australia has increased. Because of the change to the composition of wool produced in Australia, the composition of wool exported from Australia has also altered.

In 2002/3 Australia exported 75 per cent of all raw wool, scoured wool and wool top to five destinations: China, Italy, South Korea, Taiwan and India. China was the single largest export destination for Australian wool,

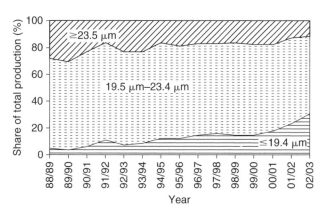

Notes: The diameter of a wool fibre is measured in microns: 1 μm = 1 micron = 1 000 000th of a metre.

Source: WoolDesk, Department of Agriculture, WA.

*Figure 14.2   Share of Australian fine wool (≤19μm), medium wool
(19.5μm to 23.4μm) and broad wool (≥23.5μm) since 1988/9*

Table 14.1   *Changes in Australia's raw wool exports (by quality) to major Asian countries and the USA*

Countries	Percentage change between 1998/9 and 2002/3				
	19μm	20–23μm	24–27μm	28μm	Total
China	563	12	−3	12	43
India	35	−26	−69	−17	−28
Japan	−98	−100	52	No	−99
South Korea	21	−55	−1	No	−19
Taiwan	211	−40	−94	−98	−43
USA	−68	−74	−89	−100	−75

Source: WoolDesk, Department of Agriculture, WA.

absorbing 40 per cent of Australian wool exports during this period. In comparison, the USA absorbed less than 1 per cent of Australian wool exports during this period.

Table 14.1 shows that between 1998/9 and 2002/3, China had become increasingly important to Australia as a third country that converts raw wool into retail product; many of the Asian countries appear to have lost some market share because of Australian wool imports to China. After 1998/9 China increased its imports of Australian wool and significantly increased the proportion of fine wool imported (Table 14.1). South Korea and Taiwan have also increased their imports of fine wool, however both countries have reduced their imports of other wool qualities. Since 1998/9 imports of Australian wool into both India and Japan have declined; within five years Japan's raw wool processing industry had disappeared. It should be noted that the signing of the AUSFTA will not improve access by these countries to the US market.

In five years imports of raw wool into the USA declined for all wool qualities (Table 14.1). Despite this, the USA remains a very important retail market for wool. It is the second largest consuming country in weight of wool product purchased at retail. It is important to note that major importing countries of Australian raw wool, such as China and Italy, are also the major suppliers of pure wool woven garments into the USA. This illustrates the importance of the trade of intermediate wool products before the product ends up on a retail shelf in the USA. Therefore the value of Australian wool exports is reliant on access by third party countries to the USA retail market.

Also, the benefits from concessions in the AUSFTA are dependent on wool fibre quality, and are explicit in US tariff codes which refer to fibre

Table 14.2   USA tariff rates and values of raw wool

	Raw wool	
	<32μm	≥32μm
NTR[a] (c/kg clean)	18.7	0
Countries	*Import value (US$'000)*	
Australia	11 373	
New Zealand	48	6263
Argentina		20
Canada	221	68
Mexico		80
UK		896
Brazil	88	
South Africa		100

Note: [a] Normal tariff rate.

Source: USITC (2004).

fineness, yarn count and fabric weight. Significant changes to the composition of wool may result in a series of reduced tariff rates that apply to products that are no longer imported.

In 2002/3 Australia exported $11.8m of raw wool, $4.3m of washed wool and $8.3m of combed top to the USA. Prior to implementation of the AUSFTA, imports of Australian raw wool fibre into the USA have been subject to tariffs for the USA Harmonized codes[1] which differentiate on fibre fineness. Data from the USA trade database shows tariffs are directed specifically at Australian raw wool imports (Table 14.2).

The tariff rates outlined in the AUSFTA show a 25 per cent reduction to the 18.7 c/kg clean tariff for raw wool (HC 51011160) and a 10 per cent reduction to the 20.6 c/kg clean tariff for scoured wool (HC 51012140) (USITC 2004). For the same products, the NAFTA and Chile–FTA achieved tariff free access to the USA for member countries.

Despite the reduction in tariffs as mentioned above, analysis of the value of raw fibre going into the USA reveals that the trend for wool imports into the USA has been approaching zero (Figure 14.3). This trend would question the need for the inclusion of these tariffs in the Agreement. The trend also indicates that the US industry that imported these wool fibre products is disappearing.

Therefore it would be reasonable to conclude that Australia has gained tariff concessions and not tariff eliminations in the AUSFTA for a set of products that are required by a rapidly disappearing US industry.

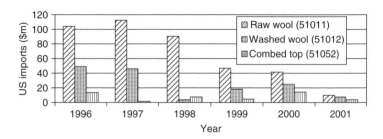

Source: TradStat (2004).

Figure 14.3   *Value of raw wool, washed wool and top imports into the USA from Australia*

It is also important to note that if the US wool processing industry is unable to supply the US spinning industry's demands for wool top, then the US spinning industry becomes dependent on the importation of wool top. So the relative importance of individual tariff rates (and concessions) is also dependent on the linkages between industry sectors, and the relative size of the industries in the importing country.

This effect is compounded by the technology used in the processing of raw wool fibre. The machinery for this processing is fibre specific, so wool carding and combing cannot be done on cotton cards or combs. Therefore the demise of the US wool fibre processing industry cannot be avoided by transferring the processing demand over to the huge US cotton processing industry.

If the USA cannot convert greasy wool to combed top for their domestic spinners, then there is no internal supply of wool fibre for these spinners, and the US industry will become totally reliant on imports. Similarly if the USA cannot convert combed top to yarn for their domestic fabric makers, then there is no internal supply of yarn for these fabric makers. If these imports are uncompetitive because of the US tariff rate applied to combed top and yarn (as part of the Textile and Apparel negotiations, not Agriculture), the Australian wool industry will lose access to the US spinning sector, and to part of its second largest retail market in the world.

Hence the importance of the AUSFTA to the Australian wool industry is not based on the tariffs for raw fibre, but on access to the US market for part-processed fibre that falls under the terms of the Textile and Apparel Products in the Agreement.

Wool, Textiles and Apparel and the AUSFTA

The significance of this discussion moving from wool fibre into Textiles and Apparel is that the negotiations for agricultural products were about getting tariffs to zero, whereas the Textile and Apparel negotiations concentrated on granting concessional tariff rates to products that were made in the industries of either economy. This definition of industries 'of either Party' is the basis for 'Rules of Origin' (ROOs) outlined in Annex 4-A of the Agreement (DFAT 2004).

ROOs centre on what constitutes an 'originating good'. A product is said to originate in the free trade area when it is grown, harvested, wholly produced or substantially transformed in the free trade area. Substantial transformation occurs when processing causes a product to shift from one tariff classification to another. ROOs have been applied in an expanded form to the AUSFTA.

An interesting twist exists in the Agreement where the Textile and Apparel sector's ROOs and the Agricultural sector overlap. For example raw wool imported from New Zealand, scoured in Australia and then exported (HC 510529) to the USA, is unable to enter at concessional tariff rates for Agricultural products. This is because the 'originating goods' rule (from the articles covering Textiles and Apparel, or Products) prevents the importation of Agricultural products into the USA at concessional tariff rates if the wool is not produced in Australia from Australian wool only.

The commentary on AUSFTA refers to the 'originating goods' sections as Yarn Forward, or Fabric Forward Rules of Origin.[2] However the example above shows that the application of ROO for Chapter 51 goods (Wool and fine Animal Hair) controls the origin of the fibre (DFAT 2004). The significance of this becomes more than an academic interest when the same FTA conditions are agreed to in another bilateral trade agreement by a third country that imports Australian raw wool and is an exporter of wool product into the USA. This will prevent the third country gaining concessional tariff access to US markets for their wool products, which will result in the loss of market share for wool, and loss of demand for Australian wool exports. However if the third country is to use US fibre (synthetic, man-made, or cotton) in the production of Textile or Apparel products, they will gain concessional tariffs from the USA, and be more competitive in the US market than the wool products from the same country. Given that prior to the creation of the AUSFTA, ROOs already existed in other FTAs including the NAFTA, USA–Chile FTA and the USA–Singapore FTA, it is not out of the question that the USA intends replicating these ROOs in each FTA it generates in the future.

So the introduction of the 'originating country' controls not only that the manufacturing of the imported product occurs in 'the country of either party' but that the imported product is manufactured from input materials from 'the country of either party'. A further constraint on Australian trade to the USA is contained in AUSFTA which limits the use of other fibres in textile and apparel products. The *de minimis* conditions (see Article 4.2.6; Rules of Origin and related matters: *De Minimis*) limit the origin of the other fibre in wool blend yarns to 93 per cent or more from 'the country of either party'. As an example, the entry of Australian wool blend yarns from combed wool (HC 510720) into the USA at the concessional tariff rates is dependent not only on the manufacturing of these yarns being done in Australia, but also on the source of the fibre in top form being Australian or American. As Australia produces very little synthetic fibre for apparel use, the synthetic fibre will have to be sourced from the USA. In addition, if changes occur in the US fibre industry that result in Australia's inability to source synthetic or elastomer, the result will be to modify the benefits Australia gets from the AUSFTA. Such was illustrated by the recent sale by DuPont of their synthetic fibre (including Lycra) Division.

The *de minimis* condition places an additional constraint on these wool blend yarns if they contain elastomers.[3] All the elastomeric fibre must be made in the USA. A summary of the scenarios presented above are outlined in Table 14.3.

The *de minimis* conditions are highly significant in the trade of wool yarns. In 2000, over 103 000 tonnes of worsted yarns containing wool were exported globally. 22 500 tonnes were classified as worsted yarns (HC 510720) containing between 50 and 85 per cent wool, the rest being synthetic yarns. Trade in worsted wool fabrics also shows that 22 per cent of product is in wool blend form. These trade figures show the significant proportions of the international market that would be modified by the *de minimis* rule that is in the FTA, and emphasizes the importance to Australia of the USA using the AUSFTA as a model trade agreement with other

Table 14.3   Products to be imported into the USA under the Yarn Forward Rules of Origin

Rule	Product exported into USA	Concession
ROO	Pure wool yarn made from 100 per cent Australian greasy wool	Yes
ROO *de minimis elastomer*	Blend wool yarn made from 94 per cent Australian and 4 per cent New Zealand greasy wool and 2 per cent Chinese elastomer	No
ROO *de minimis*	Pure wool yarn made from 92 per cent Australian and 8 per cent New Zealand greasy wool.	No
ROO *de minimis elastomer*	Blend wool yarn made from 94 per cent Australian and 4 per cent New Zealand greasy wool and 2 per cent American Elastomer	Yes

countries which have textile and apparel industries. At the same time, the benefits to the USA fibre industry are obvious.

It should also be noted that wool/elastomer blends in high quality suiting and women's knitwear are at the high end of the apparel market, and that the proportion of wool product being sold at retail as a wool blend is increasing.

Wool apparel products (Chapters 61 and 62) have the same ROOs and *de minimis* rules as the textile products (DFAT 2004). So when combined with the textile conditions, the Australian apparel product must first use yarn and fabric that satisfy the ROOs, and the apparel must also satisfy ROOs. This is the effect of the 'Yarn Forward' conditions of the Agreement.

In addition there are two Rules associated with Chapter 61 and 62 which are apparel specific. They control the origin of the visible lining material[4] in the apparel, so that the yarn and fabric of the visible lining material must be made in the 'the country of either party'. A blend wool skirt made of Australian wool and US elastomer, spun and woven in Australia and cut and sewn in Australia, will fail to gain concessional tariff entry into the USA unless the lining material is woven and finished in the USA from US yarn. Note that Australia is not a large producer of these lining fabrics or yarns.

The value of the AUSFTA to the Australian wool industry will also depend on the FTAs the USA makes with other countries. Figure 14.4 shows that US imports of pure wool lightweight fabrics from the Dominican Republic were replaced by imports from Mexico and Canada

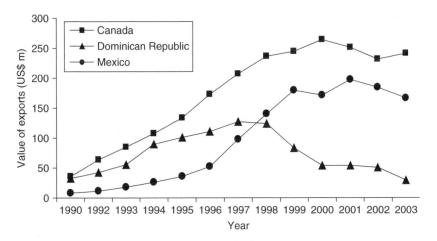

Source: TradStat (2004).

Figure 14.4   Value of pure wool lightweight fabric exported from Canada, Dominican Republic and Mexico into the USA

after the signing of the NAFTA. This shows that the USA entering into other FTAs can affect third countries imports to the USA.

The Trade Act of 2002 and the previous Trade and Development Act of 2000 both set out objectives for free trade negotiations. Both Acts include legislation for the refund of one-third of duties paid by US manufacturers on men's wool suits, on imports of imported wool fabrics, yarns and top and fibres during 1999 (Title V, Imports of Certain Wool Articles). This illustrates that any benefits of the AUSFTA can be modified through changes to the US legislation which are outside the AUSFTA.

SUMMARY AND CONCLUSIONS

A detailed, but not exhaustive, examination has been undertaken of the parts of AUSFTA which relate to the wool industry and the global textile and apparel industry that uses wool fibre. The nature of any bilateral agreement by definition will struggle with changes that occur outside the agreement, and with changes that occur in either country after the signing of the agreement. Evaluation of this Agreement should therefore include consideration of changes in the international and national environments which effect industries and economies, and how the Agreement interacts with these changes.

The industry analysis presented in this chapter illustrates that benefits from the Agreement to Australia are at risk from:

1. Changes in the Australian wool industry. The fineness of the Australian wool clip is changing, and as a result, Australia is supplying fibre into a different product range.
2. Changes in third countries. Major importing countries have responded to changes in the Australian wool supply, and their profile of wool exports products are changing.
3. Changes in the level of US industry activity. Early stage processing in the USA has all but disappeared, but claims are made that AUSFTA provides benefits from concessional tariff access to this US industry.
4. Linkages between industry sectors. The relative importance of individual tariff rates (and concessions) is also dependent on the linkages between industry sectors, and the relative size of the industries in the importing country.
5. Replication of this form of FTA by the USA with other countries. An FTA between the USA and a third country that imports Australian raw wool and exports it as a wool product into the USA, may prevent the third country gaining concessional tariff access to the US markets for the wool products.

6. The importance of overlap that occurs between agriculture and textiles in the ROOs. Because of this overlap the sectors cannot be handled independently.
7. Other agreements the USA has made. For example, the reduction in trade of lightweight wool fabrics from the Dominican Republic after the signing of the NAFTA.
8. Changes to other US legislation. Benefits of the AUSFTA can be modified through changes to the US legislation which are outside the AUSFTA.

NOTES

1. Harmonized Codes (HC) used in the six digit form in this chapter are the international codes as used by the WTO in reporting international trade between countries. The eight and ten digit form is the Harmonized Code used by the USA to record in more detail US imports and exports.
2. The Australian textile industry sought a general rule of origin based on change of tariff classification 'rather than the special "yarn-forward" rule proposed by the US side, but was unable to persuade the United States to move from this position' (ATNIA 2004).
3. Elastomeric fibres are marketed for example as Elastomer (Du Pont), Elastane or Spandex. Elastomeric fibres are available in all major synthetic fibre production regions, including the USA.
4. Suit coats, trousers and skirts mostly are lined on the inside with a lightweight silk-like material. This is the visible lining.

REFERENCES

The Australian APEC Study Centre (2001), *An Australia–USA Free Trade Agreement*, Canberra: Union Offset Printers.

Australian Bureau of Agricultural and Resource Economics (ABARE) (2003), *Australian Commodity Statistics 2003*, Canberra.

Australian Treaty National Interest Analyses (ATNIA) (2004), 'Australia–US Free Trade Agreement (AUSFTA) [2004] ATNIA 5', http://bar.austlii.edu.au/cgi-bin/disp.pl/au/other/dfat/nia/2004/5/annex1.html, 6 February.

Centre for International Economics (CIE) (2001), *Economic Impacts of an Australia–United States Free Trade Area*, Canberra: CIE.

Department of Foreign Affairs and Trade (DFAT) (2003), *Advancing the National Interest: Australia's Foreign and Trade Policy White Paper*, Canberra: Commonwealth of Australia.

DFAT (2004), 'Australia–United States Free Trade Agreement', www.dfat.gov.au, 6 February.

TradStat (2004), 'TradStat database', www.tradstatweb.com, 6 February.

United States International Trade Commission (USITC) (2004), 'Tariff database', http://dataweb.usitc.gov, 6 February.

PART VI

Conclusion

15. Regionalism, trade and economic development in the Asia-Pacific region: challenges ahead

M.A.B. Siddique

INTRODUCTION

Regional trade agreements (RTAs) are established with the main objective of increasing the flow of total trade by eliminating trade barriers between the signatory countries. These agreements are expected to bring these countries one step closer to globalization as trade barriers are reduced. However, RTAs may lead to trade friction as increased trade flows between the member economies of a regional bloc (trade creation) may take place at the expense of the non-member economies (trade diversion). There are two main facets of RTAs: bilateral and multilateral.

The advancement of RTAs in the Asia-Pacific region has gained momentum in recent years. Singapore and Japan signed an Economic Partnership Agreement in 2002. Australia established two Free Trade Agreements (FTAs) during 2003: the Singapore–Australia Free Trade Agreement (SAFTA) and the Thailand–Australia Free Trade Agreement (TAFTA), in addition to the Closer Economic Relations established with New Zealand (ANZCERTA), in force since 1998. Australia also concluded a Free Trade Agreement with the USA (AUSFTA) on 8 February 2004. Negotiations were also completed between the ASEAN 10 (Brunei, Cambodia, Indonesia, Laos, Malaysia, Myanmar, the Philippines, Singapore, Thailand and Vietnam) and China, with the ASEAN–China Free Trade Area coming into force on 1 January 2005. The United States has, on the other hand, signed nine RTAs: two with the countries included in North American Free Trade Agreement (Canada and Mexico), and seven more with Australia, Chile, Israel, Jordan, Morocco, Singapore and Bahrain. The USA also has a number of RTA discussions in progress with other countries, including an establishment of a regional trade agreement with the whole of the Americas (except Cuba) – Free Trade Area of the Americas (FTAA).

The question is whether the RTAs between these nations will damage their relationship with non-member economies in the region. The main aim of this book is to evaluate the implications of current and proposed RTAs in the Asia-Pacific region for economic development in the region, with special focus on Australia, the USA, China, India, Indonesia, Japan, South Korea, New Zealand, Singapore and Thailand.

It is argued throughout this book that RTAs in the Asia-Pacific region would have significant impacts on the material progress of the peoples of this region. However, in terms of the benefits and costs associated with the RTAs, these would vary from country to country. The main focus of the book is the impact of RTAs on major economies of the Asia-Pacific region. The book critically analyses the issues surrounding the RTAs; augments knowledge of the effects of RTAs on the major economies in the Asia-Pacific region; and documents ideas and specialized knowledge regarding RTAs. Currently, few books deal exclusively with critical issues relating to various aspects of RTAs in this region. The book not only contains new material but is quite different in approach to previous publications on the topic.

THE SCOPE AND PLAN OF THE BOOK

The book contains chapters dealing with the following issues relating to RTAs in the Asia-Pacific region:

1. RTAs – theoretical perspective;
2. RTAs and the role and goals of WTO;
3. RTAs and exchange rates;
4. RTAs, East Asia and the Pacific (Australia, China, Japan, India, South Korea, the USA and the APEC);
5. RTAs and Southeast Asia (Indonesia, Singapore and Thailand);
6. Impact of RTAs on specific sectors of an economy.

Based on chapters dealing with these issues, the book is divided into six main parts. The book commences with an introductory/review chapter examining the links between regionalism, trade and economic development with special focus on the Asia-Pacific region. The second part of the book analyses whether or not there exists any conflict between the objectives of RTAs and the role and goals of the WTO. It also examines the influence of exchange rates on the desirable impact of RTAs on the member countries. The next part of the book focuses on various RTAs in East Asia and the Pacific region which is followed by an evaluation of FTAs signed by two of the most dynamic and vibrant economies in Southeast Asia – Thailand

and Singapore. Impacts of RTAs on various sectors of an economy is the subject matter of Part V of the book. The current chapter reviews previous chapters and discusses the emerging challenges that lie ahead for further economic integration in the Asia-Pacific region.

REGIONALISM, THE WTO AND THE EXCHANGE RATE

Three chapters highlight the interface between RTAs and the WTO, and address some motivations and implications of regionalism against a setting of trade and exchange rate regimes.

With the number of RTAs growing exponentially, the question arises whether or not the objectives of the WTO will conflict with those of the RTA. In Chapter 2, Stoler examines political and economic concerns faced by the WTO in response to the growing number of RTAs. While it is acknowledged that greater benefits are realized under multilateral trade liberalization, by July 2005 only one WTO member, Mongolia, did not belong to an RTA. Stoler analyses the stimulus for negotiation of RTAs and argues that they are becoming increasingly popular due to the limited scope of the WTO. This development places intense pressure on the WTO to ensure that RTAs complement their wider objective of a multilateral trade system. Stoler raises two questions that, if answered correctly, will guarantee the RTA in question will complement the WTO's intentions. The first is whether the member countries have avoided engaging in regional commitments which they would be reluctant to broaden to a multilateral scene sooner or later; and second, whether the member countries would be prepared to extend the obligations made in the RTA to a non-discriminatory multilateral setting. It has been argued throughout this book that significant gains can be experienced by countries signing RTAs, and that the WTO system should not prevent members from realizing these rewards. Stoler is of the view that legal and political compatibility of the RTAs with the WTO's system is supremely important.

The impact of the exchange rate on gains to member countries of an RTA is often overlooked. Volatile exchange rates can lead to uncertainty regarding the prices of traded goods and then to unpredictable trade patterns. Sjaastad (Chapter 3) convincingly demonstrates that although minimal trade disruptions occur between RTA member countries under the optimum condition of fixed exchange rates, disturbances to the prices of traded goods will occur in response to changes in the exchange rates of major currencies. Countries entering into RTAs will have differing compositions of net exports and will be affected by varying degrees when the major currencies change. Because of this, prices of traded goods can diverge causing trade interruptions. Sjaastad discusses an exchange rate regime that insulates member countries from fluctuations in major currencies' exchange rates. The exchange rate rule of such a regime is defined on a basket of currencies which allows for stable trading prices between member countries. In this situation Sjaastad believes the full advantages of the RTA may be exploited.

Changing trade trends between countries or regions can have formidable effects on the success of RTAs. The inclusion and exclusion of certain regions and commodities in the RTA will depend on the structure of trade items of the member countries. In Chapter 4, Wu encapsulates the trends in trade amongst major Asia-Pacific Economic Corporation (APEC) economies. APEC has become an important contributor to world trade in recent years, and trade between APEC economies has grown substantially. Composition and patterns of trade, and intra-regional trade have also evolved significantly. While investigating these trends, Wu claims that bilateral or multilateral free trade agreements do promote trade among their members. He anticipates that further expansion of trade is possible among APEC members and hints at the formation of an APEC free trade area as an appropriate vehicle.

EAST ASIA AND THE PACIFIC

The five chapters in Part III of this book focus on specific FTAs and their economic consequences for member and non-member countries. The spotlight is thrown on Australia, Japan, China and Korea. Future FTAs are discussed in the context of the above mentioned countries, and the implications on their actions and policies examined.

The AUSFTA is likely to affect Australia's trade with its trading partners in East Asia. Yamazawa (Chapter 5) critically evaluates the impact of AUSFTA on East Asian economies, with specific emphasis given to the Japanese experience. He claims there will be no substantial effects on Japanese exports to Australia or the USA, because Japan's main exports do not compete directly with either nation's products. Yamazawa also assesses Japan's change in FTA strategy for the East Asia region. He argues that Japan should make use of bilateral and multilateral FTAs in the near future whilst East Asia moves towards an 'economic community'. Although Japan is currently pursuing FTAs with ASEAN, the ultimate outcome may be an APEC-wide FTA.

Gains attained through the use of regional integration agreements can be unevenly distributed and skewed towards the bigger economy, and thus lead to many problems associated with unequal distribution of gains. Recent surges in globalization and trade liberalization have prompted many countries, which were previously dominated by the principles of socialist/communist economies, to embrace the principles of market economies. These countries provide a unique opportunity to examine the experience of a transitional economy in global integration through RTAs. Chapter 6 covers these issues with respect to the Chinese experience. In terms of global integration, China took three important steps after the Government of the country introduced its Open Door policy in 1978: (a) trade reforms with the aim of becoming a member of the WTO; (b) market reforms with the aim of attracting foreign direct investment into the country; and (c) engaging with the neighbouring countries in order to establish FTAs which Howe describes as a 'policy of localized free trade agreements'. In this scenario Howe argues that China has incentives for increasing competition amongst ASEAN members. While implementation of globalization policies gave Chinese industries access to international markets, there are still opportunities for China to utilize FTAs. After increasing trade with ASEAN, Howe claims China would benefit from opening up to advanced countries such as Japan and Korea. In this case the FTA would expand to include not just simple tariff reductions, but also increases to FDI and trade simultaneously.

Literature dealing with the effects of FTAs focuses mainly on aggregates at the macro level rather than their distributional impact at the sectoral level such as agriculture and textile industries. It is often assumed that freer trade will bring guaranteed and well-distributed benefits. However, adverse impacts of multilateral free trade on some sectors are sometimes disregarded. In Chapter 7, Jackson evaluates the distributional effects of free trade agreements in the Asia-Pacific region with special focus on personal food security issues. He argues that traditional methodologies for assessing the impact of regional agreements are inadequate for countries which rely heavily on traditional sectors such as agriculture and fishing for generating national income and employment. Jackson cites examples from a number of countries in the Pacific Islands where 80 per cent of the population relies on agriculture for income and food security. The effect of global or regional free trade on the economies of these countries compared with countries less dependent on agriculture, would be very different. This justifies the case-by-case analysis dealing with distributional aspects of RTAs at the micro level.

Whilst FTAs can create trade and improve competition amongst member countries, non-member countries can be left behind. Thus, with the signing of FTAs gaining momentum, the non-member countries have been forced to rethink their strategies and policies. Korea is one such country. In Chapter 8, Cheong argues that if Korea doesn't embrace FTAs in the future, it risks losing competitiveness with those countries forming FTAs. Cheong's analysis of public opinion towards the Government's policy of negotiating many FTAs, demonstrates that the majority of the media and Government believe that opening up will benefit Korea's economy. As so often is the case, the agricultural sector fears adverse impacts of possible FTAs. Cheong also argues that if Korea is to achieve its goal of becoming a business hub, like Singapore and Japan, it is essential to negotiate and conclude the FTAs that would attract FDI into the country without compromising its national security.

The dismantling of trade barriers and encouragement of FDI that can follow the implementation of an FTA can increase the influence of member economies on each other. The financial sector is one area where the influences are significantly noticeable. The empirical investigation by Allen, Lim and Winduss utilizes a number of macroeconomic variables to determine the influence of the USA on the short-run and long-run stock returns in Australia. Their findings suggest that while in the absence of AUSFTA, American economic activity fails to significantly influence the Australian stock market, they expect that the degree of influence is likely to increase once the trade barriers in the financial, services and investment areas are removed after the implementation of AUSFTA.

SOUTHEAST ASIA

In Part IV of the book, Southeast Asia, and specifically Thailand and Singapore, are analysed in depth. Certain FTAs and their effects on member and non-member countries are discussed with a view to determining possible costs and benefits.

The effects of the USA–Singapore FTA (USSFTA) on Singapore and external countries needs to be evaluated with a scope that includes FTAs already completed by Singapore. The overall results of the USSFTA on Singapore will depend on creation and diversion of trade not just with the USA but also with other ASEAN countries. Tongzon (Chapter 10) employs a Computable General Equilibrium (CGE) model of the Global Trade Analysis Project (GTAP) to estimate the gains and costs of USSFTA from the perspective of Singapore and its trading partners. His findings suggest that there are negligible static effects on the Singaporean economy. However, he expects that Singapore will experience dynamic benefits resulting from increased investment, economies of scale and the effects of learning-by-doing. These are generated by Singapore becoming a more lucrative market in foreign investors' eyes as the restrictions diminish.

Regarding the implications of USSFTA for other major trading partners of the USA and Singapore, Tongzon finds that the USA's gains are relatively small, but dominant gains come in the form of a reduction in services barriers. As for ASEAN, the negative impacts of the Agreement are insignificant. FTA's that Singapore has already signed with Australia and Japan are largely unaffected, as is bilateral trade between Singapore and these two countries. Tongzon claims that with Australia and the USA having completed a FTA, the opportunity for increased cooperation between Singapore, Australia and the USA may present.

Countries with similar export patterns can be affected very differently by FTAs. Trade creation in one country may lead to trade diversion in another. Countries must consider the actions of trade partners and competitors when forming their FTA strategies, an issue considered in the context of Thailand and Indonesia by James (in Chapter 11). He looks at export competitiveness in Thailand and Indonesia with the aid of a Revealed Comparative Advantage Index (RCAI) for three digit Standard International Trade Classification (SITC) categories. His findings suggest that these two countries compete with each other in the major markets of the USA and Japan. The implication is that if one country was to negotiate enhanced market access in these markets the other stands to lose substantially – for example if Thailand succeeds in its FTA negotiations with the USA, Indonesia puts at risk nearly $10 billion in non-oil exports due to enhanced Thai competitiveness. James also examines Rules of Origin issues and finds that investment diversion and restriction of intra-industry trade may result from the exclusion of intermediate inputs. James claims that under a Japan–Thai FTA, rules of origin applied to auto parts and components may lead to diversion of investment and trade from Indonesia to Thailand. Indonesia can ill afford to let this take place.

With the WTO's goal of multilateral trade liberalization somewhat stalled, many countries have embraced bilateral trade agreements as the immediate way forward. For example, Singapore has pursued FTAs with many of its major trading partners. Australia is one of these trading partners and the motives and implications of the recently implemented Singapore–Australia FTA (SAFTA) are examined in Chapter 12. Sen concentrates on Singapore–Australia bilateral trade linkages and finds that major economic benefits will arise from the liberalization of services trade present in the SAFTA. Sen believes that the primary gain to Australia will be in the area of services trade. The SAFTA also focuses on the liberalization of investment and Sen claims that this will encourage knowledge-based investments to flow between the two countries. Sen also argues that whilst the Asia-Pacific economies could benefit from agreements like the

SAFTA, care must be taken to ensure that regional agreements do not become a stumbling block for multilateral liberalization. While SAFTA appears to be more of a building block for multilateral liberalization, it may be undermined by potential Asia–Pacific FTAs. Sen concludes by claiming that multilateral liberalization is the best outcome for trade, and this must be pursued hand in hand with regional FTAs if the full benefits of global free trade are to be realized.

SECTOR STUDIES

Part V of the book focuses on specific sectoral effects of FTAs with particular reference to agriculture and the Australian wool industry. Agriculture is often a problem sector for FTAs with the discussion often omitting externalities associated with a particular sector. Thus it is important to have a solid understanding of the economics attached to the issues relating to specific sectors.

Discrimination amongst sectors is evident in many FTAs. The partial or whole exclusion of some sectors in an FTA can cause the benefits to member countries to diminish. Hence the reasons why sectors may be left out of FTAs are likely to be non-economic. MacLaren (Chapter 13) shows these outcomes using agriculture as the prime example. This sector is often completely left out of FTAs with many reasons given as to why. Government intervention is frequently evident in the form of import protection, export assistance and domestic support, while some governments strongly feel that economics should not be applied to the agricultural sector, citing farming as a way of life and links between food production, culture and rural communities. However MacLaren claims that these are examples of public goods, and externalities exist making economic concerns relevant. The economic consequences of excluding sectors from FTAs can be considerable. For example, MacLaren finds that the exclusion of sugar, beef and dairy from the recent AUSFTA halves the benefits to the Australian economy. Hence MacLaren concludes that when a sector is left out of a FTA, a welfare loss is experienced by the member whose exports in that sector are not given preferential treatment.

Inherent in the signing of bilateral trade agreements is the inability to manage and react to changes made outside the agreement. This is certainly the case with the AUSFTA, as explored in Chapter 14, with specific reference to the Australian wool industry. Wool is an interesting and somewhat complex case in that its categorization in the AUSFTA is not clear cut. Depending on wool type and possible transformations, it may be classified in agriculture or textiles and apparel. Therefore any possible benefits to the

Australian wool industry will depend on where the wool is classified. Because of the way the wool industry is treated in the current Agreement, any benefits to the wool industry could be reversed through changes to US law and other FTAs that the USA may undertake. The authors' allege that the outcome of a bilateral trade agreement such as the AUSFTA will be unclear when third country trade is not taken into account. The authors denote this efficacy as the 'third country effect'. Australia relies heavily on the trade of intermediate wool products through third countries before the product finishes in the USA. Hence demand for Australian wool depends greatly on the third country having access to the US retail market. If the USA was to sign another bilateral agreement with an importer of Australian wool and exporter of wool products into the USA, this will prevent the country gaining concessional tariff access to the US market. This will result in a loss of competitiveness for the wool products and then a loss of import demand for Australian wool. The authors conclude that evaluation of the AUSFTA must include consideration of changes in each country's policies and industrial environments, and how these effect the terms of the Agreement.

CHALLENGES AHEAD

Although regionalism began its journey as early as in the late 1950s, it advanced with full force during the 1990s and after the turn of the century. A number of factors contributed to the accelerated rate of growth of RTAs globally and specifically within the Asia-Pacific region:

1. the sluggish progress in multilateralism initiated under the umbrella of the WTO;
2. dynamic and forceful leadership of the USA, being the global super-power, to advance the positive aspects of reducing trade barriers through RTAs;
3. collapse of the communist and socialist regimes and emergence of the transitional economies in Eastern Europe and South East Asia;
4. political will of the majority of the leaders of the transitional economies to open up their economies through a reduction in trade barriers; and
5. acceleration of the process of globalization.

The rise of regionalism within the Asia-Pacific and indeed, the world, begs the question 'Why have multilateral negotiations struggled?' Krugman (1993, pp. 73–5) offers four reasons for the slow progress in recent years.

1. The free-rider problem is hard to handle and the large number of parties make the negotiations complex.
2. The protection mechanisms have changed and become increasingly complex. Anti-dumping and other administered protection greatly complicate matters.
3. The USA's global dominance has decayed thus affecting the dynamics of negotiations.
4. There are institutional differences amongst members meaning personalized treatment is required.

These reasons may explain the drift towards trading blocs but there exist many more. A crucial question is whether trading blocs will facilitate free trade by making negotiations more productive. This proposition is common (see Summers 1991) and often cited as a major reason why regionalism could be a complement to multilateralism. However, Winters (1996) argues that the presence of sector-specific lobbies hinder the movement of regionalism towards multilateralism. Further, Laird (1999, p. 1186) claims that coalitions could form during the regionalism process, making negotiations tougher. Krugman (1993, p. 73) has further worries about the transition process – if the blocs grow large enough, they may close out the rest of the world by constructing barriers and imposing higher external tariffs. The size and large proportion of worldwide trade facilitated in the Asia-Pacific region (over 41 per cent), makes it an extremely important player, even leader, in the movement towards global free trade. Countries within the region need to ensure that the development of regionalism acts as a complement to multilateralism.

There is no doubt that the surge in RTAs in the Asia-Pacific region is a positive step and future development of the region will depend on further steps towards trade liberalization through reduction in trade barriers. However, caution must be exercised while developing expectations for economic gains for future RTAs. The scope of RTAs has become more complex during the last two decades. Tension and conflict may emerge between two dominant RTAs or between one dominant partner and another less influential partner when RTAs take place at the bilateral level. The ability to gain from RTAs depends on the bargaining power and skills of negotiators of a particular country or group of countries. As discussed by MacLaren in Chapter 13, the most recently concluded FTA between Australia and the USA excluded sugar, beef and dairy products from the agreement which simply halved the benefits. Similarly, an agreement between two RTAs, say between NAFTA and AFTA, complicate the matter to such a level that it becomes impossible to accurately assess the benefits to each party.

Another important issue that should be considered while negotiating future RTAs in the region is the degree of openness. Obviously less open economies have more to gain from RTAs. The more open economies have fewer trade barriers. The level of technological advancement is another crucial issue. More technologically advanced countries enjoy relatively more comparative advantage than the less technologically advanced nations. Thus if an RTA takes place between two technologically uneven countries, the more technologically advanced country has more to gain. It is often argued that deep integration agreements with a longer term and greater depth of coverage are more likely to lead to multilateral trade liberalization (see Crawford and Laird 2001, p. 198). Deep integration agreements go beyond the conventional border controls and focus increasingly on liberalization of services, investment, labour markets, government procurement, strengthening of technology and scientific cooperation, and harmonization of competition policies (Cernat and Laird 2005, p. 74). These fuller agreements are more effective at removing trade distortions and promoting cooperation between members for four reasons: (a) the agreements encourage coordination of macroeconomic policies; (b) the agreements present compelling incentives for cooperation due to political harmonization; (c) regulatory measures and policies are harmonized; and (d) trade flows are more extensively liberalized. If fuller agreements can satisfy these conditions they can be effective in containing the protectionist measures becoming increasingly prevalent (Drabek 2005, pp. 20–1).

The Asia-Pacific region can certainly benefit from deep integration, but diversity of its member economies' presents some challenges. It seems that deep integration agreements are more prevalent in developed economies, meaning developing countries may be left behind. Cernat and Laird (2005, pp. 85–6) are of the view that developing countries are more likely to form shallow RTAs that don't allow the full benefits of increased competition and scale, and attracting additional FDI to be realized. They further argue that the lesser level of integration may be a result of developing economies' inherent economic and political instabilities, although it may also provide useful policy discretion that would not be possible if the RTA was deeper. Developing countries need to ascertain the integration approach that best suits their economic situation. Options include joining with another developing country or a developed country. Collier *et al.* (2000, p. 129) find that blocs formed between developing countries are the most troublesome and although it may help the countries gain more attention and negotiating power, joining a bloc with a developed country is a safer option. In this case differing transition periods can be used and deeper integration promoted over time. Bhagwati and Panagariya (1996, p. xvii) observe that RTAs involving hegemons should be discouraged due to possible protectionist effects on smaller countries. The Asia-Pacific region may need to recognize these issues and certify that tension does not arise between the developed and developing countries in the region. While developing countries are under tremendous pressure to open their economies for importing capital and technology, and industrial products from developed countries, their efforts are not often reciprocated by developed countries. Developed countries are often reluctant to allow free movement of labour, agricultural and light industrial products such as footwear, clothing and textiles, from developing countries. There is constant pressure to exclude these sectors from the RTA. Agricultural sectors are particularly highly protected in most advanced countries and very often tension arises between the developed countries regarding the protection of agricultural sectors. Deep integration has the ability to enhance economic development and accelerate it in developing countries, but the issue is the extent to which harmonization should be encouraged.

The Asia-Pacific region clearly has many challenges regarding future advancement of RTAs in the region and between it and other regions. But if policymakers are guided by economic pragmatism, the region will prosper in the coming years through further reduction in trade barriers.

REFERENCES

Bhagwati, J. and A. Panagariya (1996), 'Preface', in *The Economics of Preferential Trade Agreements*, Washington, DC: The AEI Press, pp. xiii–xx.
Cernat, L. and S. Laird (2005), 'North, South, East, West: what's best? Modern RTAs and their implications for the stability of trade policy', in Z. Drabek (ed.), *Can Regional Integration Arrangements Enforce Trade Discipline? The Story of the EU Enlargement*, Hampshire, UK and New York, US: Palgrave Macmillan, pp. 69–95.
Collier, P., M. Schiff, A. Venables and L.A. Winters (2000), *Trading Blocs*, New York, US: Oxford University Press for The World Bank.
Crawford, J.-A. and S. Laird (2001), 'Regional trade agreements and the WTO', *North American Journal of Economics and Finance*, **12**, 193–211.
Drabek, Z. (2005), 'An alternative overview of regionalism', in *Can Regional Integration Arrangements Enforce Trade Discipline? The Story of the EU Enlargement*, Hampshire, UK and New York, US: Palgrave Macmillan, pp. 19–68.
Krugman, P. (1993), 'Regionalism versus multilateralism: analytical notes', in J. De Melo and A. Panagariya (eds), *New Dimensions in Regional Integration*, Cambridge, New York and Melbourne, Australia: Cambridge University Press, pp. 58–79.
Laird, S. (1999), 'Regional trade agreements: dangerous liaisons?', *World Economy*, **22** (9), 1179–1200.
Summers, L.H. (1991), 'Regionalism and the world trading system', in *Policy Implications of Trade and Currency Zones*, Kansas City, MO: Federal Reserve Bank of Kansas City, 295–301.
Winters, L.A. (1996), 'Regionalism versus multilateralism', World Bank Policy Research Working Paper 1687, Washington, DC: The World Bank.

Index